Nietzsche's
French Legacy

Nietzsche's French Legacy

➤

A GENEALOGY
OF POSTSTRUCTURALISM

Alan D. Schrift

ROUTLEDGE   New York · London 1995

Published in 1995 by

Routledge
29 West 35th Street
New York, NY 10001

Published in Great Britain by
Routledge
11 New Fetter Lane
London EC4P 4EE

Library of Congress Cataloging-in-Publication Data

Schrift, Alan D.

    Nietzsche's French Legacy: a genealogy of poststructuralism /
Alan D. Schrift.
      p.   cm.
    Includes bibliographical references and index.
    ISBN 0-415-91146-X. — ISBN 0-415-91147-8
    1. Nietzsche, Friedrich Wilhelm, 1844–1900—Influence.
    2. Philosophy, French—20th century.   I. Title.
    B2421.S36   1995
    193—dc20   95-14607
                                     CIP

For Jill

As an *artist* one has no home in Europe, except Paris....

—NIETZSCHE, *Ecce Homo*

I do not believe there is a single Nietzscheanism. There are no grounds for believing that there is a true Nietzscheanism, or that ours is any truer than others.

—FOUCAULT, "Critical Theory/Intellectual History"

A philosophy's power is measured by the concepts it creates, or whose meaning it alters, concepts that impose a new set of divisions on things and actions. It sometimes happens that those concepts are called forth at a certain time, charged with a collective meaning corresponding to the requirements of a given period, and discovered, created or recreated by several authors at once.

—DELEUZE, *Expressionism in Philosophy: Spinoza*

The time for me hasn't come yet; some are born posthumously.

—NIETZSCHE, *Ecce Homo*

... it is high time that I come again to the world as a Frenchman.

—NIETZSCHE, Draft of a letter to Jean Bourdeau
(17 December, 1888)

Contents

➤

List of Abbreviations

➤

MOST REFERENCES TO NIETZSCHE'S WRITINGS ARE INCLUDED IN THE BODY of the text denoted by the following abbreviations. Unless otherwise specified, Roman numerals denote the volume number of a set of collected works or a standard subdivision within a single work in which the sections are not numbered consecutively, Arabic numerals denote the section number rather than the page number, and "Pr" denotes Nietzsche's preface. I have generally used the translations indicated, although these translations were occasionally altered to reflect more exactly the emphasis and style of the original German texts.

A   *The Antichrist*. Translated by R. J. Hollingdale. Middlesex, England: Penguin Books, 1968.

AOM   *Assorted Opinions and Maxims*. Translated by R. J. Hollingdale in *HH*.

BGE   *Beyond Good and Evil*. Translated by Walter Kaufmann. New York: Random House, 1966.

BT   *The Birth of Tragedy*. Translated by Walter Kaufmann. New York: Random House, 1967.

D   *Daybreak*. Translated by R. J. Hollingdale. Cambridge: Cambridge University Press, 1982.

DS   *David Strauss, the Confessor and the Writer*. Translated by R. J. Hollingdale in *UM*.

EH   *Ecce Homo.* Translated by Walter Kaufmann. New York: Random House, 1967.

GM   *On the Genealogy of Morals.* Translated by Walter Kaufmann. New York: Random House, 1967.

GS   *The Gay Science.* Translated by Walter Kaufmann. New York: Random House, 1974.

H   *On the Uses and Disadvantages of History for Life.* Translated by R. J. Hollingdale in *UM.*

HH   *Human, All-Too-Human.* Translated by R. J. Hollingdale. Cambridge: Cambridge University Press, 1986.

KSA   *Sämtliche Werke. Kritische Studienausgabe in 15 Bänden.* Edited by Giorgio Colli and Mazzino Montinari. Berlin: Walter de Gruyter, 1980. (I have used the accepted convention in citing references from this edition: volume number followed by the fragment number. For example, the abbreviation "*KSA* 2: 4[78]" refers to volume 2, fragment 4[78].)

NCW   *Nietzsche Contra Wagner.* Translated by Walter Kaufmann in *The Viking Portable Nietzsche.* New York: The Viking Press, 1967.

SE   *Schopenhauer as Educator.* Translated by R. J. Hollingdale in *UM.*

TI   *Twilight of the Idols.* Translated by R. J. Hollingdale. Middlesex, England: Penguin Books, 1968.

UM   *Untimely Meditations.* Translated by R. J. Hollingdale. Cambridge: Cambridge University Press, 1983.

WP   *The Will to Power.* Translated by Walter Kaufmann and R. J. Hollingdale. New York: Random House, 1968.

WS   *The Wanderer and His Shadow.* Translated by R. J. Hollingdale in *HH.*

Z   *Thus Spoke Zarathustra.* Translated and edited by Walter Kaufmann. New York: The Viking Press, 1967.

Preface

➤

THE ORIGINS OF THIS TEXT LIE IN MY EARLIER BOOK *NIETZSCHE AND THE Question of Interpretation: Between Hermeneutics and Deconstruction.* In that work, one of the topics examined was Nietzsche's reception in France during the 1960s and 1970s, focusing in particular on the deconstructive reading of Nietzsche that is most commonly associated with Jacques Derrida. This examination led to my growing interest in recent French philosophy, beginning with Derrida and deconstruction but moving to other thinkers as well, including Michel Foucault, Gilles Deleuze, Hélène Cixous, and Jean-François Lyotard. All the while, however, I continued to read, teach, and write on Nietzsche.

As these two interests—in Nietzsche and in recent French philosophy—came increasingly together in my own thinking, my orientation toward the two interests changed. Where my earlier work addressed the French interpretations of Nietzsche, the work reflected in the present study addresses the way the French *use* Nietzsche in developing their own critical projects. This use involves a "reading" in the broadest—and perhaps most Nietzschean—sense, but certainly not a reading in the sense of a commentary or explication de texte.

As I investigated what I sometimes referred to jokingly as the French "use and abuse of Nietzsche," I noticed that most other scholars working in these areas fell into one of two groups. On the one hand, there are those who work primarily in the area of recent French thought, whether from a literary, philosophical, or social scientific disciplinary perspective. And on the other hand, there are those who would best be described as Nietzsche scholars, usually historians of philosophy whose primary research centers around issues in Nietzsche scholarship. Regarding the first group, there was a pervasive acknowledgment of Nietzsche's importance as an influence upon the development of French theory following structuralism. But this acknowledgment was, with a few notable exceptions, largely superficial. In the best cases, a book-length study might have a chapter on Nietzsche; in the worst cases, there would be a few footnotes or an isolated sentence or paragraph acknowledging an intellectual debt to Nietzsche. But rarely was there a sustained examination of Nietzsche that endeavored to show the specific ways in which Nietzsche's work either influenced, or prefigured, the analyses of the French theorists.

Regarding the second group, the Nietzsche scholarly community, the situation was no better. For here, again with a few noteworthy exceptions, regardless of whether the philosophical perspective was one informed by an Anglo-American–analytic or a phenomenological-Heideggerian back- ground, two attitudes were prevalent: either there was open hostility toward the new French readings of Nietzsche (by Deleuze, Derrida, Klossowski, Kofman, Pautrat, Lacoue-Labarthe, Rey, et al.) or these read- ings were passed over in silence. And if there was a general hesitance by mainstream Nietzsche scholarship regarding the French interpretations of Nietzsche, there was an even more critical or dismissive response to the general philosophical projects of the poststructuralists.

Both of these tendencies—to superficially address the link to Nietzsche and to ignore the general philosophical positions of poststructuralism— struck me as particularly unfortunate given the rich and multidimensional connections I saw between Nietzsche's works and the works of writers like Derrida, Deleuze, or Foucault, to name only the three most widely known. And for this reason, my goal in approaching the present study was twofold. Through a careful analysis and close reading of the texts of Nietzsche and a selection of contemporary French thinkers, I wanted to show to readers familiar with recent French philosophy the degree of specificity with which Nietzsche's ideas prefigure certain poststructuralist motifs. At the same time, I wanted to demonstrate to readers familiar with Nietzsche just how Nietzschean were some of the dominant characteristics of contemporary French philosophy. In this sense, the present text really should have two titles, not a title and a subtitle, for this text hopes to speak to two audi- ences, and to address at one and the same time what I take to be two intimately connected issues: "A Genealogy of Poststructuralism" and "Nietzsche's French Legacy."

The basic approach I follow is both historical and comparative. In successive chapters, I examine how Derrida, Foucault, Deleuze, and Cixous incorporate and make use of Nietzschean ideas within their own philosophical projects. In chapter one, I concentrate on Derrida's deconstructive critique of binary thinking, showing how the specific form of Derridean argument is previewed in Nietzsche's own critique of "oppositional thinking" which demonstrated the poverty of basing morality, philosophy, and religion on such oppositional hierarchies as good/evil, truth/error, being/becoming. In chapter two, I look at Foucault's genealogies of power relations and subject construction, showing how much Foucault draws upon Nietzsche's thinking on relations among forces and, in particular, on the relations of will to power in framing his own analyses. Chapter three examines Deleuze's account of the productivity of desire, arguing that Deleuze's affirmation of desiring-production is a post-Freudian repetition of Nietzsche's affirmation of healthy will to power and showing the ways in which Deleuze and Guattari's critique of psychoanalysis in *Anti-Oedipus* draws upon Nietzsche's link between the rise of Christianity and the rise of the modern state in *On the Genealogy of Morals*. Chapter four examines Cixous's account of the economy of gift-giving, suggesting that she brings to the fore an unacknowledged "feminine" libidinal economy which I suggest may be at work within Nietzsche's own comments on generosity and excess. In the fifth and final chapter, I take a slightly different approach by examining the recent move in France away from the Nietzscheanism of the preceding decades. Here I look first at Lyotard, whose work is shown to move away from Nietzsche in the direction of Kant and Levinas as he tries to develop an ethics and politics that will work with his postmodernist assumptions. This is followed by an examination of several of the better known "anti-Nietzscheans"—Vincent Descombes, Luc Ferry, and Alain Renaut—whose attacks upon the politics of the poststructuralists is framed in terms of the latter's "Nietzscheanism." I conclude with a reflection on what might be lost if we accept the arguments of the French anti-Nietzscheans.

While this text is in some sense very general, covering a wide range of issues as they emerge in the works of several French thinkers, it is also idiosyncratic in terms of whom I choose to discuss and, perhaps more importantly, whom I choose not to discuss. In a work purporting to discuss

"Nietzsche's French Legacy," there are many figures that one would expect to see discussed, figures whose names are only mentioned in passing, if at all, in what follows. Among this group belong, of course, the important French Nietzsche commentators, including Pierre Klossowski, Sarah Kofman, Michel Haar, Philippe Lacoue-Labarthe, Jean-Michel Rey, Bernard Pautrat, Angèle Kremer-Marietti, Jean Granier, Eric Blondel, Henri Birault, and Pierre Boudot, among others. My reasons for not discussing their work, much of which I have profited from, is that many of the issues of interest within Nietzsche *commentary* are not particularly relevant to the questions that this book seeks to address, namely questions as to how Nietzsche's ideas have been appropriated and incorporated into the ongoing projects of poststructuralism. For the same reasons, the works specifically *on* Nietzsche by the writers I do discuss (for example, Derrida's *Spurs: Nietzsche's Styles* or Deleuze's *Nietzsche and Philosophy*) are not the focus of my discussions of their work.

But there is a second group of writers who are, for the most part, overlooked in the following pages and whose absence is more problematic. I am thinking here of three in particular: Georges Bataille, Maurice Blanchot, and Luce Irigaray. For in a sense, a full treatment of Nietzsche's French legacy should include a chapter on each of these thinkers in that each is, in their own right, an innovative theorist whose work at a profound level is informed by and incorporates significant Nietzschean themes and, moreover, whose work is important enough in my opinion to warrant consideration on a par with the thinkers whom I have chosen to examine in the following chapters. My reason for excluding them, I must confess, has less to do with philosophical issues than it does with human finitude, specifically, my own: I simply do not have the broad understanding of the philosophical projects of Bataille, Blanchot, or Irigaray that I believe I have in the cases of those thinkers included here. And rather than reducing their thinking to instances of "applied Nietzscheanism," which is an injustice that my limited perspective on their projects would have forced me to commit, I have chosen instead to restrict my comments to a few passing references in the hopes that others more familiar with the works of Bataille, Blanchot, or Irigaray might be provoked to pursue these thinkers on their own as part of Nietzsche's French legacy.

In a work that evolves for as long a time as this one has, it bears the imprint of suggestions, questions, criticisms, and reflections from many people. I would like to acknowledge, in particular, two readers of the entire manuscript, Jeffrey

A. Nealon and Daniel W. Conway, whose generous gift of their time and whose thoughtful suggestions and prodding questions have made this a better work than it would otherwise have been. Many other colleagues and friends have read and commented on parts of these chapters as they developed and I would like to acknowledge and thank for their time and their comments Debra Bergoffen, Aletta Biersack, W. Joseph Cummins, Caroline Gebhard, Kathleen Higgins, David F. Krell, Bernd Magnus, Johanna Meehan, Kelly Oliver, Gayle L. Ormiston, David Owen, Richard Schacht, Jill Schrift, Peter Sedgwick, Gary Shapiro, Paula Smith, Marcia Stephenson, Maura Strassberg, and Rudi Visker. In addition, many selections from these chapters have been presented in various forums, and I thank for their attention and comments the Program Committees and members of the Nietzsche Society, the North American Nietzsche Society, and the Friedrich Nietzsche Society (UK), the Society for Phenomenology and Existential Philosophy, the International Association for Philosophy and Literature, and the faculty and students of philosophy at Queen's University at Kingston, Ontario; University of Wales, Cardiff, Wales; Institute of Philosophy, Katholieke Universiteit, Leuven, Belgium; Collegium Phaenomenologicum, Perugia, Italy; University of Warwick, England; and Grinnell College, Grinnell, Iowa. Thanks are also due to my editor at Routledge, Maureen MacGrogan for her continued support of my work, to the editorial and production staff, including Alison Shonkwiler, Jeff Hoffman, and Adam Bohannon, and to my assistants at Grinnell: Gabriel Rockhill, Scott Samuelson, Sarah Wohlford, Tanya Hedges, and Ann Musser.

I would also like to acknowledge here the financial support provided by several institutions and individuals that permitted me to complete the research for this work: the Trustees of Grinnell College, in particular Trustees Jack and Lucile Harris, sponsors of the Harris Faculty Fellowship, and Trustee Alf Johnsen, sponsor of the Grinnell Western European Studies Faculty Travel Grant; the Grinnell College Grant Board chaired by Dean Charles Duke; the National Endowment for the Humanities Summer Seminars for College Teachers; the Oregon Humanities Center, University of Oregon at Eugene, directed at the time by John Stuhr; and the Institute of Philosophy, Katholieke Universiteit, Leuven, Belgium, presided over by Carlos Steel.

I would like especially to acknowledge the encouragement and love of my parents Joan and Leonard Schrift and my family. And, finally, I would like to thank Jill, whose unwavering support and encouragement made this book possible and to whom it is dedicated.

Parts of this book have appeared in earlier versions in several articles and essays. Sections from "Reading, Writing, Text: Nietzsche's Deconstruction of Author–ity," Vol. 17, No. 2 (1985): 55–64; "Between Church and State: Nietzsche, Deleuze and the Critique of Psychoanalysis," Vol. 24, No. 2 (Summer 1992): 41–52; and "On the Gift-Giving Virtue: Nietzsche's Feminine Economy," Vol. 26, No. 2 (Summer 1994): 33–44, are reprinted with the permission of *International Studies in Philosophy*. Parts of "Genealogy and/as Deconstruction: Nietzsche, Derrida, and Foucault on Philosophy as Critique," in *Postmodernism and Continental Philosophy*, edited by Hugh Silverman and Donn Welton, Albany, 1988, pp. 193–213; and "The Becoming-Post-Modern of Philosophy," in *After the Future: Postmodern Times and Places*, edited by Gary Shapiro, Albany, 1990, pp. 99–113, are reprinted with the permission of the State University of New York Press. Sections from "Foucault and Derrida on Nietzsche and the 'end(s)' of 'man,'" in *Exceedingly Nietzsche: Aspects of Contemporary Nietzsche-Interpretation,* edited by David Farrell Krell and David Wood, London, 1988, pp. 131–49, are reprinted with the permission of Routledge and Kegan Paul. Sections from "Nietzsche and the Critique of Oppositional Thinking," *History of European Ideas*, Vol. 11 (1989): 783–90, are reprinted with kind permission from Elsevier Science Ltd., The Boulevard, Langford Lane, Kidlington OX5 1GB. Sections from "On the Gynecology of Morals: Nietzsche and Cixous on the Logic of the Gift," in *Nietzsche and the Feminine,* edited by Peter J. Burgard, Charlottesville, 1994, pp. 210–29, are reprinted with the permission of the University Press of Virginia. Sections from "Reconfiguring the Subject: Foucault's Analytics of Power," in *Reconstructing Foucault: Essays in the Wake of the 80s,* edited by Ricardo Miguel-Alfonso and Silvia Caporale-Bizzini, Amsterdam, Holland, 1995, pp. 185–99, are reprinted with the permission of Rodopi Press. Sections from "Nietzsche's French Legacy," in *Cambridge Companions to Philosophy: Friedrich Nietzsche*, edited by Bernd Magnus and Kathleen Higgins, are reprinted with the permission of Cambridge University Press. Sections from "Putting Nietzsche to Work: The Case of Gilles Deleuze," in *Nietzsche: A Critical Reader,* edited by Peter Sedgwick, are reprinted with the permission of Basil Blackwell Publishers. I thank the editors and publishers of these works for their kind permission to republish these sections.

Introduction

➤

What charity and delicate precision those Frenchmen possess! Even the most acute-eared of the Greeks must have approved of this art, and one thing they would even have admired and adored, the French *wittiness* of expression.

—NIETZSCHE, *The Wanderer and His Shadow*

The moment Germany rises as a great power, France gains a new importance as a *cultural power*. A great deal of current spiritual seriousness and *passion* has already emigrated to Paris; the question of pessimism, for instance, the Wagner question, virtually every psychological and artistic question, is speculated on with incomparably more subtlety and thoroughness there than in Germany.

—NIETZSCHE, *Twilight of the Idols*

In relation to academic philosophical discourse, which has constantly referred him back to himself, Nietzsche represents the outer frontier. Of course, a whole line of Western philosophy may be found in Nietzsche. Plato, Spinoza, the eighteenth-century philosophers, Hegel ... all this goes through Nietzsche. And yet, in relation to philosophy, Nietzsche has all the roughness, the rusticity, of the outsider, of the peasant from the mountains, that allows him, with a shrug of the shoulders and without seeming in any way ridiculous, to say with a strength that one cannot ignore: "Come on, all that is rubbish."

—FOUCAULT, "The Functions of Literature"

IN HIS INTRODUCTION TO HENRI LICHTENBERGER'S *THE GOSPEL OF Superman: The Philosophy of Friedrich Nietzsche*—the first work on Nietzsche to be translated from French into English—J. M. Kennedy commented that "there seems to be something in the French character and the French language which, while allowing for the clear exposition of original thought, allows likewise for the no less clear interpretation of ideas which have at first been presented to the world through the medium of a more obscure or less pliable tongue."[1] It is difficult to imagine many readers of recent French philosophy or French scholarship on Nietzsche agreeing with Kennedy's assertion. In fact, the opposite sentiments are more often expressed in the English-speaking philosophical community, namely that the French are unnecessarily obscure and that their works—both primary and secondary—border on the unreadable.[2]

In the chapters that follow, I would like to challenge this view, and I would like to do so precisely in terms of the diverse links that can be made between the works of several recent French thinkers and the works of Nietzsche. Nietzsche often noted the posthumous character of his work, predicting that a century hence, he would find his rightful heirs, the "philosophers of the future" to whom his works were addressed. That Nietzsche would find his rightful heirs among the French, with whose culture and language he felt a special kinship, would neither have surprised nor displeased him.[3] Nietzsche often remarked that he felt more at home with the French than with Germans.[4] More than once, he regretted having to write in German rather than in a more fluid, playful, musical language like French.[5] And more than once, he felt his spiritual kin to reside west of the Rhine, preferring the philosophical companionship of Montaigne, Voltaire, and La Rochefoucauld to that of Leibniz, Kant, or Hegel.

Whatever the reasons for Nietzsche's fond feelings for the French, there can be little doubt that for most of the past three decades, Nietzsche's texts have been received more enthusiastically in Parisian intellectual circles than anywhere else.[6] Numerous commentators on and critics of recent French philosophy have noted this fact and, more than any other figure, Nietzsche is cited as the philosopher who anticipates and previews the philosophical themes that have dominated contemporary French thought.[7] Some of Nietzsche's French readers came to his texts directly; others came through Heidegger, and still others through Bataille. All were profoundly influenced by Deleuze's groundbreaking 1962 study *Nietzsche et la philosophie*.[8] And as is the case with his German and English interpreters, the diversity of interpretations among his French readers is extreme.

This fact is sometimes lost in the often contentious discussions of the "French Nietzsche" and, more generally, of the work of the poststructuralists. Among the French Nietzscheans—for example, among those who attended the Royaumont (1964) and Cerisy (1972) conferences—one can locate readings of Nietzsche that are Heideggerian, deconstructive, hermeneutical, rhetorical, historical, philological, genealogical, materialist, psychoanalytic, etc.[9] And writers addressing related issues—for example, Sarah Kofman and Jean Granier on the question of perspectivism and interpretation, or Jacques Derrida and Eric Blondel on the role of metaphor—often adopt very different approaches to reading Nietzsche, which result in very different conclusions. In his preface to the volume that first presented the "new Nietzsche" to an English-speaking audience, David B. Allison noted the absence of "any particular orthodoxy" in the selections he had collected.[10] As the following chapters demonstrate, this observation of the absence of any "orthodoxy" or "united front" should be extended to the writers discussed in the present work. Having said this, however, one should be careful not to allow this diversity of interpretive perspective to obscure the fact that one of the most basic themes shared within recent French thought is precisely the appeal to "Nietzsche." Indeed, I would go so far as to say that if one wishes to distinguish what—in the English-speaking world—is called "poststructuralism" from its structural and existential predecessors, perhaps the most obvious way to do so is precisely in terms of the appearance of Nietzsche as an important reference for virtually all those writers who would be characterized as "poststructuralist."[11]

A very brief historical sketch of the past half-century of French philosophy will make this clear. The first important twentieth-century philosophical development in France, existentialism, is associated most closely with the works of Jean-Paul Sartre and Maurice Merleau-Ponty. Drawing their inspiration initially from Husserl and Heidegger, and later from Marx, existentialism in its phenomenological or Marxist forms dominated the French philosophical scene during the 1940s and 1950s. While Nietzsche was, of course, "in the air" during this time, the effect that his thought had on the literary and cultural avant garde (for example, his effect on people like Bataille, Klossowski, Camus, Malraux, Blanchot, etc.) far exceeded his direct impact on French philosophical discourse in the years between the wars and the immediate post-war years. During this period, his place as a "philosopher" was decidedly subordinate to that of the "three H's": Hegel, Husserl, Heidegger.

Inspired by Ferdinand de Saussure's work in linguistics, poststructuralism's immediate predecessor, structuralism, emerged in the late 1950s and came into prominence in French circles in the early 1960s. United by a profound distrust of phenomenology and its privileging of subjectivity, structuralists like Claude Lévi-Strauss, Jacques Lacan, and Louis Althusser drew on the methodology of Saussurean linguistics and applied it to their respective investigations of the "human sciences" of anthropology, psychoanalysis, and political economy. While this is not the place to examine in any detail structuralism's critique of existentialism, two features of the structuralist challenge are relevant to the present discussion. First, where the existentialists emphasized human historicity (Merleau-Ponty's notion of existential phenomenology as a descent of the transcendental into history) and the futural character of human being (Sartre's self as "project"), the structuralists clearly privileged the synchronic analysis of isolated moments in the diachronic evolution of structural systems. And second, where the existentialists privileged consciousness in their analyses of the data of human existence, the structuralists rejected any notion of an autonomous consciousness, focusing their analyses instead on the dissolution of the subject as a moment in the structural functioning of social, cultural, and material systems.

The structuralist rediscovery of Freud and Marx along with Heidegger's retrieval of Nietzsche,[12] set the stage for the emergence of poststructuralism as a distinctly *philosophical* response to the privileging of the human sciences that characterized the work of the structuralists. Pierre Bourdieu addresses this point in the preface to the English translation of his *Homo Academicus*.[13] He notes that the influence of philosophy had declined steadily within French academic institutions in the wake of the structuralists focusing their critical attention on the discursive and analytic practices of the human sciences. Bourdieu then suggests—in reference specifically to Foucault, but the observation holds for Derrida and Deleuze as well—that Nietzsche's appeal to the new generation of philosophically oriented intellectuals lay to a large extent in Nietzsche's having been overlooked by the more "traditional" philosophers who comprised the philosophical establishment in France.

While Bourdieu's observation of the poststructuralists' desire to keep their distance from "the philosophical high priests of the Sorbonne"[14] is important in the context of the present study of Nietzsche, it has a more general significance that has not been sufficiently recognized. That is to say, while there are many different accounts of the relation between structuralism and poststructuralism, what is not often acknowledged is that for all the poststructuralist rhetoric concerning the "end of philosophy," one of the most obvious differences between the discourses of structuralism and poststructuralism is the degree to which the latter's discourse *remains philo-*

sophical. And it seems to me that the role Nietzsche plays in this renewal of philosophical discourse is not insignificant.

As Bourdieu remarks, it was precisely Nietzsche's "marginal" status as a philosopher that made him "an acceptable philosophical sponsor" at a time—the late 1950s and early 1960s—when it was not in fashion in France to be a "philosopher."[15] In fact, both Deleuze and Foucault acknowledge the emancipatory role Nietzsche played at the time. In a 1983 interview, for example, Foucault commented that

> The actual history of Nietzsche's thought interests me less than the kind of challenge I felt one day, a long time ago, reading Nietzsche for the first time. When you open *The Gay Science* after you have been trained in the great, time-honored university traditions—Descartes, Kant, Hegel, Husserl—and you come across these rather strange, witty, graceful texts, you say: Well I won't do what my contemporaries, colleagues or professors are doing; I won't just dismiss this. What is the maximum of philosophical intensity and what are the current philosophical effects to be found in these texts? That, for me, was the challenge of Nietzsche.[16]

Unlike the rigid, scientist, and constraining systems of structuralism, Nietzsche appeared to his new readers to be both philosophically inspired and philosophically inspiring.

Moreover, by addressing questions concerning human existence without centering his reflection on human consciousness, Nietzsche indicated how one might respond to structuralism's sloganistic "death of the subject" by showing a way to raise anew questions of individual agency without succumbing to an existentialist voluntarism or subjectivism. At the same time, the poststructuralists saw in the notion of eternal recurrence[17] a way to again entertain questions of history and historicity, questions that had been devalued within the structuralists' ahistorical emphasis on synchronic structural analyses.[18] In this way, I would like to suggest that Nietzsche's emergence as a philosophical voice played an unparalleled role in the development of poststructuralism as a historical corrective to the excesses of both its predecessor movements. That is to say, where the structuralist's responded to existentialism's privileging of consciousness and history by eliminating them both, the poststructuralists took from structuralism insights concerning the workings of linguistic and systemic forces and returned with these insights to reinvoke the question of the subject in terms of a notion of constituted-constitutive-constituting agency situated and operating within a complex network of socio-historical and intersubjective relations.

Examining the various appearances of Nietzsche within poststructuralist French thought reveals two sorts of projects. In the first, we can situate those works in which Nietzsche's texts, and his philosophy in general, appear as the "object" of interpretation. These works reflect contemporary philosophical approaches in various degrees and primarily take traditional scholarly forms—historical, critical and/or thematic monographs, collections of essays, etc.—that put forward interpretations of Nietzsche's philosophy, often focusing on the major Nietzschean themes of eternal recurrence, will to power, nihilism, *Übermensch,* and so on.[19]

In the second group, we can locate those writers who make "use" of "Nietzsche" as they develop their own philosophical positions. In the works of these writers, Nietzsche appears as a reference point, someone whose works or ideas have inspired his descendents to develop them into forms that are useful for their own philosophical-critical ends. The goal of this second group of writers is not to offer "interpretations" of Nietzsche's philosophy, although that may in fact result from their productions. Instead, they use those Nietzschean motifs they find advantageous in the development of their own critical projects.[20]

In the following chapters, we examine some of these productions, showing how Nietzsche's legacy has been played out in several of the most important and influential figures to emerge in recent French philosophy. At the same time, we offer a genealogy of poststructuralism that traces its Nietzschean affiliations. I say *a* genealogy of poststructuralism, not *the* genealogy of poststructuralism, because genealogies, like styles, are always multiple. That is to say, one could write a similar book about the thinkers discussed here in terms of a Freudian heritage, a Heideggerian heritage, a May '68 heritage, etc. For the point is that what is called "poststructuralism" is not a monolithic theory with a rigid and uniform set of shared assumptions or axioms. It is instead a loose association of thinkers whose works draw from several shared sources, one of the most significant of which, I will demonstrate, is Nietzsche. Nietzsche's critique of truth, his emphasis on interpretation and the differential relations of power and knowledge, and his attention to questions of style in philosophical discourse have become central motifs within the works of the poststructuralists, who have developed these Nietzschean themes in a number of ways: by attending to questions of language, power, and desire in ways that emphasize the context in which meaning is produced while making problematic all universal truth and meaning claims; by challenging the assumptions that give rise to binary, oppositional thinking, often opting to affirm that which occupies a position of subordination within a differential network; by questioning the figure of the humanistic human subject, challenging the assumptions of autonomy and transparent self-consciousness while situating the subject as a complex intersection of discursive, libidinal, and social forces and practices; by resisting the impulse toward claims of universality and unity, preferring instead to acknowledge difference and fragmentation.

By examining these themes in the philosophical and critical projects of several of the leading voices of poststructuralism, the following chapters both clarify the views of the poststructuralists and demonstrate the degree to which they belong within a Nietzschean legacy. A century earlier, Nietzsche remarked that he found the most recent Frenchmen "charming company," noting that it would be hard to find anywhere in past history "such inquisitive and at the same time such delicate psychologists as in contemporary Paris" (*EH*, II, 3). More significantly, perhaps, he included the French among his most "natural readers and listeners" (*EH*, III, CW3).[21] Nietzsche reflected a great deal on what it meant to be a good reader, and he both took pride in and despaired of the fact that his works were able to find so few good readers. "We honour the great artists of the past," he wrote in *Assorted Opinions and Maxims*, "less through that unfruitful awe which allows every word, every note, to lie where it has been put than we do through active endeavours to help them to come repeatedly to life again" (*AOM*, 126). There can be little doubt that the efforts of those thinkers I discuss as "Nietzsche's French legacy" have been successful in bringing Nietzsche's words "repeatedly to life again" and to their collective efforts is due the credit of bringing Nietzsche to the center of contemporary intellectual reflection. It is in this sense that I argue that they deserve to take their places among the philosophers of the future to whom Nietzsche addressed his writings, philosophers who, appropriating Nietzsche's description of an earlier generation of French philosophers with whom he felt a special kinship, create "*real ideas... ideas of the kind that produce ideas*" (*WS*, 214).

Derrida:
The Critique of Oppositional Thinking
and the Transvaluation of Values

➤

This is not the censorship but the *criticism* of reason, whereby not its present *bounds* but its determinate [and necessary] *limits*, not its ignorance on this or that point but its ignorance in regard to all possible questions of a certain kind, are demonstrated from principles, and not merely arrived at by way of conjecture.

—KANT, *Critique of Pure Reason*

[O]ppositional thinking... is out of step with the most vital modes of post-modern knowledge.

—LYOTARD, *The Postmodern Condition*

THERE CAN BE NO QUESTION THAT FRIEDRICH NIETZSCHE STANDS AS ONE OF THE central figures to whom Jacques Derrida traces his own intellectual genealogy. Throughout his career, Nietzsche appears at crucial points in the development of Derrida's thought and, among the themes which Derrida credits Nietzsche for having first addressed, one finds "the systematic mistrust as concerns the entirety of metaphysics, the formal vision of philosophical discourse, the concept of the philosopher-artist, the rhetorical and philological questions put to the history of philosophy, the suspiciousness concerning the values of truth ('a well applied convention'), of meaning and of Being, of the 'meaning of Being,' the attention to the economic phenomena of force and of the difference of forces, etc."[1]

In his earlier works, particularly up to and including *La carte postale* (1980), Derrida appeals regularly to Nietzsche in his own attempt to deconstruct the logocentric tendencies of metaphysical thinking. More specifically, Nietzsche often appears in the Derridean text as an alternative to the nostalgic longing for full presence that Derrida locates at the core of Western metaphysics.[2] In fact, "Nietzsche" comes to serve a talismanic function as a proper name for the very possibility of thinking otherwise, a shorthand marker for the *other* of logocentrism.[3] The most famous example here is, of course, the concluding paragraphs of "Structure, Sign, and Play in the Discourse of the Human Sciences," where "Nietzsche" appears as the name of that *other* interpretation of interpretation, of structure, of sign, of play that, unlike the interpretations of logocentrism, is able to affirm the play of interpretation in a way that "*determines the noncenter otherwise than as loss of the center.*"[4] But as we will see, this is by no means the only example.

Otherwise than Being, or Nietzsche contra Heidegger

In *Spurs: Nietzsche's Styles*, as I have argued elsewhere, Derrida again offers Nietzsche as an example of thinking otherwise, this time with respect to the nostalgic tendencies he locates in Heidegger's thinking.[5] While his next text "on" Nietzsche—*Otobiographies: The Teaching of Nietzsche and the Politics of the Proper Name*[6] —takes the problematic of the name itself as its central focus, Derrida returns to the Heideggerian landscape in a subsequent Nietzschean text— "Interpreting Signatures (Nietzsche/Heidegger): Two Questions"[7] —in which he addresses the question of the unity of the proper name as this question is prompted by the opening of Heidegger's preface to his two-volume *Nietzsche*: "'*Nietzsche'—der Name des Denkers steht als Titel für* die Sache *seines Denkens* ['Nietzsche'—the name of the thinker stands as the title for *the matter* of his thinking]."[8] According to Derrida, the placing of Nietzsche's name between quotation marks signals Heidegger's metaphysical "desire" to impose a unitary interpretation on that "totality" he calls "the history of metaphysics." In response to Heidegger's "interpretive decision" to impose the unity of the proper name "Nietzsche" on a writing machine that remains multiple, Derrida replies:

> who ever has said that a person bears a single name? Certainly not Nietzsche. And likewise, who has said or decided that there is something like a Western metaphysics, something which would be capable of being gathered up under this name and this name only? What is it—the oneness of a name, the assem-

bled unity of Western metaphysics? Is it anything more or less than the desire (a word effaced in Heidegger's Nietzsche citation) for a proper name, for a single, unique name and a thinkable genealogy? Next to Kierkegaard, was not Nietzsche one of the few great thinkers who multiplied his names and played with signatures, identities, and masks? Who named himself more than once, with several names? And what if that would be the heart of the matter, the *causa*, the *Streitfall* [point of dispute] of his thinking?[9]

It has been a common gesture in France to appeal to Nietzsche when distancing oneself from the Heideggerian project of recuperating Being from its metaphysical oblivion. And Derrida, perhaps more than anyone else, chose Nietzsche's texts as a site on which to confront Heidegger's thinking. This confrontation was not restricted to the politics or metaphysics of signatures and proper names, however. Nor was it restricted to his few brief texts "on" Nietzsche. In fact, the central position Nietzsche was to occupy in Derrida's *Aus-einander-setzung* with Heidegger and the history of philosophy in general was made clear as early as *Of Grammatology*, as we see in the following remark whose importance warrants a lengthy citation:

Radicalizing the concepts of *interpretation, perspective, evaluation, difference,* and all the "empiricist" or nonphilosophical motifs that have constantly tormented philosophy throughout the history of the West, and besides have had nothing but the inevitable weakness of being produced in the field of philosophy, Nietzsche, far from remaining *simply* (with Hegel and as Heidegger wished) *within* metaphysics, contributed a great deal to the liberation of the signifier from its dependence or derivation with respect to the logos and the related concept of truth or the primary signified, in whatever sense that is understood. Reading, and therefore writing, the text were for Nietzsche "originary" operations... with regard to a sense that they do not first have to transcribe or discover, which would not therefore be a truth signified in the original element and presence of the logos, as *topos noetos*, divine understanding, or the structure of a priori necessity. To save Nietzsche from a reading of the Heideggerian type, it seems that we must above all not attempt to restore or make explicit a less naive "ontology," composed of profound ontological intuitions acceding to some originary truth, an entire fundamentality hidden under the appearance of an empiricist or metaphysical text. The virulence of Nietzschean thought could not be more completely misunderstood. On the contrary, one must *accentuate* the "naiveté" of a breakthrough which cannot attempt a step outside of metaphysics, which cannot *criticize* meta-physics radically without still utilizing in a certain way, in a certain type or a cer-tain style of *text*, propositions that, read within the philosophic corpus, this is to say according to Nietzsche ill-read or unread, have always and will always be "naivetés," incoherent signs of an absolute appurtenance. Therefore, rather than protect Nietzsche from the Heideggerian reading, we should perhaps offer him up to it completely, underwriting that interpretation without reserve; in a *certain way* and up to the point where, the content of the Nietzschean discourse being almost lost for the question of being, its form regains its absolute strangeness, where his text finally invokes a different type of reading, more faithful to his type of writing: Nietzsche has *written what* he has written. He has written that writing—and first of all his own—is not originally subordinate to the logos and to truth. And that this subordination has *come into being* during an epoch whose meaning we must deconstruct. Now in this direction (but only in this direction, for read otherwise, the Nietzschean demolition remains dogmatic and, like all reversals, a captive of that metaphysical edifice which it professes to overthrow. On that point and in that *order of reading*, the conclusions of Heidegger and Fink are irrefutable), Heideggerian thought would reinstate rather than destroy the instance of the logos and of the truth of being as "primum signatum."[10]

In this passage, we see the complexity of Derrida's position vis-à-vis both Nietzsche and Heidegger. While the historical moment in which Heidegger's interpretation appeared can explain his intention to save Nietzsche from a biologistic, vitalist, or racist reading that remains focused on the theme of life, Derrida notes elsewhere that Heidegger can save Nietzsche from the Nazis only by losing him to the history of meta-physics.[11]

For his part, Derrida confesses to having no interest in "saving" Nietzsche from his fate in the hands of Heidegger. Nevertheless, he wants to show how Nietzsche's text exceeds the Heideggerian reading of it. In a recent interview, he has made the point explicitly:

It is important in this context to take Heidegger's Nietzsche and show that there are *other* possibilities in Nietzsche which are not programmed by a his-tory of metaphysics, that there are moves which are stronger, which go further than what Heidegger calls the history of the completion of metaphysics; moves which actually put in question Heidegger himself: his reading of

Nietzsche in particular and his philosophical orientation in general. Briefly, there exists a reserve in Nietzsche which allows one to read Heidegger's own thought genealogically.[12]

As the passage cited earlier from *Of Grammatology* indicates, Derrida locates this reserve in Nietzsche's affirmation of "*interpretation, perspective, evaluation, difference*," for it is this affirmation that exceeds a metaphysical determination governed by the logos or truth and, in so doing, exceeds the Heideggerian reading. "There is, for Nietzsche, no entity which is not interpretable as both an active and a reactive form of life. It is this which distinguishes Nietzsche from Heidegger: everything is, for Nietzsche, interpretation."[13]

But from remarks such as these, it would be wrong to conclude, as did Hans-Georg Gadamer, for example, in his ill-fated "dialogue" with Derrida in Paris at their 1981 Goethe Institute meeting, that Derrida had *simply* chosen Nietzsche over Heidegger. Gadamer's treatment of the Nietzsche-Heidegger-Derrida relationship is instructive, for it exemplifies a common misperception of Derrida's position. In their encounter, Gadamer remarked that

> Derrida has argued against the later Heidegger that Heidegger himself has not really broken through the logocentrism of metaphysics. Derrida's contention is that insofar as Heidegger asks about the essence of truth or the meaning of Being, he still speaks the language of metaphysics that looks upon meaning as something out there that is to be discovered [*vorhandenen und aufzufindenen*]. This being so, Nietzsche is said to be more radical.[14]

In response to Derrida's apparent conclusion in favor of Nietzsche's "radicality," Gadamer replies that he finds that the "French followers of Nietzsche have not grasped the significance of the seductive and tempting challenge of Nietzsche's thought. Only in this way, [he continues,] could they come to believe that the experience of Being that Heidegger tried to uncover behind metaphysics is exceeded in radicality by Nietzsche's extremism."[15] In other words, the only way the French could have concluded that Nietzsche is more radical than Heidegger would be if they misunderstood one or both of these thinkers. The question of Nietzsche's radicality is thus, for Gadamer, not an open one. There is a correct answer, and the French, Derrida included, do not have it.

While Gadamer is willing to acknowledge a "deep ambiguity" in Heidegger's "image of Nietzsche," he fails here to acknowledge an equally deep ambiguity in Derrida's relationships to Heidegger and Nietzsche. On several different occasions, Derrida has said that there can be no simple choice between Heidegger and Nietzsche. The undecidability of this choice is one of the threads woven throughout *Spurs*, Derrida's most explicit *Aus-einander-setzung* with Nietzsche/Heidegger. It appears in other Derridean texts as well. Consider the following remark from "Structure, Sign, and Play in the Discourse of the Human Sciences:"

> Nietzsche, Freud, and Heidegger, for example, worked within the inherited concepts of metaphysics. Since these concepts are not elements or atoms, and since they are taken from a syntax and a system, every particular borrowing brings along with it the whole of metaphysics. This is what allows these destroyers to destroy each other reciprocally—for example, Heidegger regarding Nietzsche, with as much lucidity and rigor as bad faith and misconstruction, as the last metaphysician, the last "Platonist." One could do the same for Heidegger himself, for Freud, or for a number of others. And today no exercise is more widespread.[16]

It would appear that Gadamer came to Paris with the intention of engaging in just this sort of exercise.[17] But this is not the point I want to emphasize. Instead, I want to draw attention to Gadamer's failure to acknowledge that while Derrida does at times affirm that Nietzsche exceeds Heidegger in "radicality," there are other occasions where Derrida credits Heidegger with being the "more radical." In fact, we find an example of his privileging Heidegger shortly before the passage just cited from "Structure, Sign, and Play." There, in the context of discussing Nietzsche, Freud, and Heidegger as exemplars of decentering or "thinking the structurality of structure," Derrida follows brief references to Nietzsche's critique of metaphysics and Freud's critique of consciousness as self-presence by noting that we find the discourse of decentering structure "more radically [in] the Heideggerian destruction of metaphysics, of onto-theology, of the determination of Being as presence."[18]

Nevertheless, it certainly warrants noticing, again as did Gadamer at the Paris meeting, that on occasions like those cited above, Derrida does argue that Nietzsche's texts exceed Heidegger's in radicality. And on those occasions, both with respect to Heidegger and in the broader context of his deconstructive reading of the history of philosophy in general, Derrida draws upon what he calls, in *Of Grammatology*, "the axial intention of [Nietzsche's] concept of interpretation": the emancipation of interpretation from the constraints of a truth "which always implies the *presence* of the signified (*aletheia* or *adequatio*)."[19] Freeing interpretation from the constraints of a truth, freeing thought from the constraints of the logos, was an essential part of the Nietzschean project and, contrary to Heidegger's totalizing interpretation of the history of metaphysics, Derrida concludes that Nietzsche's "active forgetting of Being... would not have the metaphysical form imputed to it by Heidegger."[20]

The Critique of Philosophical Binarism

Derrida of course draws upon Nietzsche in many contexts other than his confrontation with Heidegger. Moreover, his attraction to Nietzsche depends upon more than just a vague affiliation between certain Derridean and Nietzschean themes. As I will show, there is a profound methodological affinity between Derrida and Nietzsche in terms of a rejection of the binary logic that they both view as a mainstay of the philosophical tradition. The "typical prejudice" and "fundamental faith" of all metaphysicians, Nietzsche wrote in *Beyond Good and Evil*, "is *the faith in opposite values*" (*BGE*, 2). Throughout his critique of morality, philosophy, and religion, Nietzsche attempted to dismantle such oppositional hierarchies as good/evil, truth/error, being/becoming. This refusal to sanction the hierarchical relations among those privileged conceptual oppositions transmitted within the Western metaphysical tradition pervades the contemporary French philosophical scene, and it is one of the primary points of convergence between Nietzsche and contemporary French philosophical thought in general. This critique of binary, oppositional thinking is, of course, most closely identified with Derrida's critical project, and it is on this issue, so central to the critical method that has come to be called "deconstruction," that we can locate most clearly Derrida's intellectual debt to Nietzsche.

For Derrida, the history of philosophy unfolds as a history of certain classical philosophical oppositions: intelligible/sensible, truth/error, speech/writing, literal/figurative, presence/absence, etc. These oppositional concepts do not coexist on equal grounds, however; rather, one side of each binary opposition has been privileged while the other side has been devalued. Within these oppositions, a hierarchical "order of subordination"[21] has been established and truth has come to be valued over error, presence has come to be valued over absence, and so on.

In his early works, Derrida takes as his task the dismantling or deconstruction of these binary oppositions.[22] In *Positions*, he discloses his critical strategy:

I try to keep myself at the *limit* of philosophical discourse... the limit on the basis of which philosophy became possible, defined itself as the *episteme*, functioning within a system of fundamental constraints, conceptual oppositions outside of which philosophy becomes impracticable.... To "deconstruct" philosophy, thus, would be to think—in the most faithful, interior way—the structured genealogy of philosophy's concepts, but at the same time to determine—from a certain exterior that is unqualifiable or unnameable by philosophy—what this history has been able to dissimulate or forbid, making itself into a history by means of this somewhere motivated repression.[23]

Philosophy, in other words, has organized itself as a discipline around the institutionalized practices of oppositional thinking. Plato's metaphor of the "Divided Line" is in more ways than one the defining gesture of philosophical thinking: not only did it set up two oppositional pairs (Being-becoming [or intelligible-visible] and knowledge-opinion) as the privileged concepts that established the framework for all subsequent metaphysical and epistemological discourse respectively, but the metaphor itself codified the disjunctive, oppositional framework already in wide circulation among the Presocratics as the defining gesture of philosophy itself. To deconstruct philosophy is, therefore, to trace precisely the evolution of these hierarchical oppositions *as* the "history of philosophy" and, at the same time, to locate alternatives for philosophical thinking and discourse that the institutionalization of oppositional thought has refused to allow.

The critical practice of deconstructing these oppositions involves a biphasic movement that Derrida has called "double writing" or "double science." In the first phase, he overturns the hierarchy and argues for the value of those poles traditionally subordinated within the history of philosophy. Derrida is often read simply as privileging, for example, writing over speech, absence over presence, or the figurative over the literal. But such a reading is overly simplistic; like Heidegger before him,[24] Derrida realizes that in overturning a metaphysical hierarchy, one must avoid reappropriating the hierarchical structure. It is the hierarchical oppositional structure itself that is metaphysical, and to remain within the binary logic of metaphysical thinking reestablishes and confirms the closed field of these oppositions.[25]

To view deconstruction as a simple inversion of these classical philosophical oppositions ignores the second phase of deconstruction's "double writing": "we must also mark the interval between inversion, which brings low what was high, and the irruptive emergence of a new 'concept,' a concept that can no longer be, and never could be, included in the previous regime."[26] These new "concepts" are the Derridean "undecidables" (e.g., "*différance*," "trace," "*supplément*," "*pharmakon*," "hymen," "spacing"): marks that in one way or another resist the formal structure imposed by the binary logic of philosophical opposition while exposing the optional character of those choices that the tradition has privileged as dominant. Throughout Derrida's early work, we find as a recurrent motif his charting the play of these undecidables: the play of the trace, which is both present and absent; the play of the *pharmakon*, which is both poison and cure; the play of the *supplément*, which is both surplus and lack.

When marking the interval between philosophy's classical hierarchical oppositions and the undecidables, Derrida marks the limits of the binary logic that has guided the history of metaphysics. In so doing, he displays another sort of logic that he calls the "logic of supplementarity."[27] This "other" logic has been repressed and excluded by the history of philosophy. Whereas binary logic operates within the limits of a disjunctive "either... or..." Derrida's undecidable logic of supplementarity is a conjunctive logic of "both... and..." that resists and disorganizes classical binary thinking. The fundamental laws of binary logic are the principles of identity (A=A) and non-contradiction (not [A and not-A]). The movement of the undecidables exhibits a different principle: *both* A *and* not-A. The *pharmakon*, for example, "acts as both remedy and poison... [it] can be—alternatively or simultaneously—beneficent or maleficent."[28] "*Pharmakon*" plays between the poles of remedy and poison, and to render *pharmakon* as either "remedy" or "poison," as the binary thinking of the history of metaphysics is prone to do, cancels out the resources of signification reserved in that sign.

Thus, when Socrates drinks the *pharmakon* at the conclusion of the *Phaedo* (115d–117c), the metaphysical tradition is quick to interpret this *pharmakon* as a "poison." In so doing, the tradition must suppress Socrates's final speech in the *Apology* (40c–41d), where he claims we have reason to hope that death is a good that a virtuous man need not fear, while it forces us to regard as *ironic* his last words, concerning the debt his death will incur with Asclepius (*Phaedo* 118a). This overdetermination of the meaning of *pharmakon* (=poison) is, for Derrida, exemplary, and his focus on the movement of the *pharmakon* exposes the limits of metaphysical thinking:

because *pharmakon* is *both* remedy *and* poison, both a remedial poison and a poisonous remedy, its movement cannot be thought in the binary fashion that characterizes the metaphysical tradition. Derrida refuses to determine a univocal meaning for the *pharmakon* or the other undecidables; instead he emphasizes the tension and oscillating play that guides their use. His point, it must be stressed, is not to reify these terms nor to privilege them as foundational. Rather, he marks these terms in a way that inscribes his writing in the tradition of critical philosophy called for by Kant, emphasizing the "determinate [and necessary] *limits*" of this binary logic while indicating "its ignorance in regard to all possible questions of a certain kind."[29]

Whether or not Derrida should be viewed as a transcendental thinker in the Kantian tradition has been a topic debated for several years. In linking Derrida with Kant, I do not mean to imply that Kant was a deconstructionist or that Derrida is a Kantian. But I do want to bring out a similarity between one aspect of Kant's project of "critical philosophy" and Derrida's strategy of deconstruction. Both Kant and Derrida endeavor to show the *limits* of a certain type of philosophical discourse. In so doing, they each disclose an area of inquiry about which the traditional discourse of philosophy is silent. In the introduction to her *Derrida and the Economy of Différance*,[30] Irene E. Harvey points out the similarities between Kantian critique and deconstruction in order to support her ultimate conclusion that, in fact, these similarities belie much more profound differences. For reasons that will be articulated below, I am more inclined to the position of Christopher Norris, who concludes that Derrida uses "the form of 'transcendental' reasoning which Kant first brought to bear upon the central problems of philosophy." And for this reason, Norris argues "that deconstruction is a Kantian enterprise in ways that few of its commentators have so far been inclined to acknowledge." [31]

The transcendental character of Derrida's thought also has been a central issue in the work of Rodolphe Gasché and Richard Rorty. Gasché, in *The Tain of the Mirror: Derrida and the Philosophy of Reflection*, argues that Derrida goes beyond both Kant and Heidegger in that his structures are "quasitranscendentals," which are

> no longer simply transcendentals, for they represent neither a priori structures of the subjective cognition of objects nor the structures of understanding of Being by the *Dasein*. The quasitranscendentals are, on the contrary, conditions of the possibility and impossibility concerning the very concep-

tual difference between subject and object and even between *Dasein* and Being.[32]

Where Harvey distinguished Derrida from Kant in terms of the former's "radicality,"[33] Gasché argues instead that what distinguishes Derrida's quasitranscendentals as "conditions of the possibility and impossibility of the logic of philosophy as a discursive enterprise" is "a certain irreducible erratic contingency."[34] Rorty, on the other hand, responds to both Norris and Gasché in "Is Derrida a Transcendental Philosopher?" as he suggests that instead of a "much-misunderstood transcendental 'philosopher of reflection',," we might better view Derrida as "a much-misunderstood nominalist, a sort of French Wittgenstein."[35]

Whatever position one takes on this question, it is impossible to avoid noting the transcendental character of Derrida's introduction of many of his "undecidables" as he argues for their introduction in terms of conditions of possibility or impossibility.[36] We should also not overlook the structural similarities between his and Kant's respective projects of philosophical *critique*. For example, we can also locate in Kant a rejection of binary thinking. When discussing the antinomies of pure reason, Kant locates a moment of what we can only call *'undecidability'* in the choice between the dogmatic and skeptical solutions to the antinomies:

since the arguments on both sides are equally clear, it is *impossible to decide between them*.... There can therefore be no way of settling it once and for all and to the satisfaction of both sides, save by their becoming convinced that the very fact of their being able so admirably to refute one another is evidence that they are really quarreling about nothing.[37]

It was, according to Kant, the task of critical philosophy to convince the two sides that it is not their solutions that are flawed; rather, the error lies in the nature of the questions that elicit their respective conclusions. The "critical solution" will thus "not consider the question objectively," but will proceed "in relation to the foundation of the knowledge upon which the question is based."[38]

Deconstruction shares with Kantian critique the aim of problematizing the foundational assumptions that make possible all questions of a certain kind. Yet we should recognize that the scope of Derrida's project exceeds Kant's. For Kant, the issues addressed were *internal* to philosophy—the "critical solution" was a solution to a local problem within philosophical discourse that this discourse had given to itself inasmuch as the dogmatist and the skeptic had, as it were, arrived together at a dead end. For Derrida, on the other hand, deconstruction "attacks not only the internal edifice, both semantic and formal, of philosophemes." In addition, it goes on to challenge what is wrongly assigned to philosophy as "its external housing, its extrinsic conditions of practice: the historical forms of its pedagogy, the social, economic or political structures of this pedagogical institution. It is because deconstruction interferes with solid structures, 'material' institutions, and not only with discourses or signifying representations, that it is always distinct from an analysis or a 'critique.'"[39]

Nevertheless, when Derrida resorts to the "logic of paleonymy," to the provisional and strategic *conservation* of the old names of the Western philosophical tradition, he approximates the goal of Kantian critique. By using the tradition against itself, Derrida seeks both to expose the foundational choices of the philosophical tradition and to bring into view that which the tradition has repressed, excluded, or, in Derridean terminology, marginalized. Deconstruction cannot, he writes,

> proceed immediately to a neutralization: it must, by means of a double gesture, a double science, a double writing, practice an *overturning* of the classical opposition *and* a general *displacement* of the system. It is only on this condition that deconstruction will provide itself the means with which to *intervene* in the field of oppositions that it criticizes.[40]

Derrida maintains both that no complete escape from the closure of metaphysics is possible and that philosophy itself provides the condition for the possibility of its own deconstruction.[41] The strategy of marginal, double writing thus permits the deconstructionist critique to circumvent the border between what is within the philosophical tradition and what is external to that tradition. By seizing concepts within the tradition and marking a movement of these concepts that the tradition *both* authorizes *and* excludes, deconstruction succeeds in inhabiting the closed field of metaphysics' binary oppositions without at the same time confirming that field. In so doing, it displays those choices, neither made explicit nor explicitly made, by means of which the tradition constitutes itself *as* a tradition.

An example may be helpful here, and we can return to the use Derrida makes of the *pharmakon*, this time in terms of the remark in the *Phaedrus* that writing is a *pharmakon* (274e–275a). Again the polysemy of *pharmakon* (writing as a remedy for the weakness of memory and as a poison that infects the purity of speech) is overdetermined, as the tradition has read Socrates to be condemning writing as inferior to and derivative from speech. Derrida highlights this overdetermination to show how the privileging of the spoken word over the written word follows from the determination of metaphysics as the metaphysics of presence. The immediate presence of meaning in the spoken word is the ideal of Western metaphysics, which must then devalue the written word as a secondary, derivative *re*-presentation of speech. By engaging in the strategy of double writing, Derrida first uses the *pharmakon* to question the privileging of speech over writing; he then proceeds to question the assumptions of the metaphysics of presence that make the binary opposition of speech/writing possible. After he shows that the primacy of speech over writing is itself grounded on the oppositions of presence over absence and immediacy over representation, he can then demonstrate that the spoken word is itself a phonic signifier of a mental signified. As a result, we must conclude that the spoken word is no more immediate a presentation of sense than the written word, and the grounds for the tradition's privileging speech over writing are thereby shown to be illegitimate. This demonstration makes possible his substitution of the notion of the "trace," always differing and deferring, for the concept of the sign, and it is a typical example of Derrida's strategy of using the binary concepts of the metaphysical tradition both in order to deconstruct or neutralize that tradition and to intervene into that tradition with the introduction of a supplementary "non-concept" that thwarts any metaphysical determination.

Nietzsche's Protodeconstruction of Oppositional Thinking

We noted above that on several occasions, Derrida cites Nietzsche as a precursor to deconstruction. In the essay "*Différance*," for example, in his quick review of several of the precursors of deconstruction (Saussure, Freud, Nietzsche, Heidegger, Levinas), he comes close to fully recognizing Nietzsche's anticipation of the deconstructive gesture marked by "*différance*" insofar as "all of Nietzsche's thought [is] a critique of philosophy as an active indifference to difference, as the system of adiaphoristic reduction or repression."[42] What I would like to suggest is that Nietzsche anticipates not only the general outline of this deconstructive critique. Rather, if we attend to the details of Nietzsche's own thinking, we can see with some degree of specificity the same critique of oppositional thinking anticipated in his assessment of traditional values as he often proceeds by disassembling the privileged hierarchical relation that has been established among the values in question.

Like Derridean deconstruction, Nietzsche's disassembling operates in two phases. The first phase overturns the traditionally privileged relation between the two values while the second seeks to displace the opposition altogether by showing it to result from a prior value imposition that itself requires critique. For example, regarding the genealogy of the will to truth, we find Nietzsche inverting the traditional hierarchy of truth over falsity. Investigating the origin of the positive value placed upon truth, Nietzsche finds that it is simply a moral prejudice to affirm truth over error or appearance (see *BGE*, 34). To this, he suggests that error might be *more* valuable than truth, that error might be a necessary condition of life. His analysis does not stop here, however, as Heidegger assumed when he accused Nietzsche of "completing" the history of metaphysics through an "inversion"—albeit not a simple inversion[43]—of Platonism. By adopting a perspectival attitude and denying the possibility of an unmediated, non-interpretive apprehension of "reality," Nietzsche displaces the truth/falsity opposition altogether. The question is no longer whether a perspective is "true" or "false"; the sole question that interests Nietzsche as genealogist is whether or not a perspective enhances life.[44]

Nietzsche discovers a certain faith in binary thinking at the center of philosophical discourse. By genealogically uncovering the will to power whose imposition of a certain value gave rise to the two poles of the opposition in question, genealogy obviates the force the opposition is believed to have. The clearest example of this strategy is his deconstruction of the good-evil opposition. Nietzsche moves *beyond* good and evil precisely by showing that both "good" and "evil" owe their meaning to a certain type of will to power—the slavish, reactive will to power of herd morality. To simply invert the values of slave morality, making "good" what the slave judges to be "evil," is no less reactive than the original imposition of value by the slave, who judges all that differs from himself to be "evil" and defines the good in reactionary opposition to what is other than himself.

A reading of Nietzsche as an "immoralist" or "nihilist" remains at this level of mere inversion, failing to acknowledge Nietzsche's insight that by conforming to the oppositional structure, one inevitably confirms its validity and its repressive, hierarchizing power. But a reading of Nietzsche as the "transvaluer of values" locates a second movement in the Nietzschean critique of morality. This second movement flows from the *active* imposition of new values arising from a healthy will to power that has displaced the hierarchy of good/evil altogether. In rejecting the binary structure of moral evaluation, Nietzsche's transvaluation inaugurates a playful experimentation with values and multiplication of perspectives that he labels "*Ausdeutung der That*," "active interpretation" (*KSA*, 12: 9[48]; see also 9[44]).[45] The affirmation of perspectival multiplicity thus emerges as the life-enhancing alternative for those with a will to power sufficient to go beyond the reactive decadence of binary morality. The outcome of this life-enhancing multiplicity—as we see in Nietzsche's own interpretive practices in, for example, *On the Genealogy of Morals*, as well as Derrida's reiteration of these practices—is a productive style of reading that does not merely "protect" but "opens" texts to new interpretive possibilities.[46]

There is a further similarity between Nietzsche's and Derrida's strategies, and this concerns the relation between these binary oppositions and language. Regarding the origin of both our moral and epistemological values, Nietzsche writes that "*language*, here as elsewhere, will not get over its awkwardness and will continue to talk of opposites where there are only degrees and many subtleties of gradation" (*BGE*, 24). For this reason, as Nietzsche puts it, "we really ought to free ourselves from the seduction of words" (*BGE*, 16). The basic presuppositions of the metaphysics of language involve us in a "rude fetishism" (*TI*, "'Reason' in Philosophy," 5) that tends to dichotomize our world into truths and appearances, causes and effects, subjects and objects. It is "only owing to the seduction of language (and of the fundamental errors of reason that are petrified in it) [that we] conceive and misconceive all effects as conditioned by something that causes effects, by a 'subject,'... But there is no such substratum; there is no 'being' behind doing, effecting, becoming; 'the doer' is merely a fiction added to the deed—the deed is everything" (*GM*, I, 13).[47]

Nietzsche's awareness of language's power to seduce us to a faith in all sorts of metaphysical presuppositions leads him to call for a deconstruction of our grammatical habits. This call motivates much of the First Essay of *On the Genealogy of Morals*, and it is punctuated by the First Essay's closing note, which suggests the following question in order to "advance *historical* studies *of morality*": "'*What light does linguistics, and especially the study of etymology, throw on the history of the evolution of moral concepts?*'" Elsewhere, he urges us not to forget that language is a "mere semiotic" (*KSA*, 13: 14[79, 122]; *WP*, 634, 625), a simplified, falsified, humanly-created sign system. To this "semiotic" we must bring the critical tools of genealogy; we must decipher linguistic concepts as symptoms of the forces that have achieved mastery by means of these "grammatical blunders."

"Shouldn't philosophers be permitted to rise above faith in grammar?" Nietzsche asks (*BGE*, 34). If they rise above this faith and subject it to rigorous genealogical scrutiny, they will discover even the belief in God to be a philosophical article of faith derived from our linguistic situation. For what else is the cosmological argument but a linguistic inference from deed to doer (see *BGE*, 17, 54), and why else would Nietzsche enigmatically confess that he fears we will not get rid of God so long as we continue to believe in grammar (*TI*, "'Reason' in Philosophy," 5)? The death of God and deconstruction of divine authority are prerequisites for a transvaluation of values. So, too, our faith in the authority of language must be suspended if a transvaluation is to be possible. And, as we will see in the next section, Nietzsche's genealogical suspicion concerning the inference from deed to doer, lays the ground for another linkage between his thinking and Derrida's, this time concerning the deconstruction of the authority of the (literary) subject.

Deconstructing the Authorial-Authoritarian Subject

This question of authority and its legitimation is a central issue in Nietzsche's writings, and one to which insufficient attention has been paid. Whether he is dismantling the authority of the moral-theological tradition, deconstructing the authority of God, or excising the hidden metaphysical authority within language, Nietzsche's refusal to legitimate any figure of authority remains constant. This holds for his own authority as a writer, the authority of his "prophet" Zarathustra, and the authority of the *Übermensch*.[48] As he remarks apropos moral authority, "in the presence of morality, as in the face of any authority, one is not *allowed* to think, far less to express an opinion: here one has to *obey!* As long as the world has existed no authority has yet been willing to let itself become the object of critique" (*D*, Pr3). Because authority demands obedience, a philosophy of the future will necessitate a critique of authority. If values are to be transvalued, obedience to the previous values must be undermined. The whole Nietzschean project of genealogy directs itself toward deconstructing the foundations of the dominant values of modernity, which is to say that Nietzsche's project of a transvaluation of values presupposes a delegitimation of the existing (moral) authority.

While not sufficiently attended to in Nietzsche's writings, the question of authority has, of course, been a central question in recent French thinking. And here as elsewhere we can see, both in broad outline and with a certain degree of specificity, how Nietzsche's ideas are developed in Derrida's thought on literary authority and its relation to the deconstruction of the subject. While the critique of the subject in recent French thought is most closely identified with the work of Michel Foucault, Derrida also has addressed the question of the authoritarian domination that accompanies the modern concept of the subject. Derrida develops his deconstructive critique of the subject as a privileged center of discourse in the context of his project of delegitimizing authority, whether that authority emerges in the form of the author's domination of the text[49] or the tradition's reading of the history of philosophy. In fact, as Derrida himself notes in *Positions*, from his earliest published texts, his project of delegitimation was an attempt "to systematize a deconstructive critique precisely against the authority of meaning, as the *transcendental signified* or as *telos*..." [50]

In Derrida's reading of Nietzsche, the deconstruction of authority emerges alongside his supplementation of binary logic with undecidability. We saw above that Derrida "uses" Nietzsche as an exemplar of undecidability to frustrate the logocentric longing to choose between one or the other alternative within a fixed binary opposition. A case in point is Derrida's 1968 lecture "The Ends of Man." At the conclusion of this lecture, Derrida brings the undecidable logic of supplementarity to the two strategies that have appeared in connection with the deconstruction of metaphysical humanism. The first strategy proceeds by means of a return to the origins of the metaphysical tradition and uses the resources of this tradition against itself. In adopting this strategy, "one risks ceaselessly confirming, consolidating, *relieving* [*relever*] at an always more certain depth that which one allegedly deconstructs."[51] The second deconstructive strategy affirms an absolute break with tradition, seeking to change ground in a discontinuous and irruptive fashion. However, such a strategy fails to recognize that one cannot break with the tradition while retaining its language. The inevitable consequence of this blindness to the powers of language is a naive reinstatement of a "new" ground on the very site one sought to displace.

According to Derrida, the first of these styles of deconstruction is that of Heidegger, while the second is the style that prevailed in France in the sixties and into the seventies. When applying these deconstructive strategies to Nietzsche and the "end of man," two very different interpretations result.

For Heidegger, Nietzsche emerges as the last great metaphysician, in whose writings the end of man appears as the culmination of metaphysical voluntarism. *Übermensch*, as pure will, thus assumes for Heidegger the form of a metaphysical repetition of humanism. For the French, as perhaps is most clear in the case of Michel Foucault's *The Order of Things* (whose French title, we should recall here, is *Les mots et les choses*, "Words and Things"), Nietzsche emerges not as repetition but as the first break from modernity. In his final reference to Nietzsche in *The Order of Things*, Foucault couples Nietzsche's death of God with the end of man, an end that is marked by the laughter of the *Übermensch* at the going-under of the last man. Recalling that in *Thus Spoke Zarathustra* ("The Ugliest Man"), God is reported to have died of pity upon encountering the last man, Foucault writes:

> Rather than the death of God—or, rather, in the wake of that death and in a profound correlation with it—what Nietzsche's thought heralds is the end of his murderer; it is the explosion of man's face in laughter, and the return of masks; it is the scattering of the profound stream of time by which he felt himself carried along and whose pressure he suspected in the very being of things; it is the identity of the Return of the Same with the absolute dispersion of man.[52]

Derrida, on the other hand, warns that we must refrain from choosing one strategy rather than the other. The two strategies supplement one another, and we are now at a point where there is no question of a simple choice between them. In other words, we must choose *both at once*, thereby effecting a change of ground while returning to the origins. To do so is to effect a change of *style* in philosophical writing. Derrida marks this change of style when he confronts Nietzsche's position on the "end" of "man," a position he finds equivocal. That is to say, there is more than one "end" of "man" in Nietzsche. Insofar as style is always *plural*,[53] to read Nietzsche's texts requires that we be prepared for multiple readings. In the case at hand, we find that there are at least *two* ends of man: the end as *eschaton* and the end as *telos*. And Nietzsche confronts us with these equivocal ends at the conclusion of *Thus Spoke Zarathustra*, where we find (the last) man meeting his end in the choice between the higher man (*höherer Mensch*) and the *Übermensch*. This equivocation on the "end" of "man" points to Derrida's own view of the undecidable place of the subject within philosophical discourse. Unlike Heidegger and the Foucault of *The Order of*

Things, Derrida refuses to do away with the subject. Instead, he seeks to situate the subject. As he puts it—in an admittedly different context—"I believe that at a certain level both of experience and of philosophical and scientific discourse, one cannot get along without the notion of the subject. It is a question of knowing where it comes from and how it functions."[54]

To help answer these questions, I suggest we return to Nietzsche's texts and examine his attempt to deconstruct his own subjectivity as an author. Nietzsche noted, in the preface to the second edition of *Daybreak*, that "in the face of any authority, one is not *allowed* to think, [instead] one has to— *obey!*" (*D*, Pr3). Insofar as the author has come to occupy a position of authority within the traditional view of interpretation, we should not be surprised to find in his affirmation of the *activity* of interpretation that Nietzsche expresses an antipathy toward any factor, including the author, that tends to inhibit this activity and limit its play. Throughout the two volumes of *Human, All-Too-Human*, for example, Nietzsche cautions against confusing the work with its author. Once the text has been written, it lives a life of its own, and by bringing the text into the public domain the author relinquishes all authority over what it is to mean: "When his book opens its mouth, the author must shut his" (*AOM*, 140; see also *AOM*, 157 and *HH*, 197, 208).

Throughout his writings, Nietzsche continues to question the privileged position of the author within the space of interpretation. In the third chapter of *Ecce Homo*, entitled "Why I Write Such Good Books," he openly acknowledges and affirms the consequences of the self-deconstruction of his own literary authority. In the opening sentence, Nietzsche separates himself from his texts: "I am one thing, my writings are another." From here he proceeds to confront the question of "being understood or *not* understood." In the pages that follow we find Nietzsche proudly proclaiming a number of reasons for his writings not being understood, reasons that reflect the problematic relation of the author to his text. To understand Nietzsche's writings as Nietzsche understands them, one would have to be Nietzsche:

> Ultimately, nobody can get more out of things, including books, than he already knows. For what one lacks access to from experience one will have no ear. Now let us imagine an extreme case: that a book speaks of nothing but events that lie altogether beyond the possibility of any frequent or even

rare experience—that it is the *first* language for a new series of experiences. In that case, simply nothing will be heard, but there will be the acoustic illusion that where nothing is heard, *nothing is there*. (*EH,* III, 1)

This extreme position indicates that there are different ways in which one's writings are not understood. Granted Nietzsche's perspectivism, no one could possibly understand his text as he does. Yet such an understanding would not, in his view, even be desirable. One might recall here Zarathustra's remark to his followers:

> An experimenting and questioning was my every move; —and verily, one must also *learn* to answer such questioning: That however—is my taste:
> —not good, not bad, but *my* taste of which I am no longer ashamed and which I have no wish to hide.
> "This—is *my* way,—where is yours?" thus I answered those who asked me "*the* way." For the way, that does not exist. (*Z,* "On the Spirit of Gravity," 2)

Nietzsche does not lament the lack of an identical reproduction of meaning in his readers. Instead, he takes pride in the fact that his contemporary readers "lack the ears" to hear what speaks within his text and he absolves himself of responsibility for having caught no fish with the bait his writings set out.[55]

To be caught by Nietzsche's fish hooks, to experience his writings in the affirmative sense, would result in the reader's being incited to act, to take action toward a transvaluation of values. This does not mean that one must duplicate the Nietzschean transvaluation, however. Instead, Nietzsche invites his readers to bring their own perspectives to the task of transvaluation and he recognizes that whatever he has written will be transformed in the process of perspectival appropriation. As an author, Nietzsche thus relinquishes his position of authority in favor of a position more conducive to provoking healthy performative responses on the part of his readers. In the concluding section of *Beyond Good and Evil,* one finds Nietzsche expressing a fear that his writings are becoming truths. The reason for Nietzsche's concern is that the communication of truth runs counter to his conception of his function as an author insofar as all truths, including his own, if they are accepted *as* truths, can only serve to inhibit the healthy response of transvaluation that his writings seek to "communicate."

Nietzsche was well aware that adopting a posture as an authority ran counter to much that his positive philosophy advocated in the call to trans-value values. In a remark from the *Nachlass*, he articulates a position whose echoes can be heard in much recent French thinking:

> We see: an authority speaks—who speaks?—One may forgive human pride if it sought to make this authority as high as possible in order to feel as little humiliated as possible under it. Therefore—God speaks!
>
> One needed God as an unconditional sanction, with no court of appeal, as a "categorical imperative"—or, if one believed in the authority of reason, one needed a metaphysic of unity, by virtue of which this was logical.
>
> Now suppose that belief in God has vanished: the question presents itself anew: "who speaks?"—My answer, taken not from metaphysics but from ani-mal physiology: *the herd instinct speaks*. It *wants* to be master: hence its "thou shalt!"—it will allow value to the individual only from the point of view of the whole, for the sake of the whole, it hates those who detach themselves—it turns the hatred of all individuals against them. (*KSA*, 12: 7[6], p. 279; *WP*, 275)[56]

We find in Nietzsche's remark that *authority* speaks, first the authority of God and then the authority of the herd. Nietzsche's *Übermensch*, who her-alds the demise of God and the last/herd man, will be subject to no author-ity and, inasmuch as both divine and human subjectivity function within a network of relations of power, authority, and submission, the *Übermensch* will not be a subject at all.

Nietzsche's self-deconstruction of his own authorial-authoritarian sub-jectivity provides the link between his critique of the traditional view of interpretation and the critique of the philosophical subject. In emphasizing the dynamic character of the interpretive process, Nietzsche rejects the view of interpretation as a relationship between a subject and an object. For Nietzsche, both "subject" and "object" are themselves already interpreta-tions (see *KSA*, 12: 7[60]; *WP*, 481), and when he writes that "one may not ask: 'who then interprets?'" (*KSA*, 12: 2[151]; *WP*, 556), it is only because such a question already mislocates the process of interpretation. Likewise, one may not ask "what then is interpreted?" Interpretation is not grounded in either the subject or the object; it exists in the *between*, in the space that separates them. Within this space, subject and object can function only as limits, and the attempt to focus the interpretive process in the direc-tion of either will serve only to obscure the dynamics of this process and put an unjust end to its interminable play.

When, for his part, Derrida appeals to Nietzsche and the play of inter-pretive forces, he indicates a means of escape from the closure of authority by adopting a style of writing that affirms multiplicity, play, and difference rather than the traditional logocentric values of subjectivity, univocity, autonomy, and self-identity. The similarity of style in their respective cri-tiques thus betokens a basic similarity in the way they try to subvert the notion of authority. Nietzsche opposes the "tyranny of the true" (*D*, 507) and he expresses concern that his writings take the appearance of procla-mations of truth (see *BGE*, 296). Likewise, Derrida is sensitive to the ten-dency to privilege undecidables and reify them into foundations for a new philosophical system. For this reason, he moves from one to another, uti-lizing each for a particular, *strategic* purpose and then leaving them behind. These undecidables have the power to subvert, but they lack the power to command and they can exercise no authority.[57]

In *Of Grammatology*, when Derrida deconstructs the writer as a sovereign subject in command of the reserve within language, or when he fractures the "subject of writing" in his discussions of Freud, a Nietzschean "sub-ject" emerges. The classical subject, as a privileged center, thus disappears within the *system* of relations that is writing (*écriture*): "The 'subject' of writing does not exist if we mean by that some sovereign solitude of the author. The subject of writing is a *system* of relations between strata: the Mystic Pad, the psyche, society, the world."[58] In dispersing the subject within a system of textual relations, Derrida adopts a Nietzschean strategy of refusing to hypostasize the subject. For Nietzsche, this refusal is grounded in the affirmation of a multiplicity of perspectives, of seeing the world with new and different eyes, that animates his philosophy of will to power as active force within the infinite play of becoming. For Derrida, the refusal is grounded in his account of the infinite iterability of the mark and a theory of contextuality that views the person writing or reading as always already inscribed in a textual network that cannot and will not be dominated absolutely.

What links these two refusals is the emphasis on fluidity of relations, as both Nietzsche and Derrida view the classical concept of the subject as func-tioning in a way that engenders separation and fixation. In Nietzsche's case, it is the play of relations of forces and the accumulation of power within this play that is blocked by the hypostasization of the subject: the concept of the subject performs only a *preservative* function and to enhance one's life within the innocent, infinite play of becoming, one must refrain from conceiving the subject as a static, enduring substance (see *GM*, I, 13). In Derrida's case, it is the relational "system" of writing/play that resists the classical notion of a subjectivity that functions as a center and limit to this play/writing.

Derrida himself acknowledges Nietzsche for pointing the way to an affirmation of the decentered play of writing that disrupts the metaphysics of presence which guides the logocentric tradition. Nietzschean affirmation is

> the joyous affirmation of the play of the world and of the innocence of becoming, the affirmation of a world of signs without fault, without truth, and without origin which is offered to an active interpretation. *This affirmation then determines the noncenter otherwise than as loss of the center.* And it plays without security, [surrendering] itself to *genetic* indetermination, to the *seminal* adventure of the trace.... [N]o longer turned toward the origin, [it] affirms play and tries to pass beyond man and humanism, the name of man being the name of that being who, throughout the history of metaphysics or of ontotheology— in other words, throughout his entire history—has dreamed of full presence, the reassuring foundation, the origin and the end of play.[59]

Grammatology, the "science" of writing, therefore, will not be a science of man. "Man," the name bestowed on the subject as center, as the full presence of consciousness in being, must be decentered if there is to be a logic of the *grammē*, which is to say, "man" must be deconstructed, must be allowed to play. In Derrida's call for play we can hear the echo of Zarathustra's message to the higher men in the fourth book of *Thus Spoke Zarathustra*, in which the recurring theme is the invitation to learn to dance and laugh:

> You higher men, the worst about you is that all of you have not learned to dance as one must dance—dancing away over yourselves! What does it matter that you are failures? How much is still possible! So *learn* to laugh away over yourselves! Lift up your hearts, you good dancers, high, higher! And do not forget good laughter. This crown of him who laughs, this rose-wreath crown: to you, my brothers, I throw this crown. Laughter I have pronounced holy; you higher men, *learn* to laugh! (*Z*, "On the Higher Man," 20)

Zarathustra himself learns this lesson during the Ass Festival, as his companions teach him that he is perhaps succumbing to their entreaties to exercise his authority over them through his teachings. But insofar as the higher men cannot accept Zarathustra's ultimate renunciation of his authority over them, insofar as they cannot hear him when he says "I am a law only for my kind, I am no law for all" (*Z*, "The Last Supper"), he must leave them behind. And so *Thus Spoke Zarathustra* ends, with Zarathustra alone again, having again renounced his position of authority, a troubling renunciation that has been repeated through the writings and throughout the career of Jacques Derrida.

Conclusion

Derrida's deconstruction of binary opposites shows that what has emerged as "necessary" and "a priori" within the history of philosophy is in fact a series of contingent and optional choices that could have been made otherwise. Like Nietzsche, who a century earlier challenged as "moral prejudices" (*BGE*, 34) what were taken to be necessary assumptions (for example, that truth is more valuable than error), Derrida's deconstructions make it possible to challenge radically the basic philosophical assumptions upon which the history of the West has been erected. While we may ultimately renew our choice to privilege good over evil, or truth over error, we can no longer accept as natural and necessary the evaluation of the intelligible over the sensible, man over woman, or white over non-white. And perhaps it is on that ground that the importance and lasting value of deconstruction should be judged.

CHAPTER TWO

Foucault:
Genealogy, Power, and the
Reconfiguration of the Subject

➤

For myself, I prefer to utilize the writers I like. The only valid tribute to thought such as Nietzsche's is precisely to use it, to deform it, to make it groan and protest. And if commentators then say that I am being faithful or unfaithful to Nietzsche, that is of absolutely no interest.

—FOUCAULT, "Prison Talk"

If I wanted to be pretentious, I would use "the genealogy of morals" as the general title of what I am doing. It was Nietzsche who specified the power relation as the general focus, shall we say, of philosophical discourse—whereas for Marx it was the productive relation. Nietzsche is the philosopher of power, a philosopher who managed to think of power without having to confine himself within a political theory in order to do so.

—FOUCAULT, "Prison Talk"

Foucault's originality among the great thinkers of our century lay in his refusal to convert our finitude into the basis for new certainties.

—PAUL VEYNE, "The Final Foucault and His Ethics"

IN THE ESSAY "WHAT IS AN AUTHOR?" MICHEL FOUCAULT ISOLATES A RARE kind of author-function that he calls a "founder of discursivity." Founders of discursivity, he writes,

> are unique in that they are not just the authors of their own works. They have
> produced something else: the possibilities and the rules for the formation of
> other texts. In this sense, they are very different, for example, from a novelist,
> who is, in fact, nothing more than the author of his own text. Freud is not
> just the author of *The Interpretation of Dreams* or *Jokes and Their Relation to*

the Unconscious; Marx is not just the author of the *Communist Manifesto* or *Das Kapital:* they both have established an endless possibility of discourse.[1]

Founders of discursivity initiate a new set of discursive practices and, unlike the founder of a science (Foucault gives as examples Cuvier and Saussure), a founder of discursivity's own discourse remains heterogeneous to the subsequent transformations of the discursive practices they initiate. This is to say, their works are not corrected, but applied; they become incorporated into the ongoing discourse while at the same time remaining an object of study and a source of inspiration separate from the discursive transformations in which they participate. Thus, while psychoanalytic discourses as we find them in Lacan, Guattari, or Irigaray have gone beyond the discourse of Freud, these discourses nevertheless continue to return to the works of Freud, both as resources to be reappropriated and as texts to be reinterpreted. Similarly, thinkers as diverse as Althusser, Habermas, Adorno, or Thompson continue to return to Marx not in an appeal to authority but in order to bring into the present what in their respective views remains important in Marx's thought.

Foucault's remark cited as the second epigraph to this chapter suggests that he might credit Nietzsche with founding the discursive practices at work today concerning power relations. I would like to suggest, however, that it is Michel Foucault himself who has come to occupy a place on the contemporary intellectual scene as a founder of discursivity whose works have initiated and continue to inform a wide range of discursive practices concerning the functioning of power in contemporary societies. This is not to say that one should appropriate uncritically Foucault's remarks concerning how to analyze relations of power. But as I hope to show in what follows, it is to say that today, whether one writes with or against Foucault, the rules that frame how one can speak about power are indelibly marked by Foucault's own discursive practices. And while Foucault's discourse may itself bear the constant imprint of Nietzschean thinking, it is largely because of the form this imprint has taken within Foucault's own works that Nietzsche's thinking on power retains much of its currency.

Nietzschean Continuities

Let me begin by setting a context in which I think Foucault's analytics of power should be placed. This context involves two components, both of which were touched upon in the introduction. First, the disillusionment of the French Left with the possibility of a successful revolution of the Left,

a disillusionment punctuated by the events of May '68 and the retrench-
ments of power that followed. As Paul Bové has noted, "Foucault argues
that many of the 'oppositional' rhetorics [and, in particular, the rhetorics
of Marxism and psychoanalysis —AS] are in complicity with the hegemony
of power."[2] The state, Foucault claimed in a 1976 interview, "consists in
the codification of a whole number of power relations which render its functioning possible."[3] Revolutions, he continued, involve "subversive recodi-
fications of power relations" which, however, tend to leave untouched the
very relations of power that make possible the functioning of the state apparatus. As the twentieth century progresses toward its conclusion, it has
become increasingly difficult to ignore the historical tendency of revolutions of the Left evolving into regimes of the Right. To examine our century is to find the oppressed overthrowing their oppressors, all too often only
to take their places without challenging the fundamental social logics that
initially made possible their own oppression. To put this in a Foucaultian
idiom, about which more will be said in a moment, those who are reputed
to be the possessors of power may change, but the fundamental *forms* of
relations of power remain largely unaltered.

For many post-Sartrean French Left intellectuals, this tendency, writ
large for the French first in Hungary and then in Prague, made it difficult to
align themselves with Marxism. It was also a primary motive for what I take
as the second component of the Foucaultian context: the attraction to
Nietzsche. While Nietzsche has been associated with both politics of the
Left and regimes of the Right, it is not Nietzsche's politics but his recognition of the power–knowledge–truth nexus and his revolutionary philosophical position outside both Marxism and phenomenology—the two
hegemonic orthodoxies of Foucault's youth—that attracted Foucault.[4]
Foucault rivals Gilles Deleuze as the most Nietzschean of contemporary
French philosophers. Like Deleuze, Foucault attributed to his reading of
Nietzsche a transformative power that helped him to escape from what he
perceived to be the traps of French social and intellectual life.[5] And again like
Deleuze, Nietzsche's power to transform appears, albeit in different guises,
at every stage of Foucault's thought and career.

It has become common to divide Foucault's thinking into three discrete and distinct moments: an archaeological period (*Madness and
Civilization, The Birth of the Clinic, The Order of Things, The Archaeology
of Knowledge*) that focused on relations of knowledge, language, truth,
and the discursive formations that made them possible; a genealogical

period (*Discipline and Punish*, *The History of Sexuality*, *Volume One*) that
focused on the question of power; and an ethical period (*The History of
Sexuality*, *Volumes Two and Three*), that focused on the construction of the
ethical/sexual subject or self. This orthodox periodization is difficult to
maintain, however, in the light of Foucault's numerous comments that
explicitly challenge its neat divisions. For example, when his thought
turned, with *Discipline and Punish*, away from "discourse" and "language" and toward "power," he remarked in an interview that "When I
think back now, I ask myself what else it was that I was talking about, in
Madness and Civilization or *The Birth of the Clinic*, but power."[6] Later,
when asked to relate the first volume of *The History of Sexuality* to his earlier works, he commented that in his studies of the prison and of madness,
"the question at the center of everything was: what is power? And, to be
more specific: how is it exercised, what exactly happens when someone
exercises power over another?"[7] And later still, when his attention turned
specifically to sexuality and the construction of the ethical subject, he was
again able to reinvent his earlier work as a consistent investigation of subjectivation, *assujettissement*—the transformation of human beings into
subjects of knowledge, subjects of power, and subjects to themselves—
concluding that "it is not power, but the subject, which is the general
theme of my research."[8]

It is particularly ironic that Foucault has often been portrayed as the
philosopher of discontinuity, especially if one considers the many self-inter-
pretations he offered that stressed the continuity of his thinking. For example, in an important interview with Pierre Boncenne in 1978, Foucault
responded directly to the question of discontinuity. While distancing himself from *The Order of Things*, a work he called "the most difficult, the most
tiresome book I ever wrote [that was] seriously intended to be read by about
two thousand academics who happen to be interested in a number of problems concerning the history of ideas," he remarked that his approach "was
quite the opposite of a 'philosophy of discontinuity'" insofar as it sought to
problematize the self-evidence of certain "ruptures" in the history of biology, political economy, and general grammar.[9]

Foucault's eliding of the supposed ruptures in his thinking has not prevented a certain orthodox division of the Foucaultian corpus, however. The
reason for this division rests not on massive ruptures in Foucault's thinking
but rather on the fact that as Foucault's work evolved, each new turn in his
thinking problematized his previous position, thus leading him to orient

his thought toward different foci. Language/discourse, truth, power, and the subject are perhaps the four foci to which discussions of Foucault most typically appeal, and they are in fact the signposts he himself frequently offered in interviews and other glosses on his own career.

While one could organize his thought around these signposts in various ways, giving precedence to one rather than another at different points in his career, must we view this shifting emphasis as a sign of discontinuity? Might the changes of focus be viewed instead in a more holistic fashion? That is to say, might these four foci function *together* as the privileged nodes in that analytic grid that emerges within Foucault's thought as a whole? Foucault himself acknowledged on many occasions that thinking and writing are activities that lead one to move, not remain the same, and he came to define philosophy itself as a kind of intellectual *askesis*, "an exercise of oneself in the activity of thought" which consists "in the endeavor to know how and to what extent it might be possible to think differently."[10]

In the context of the present discussion, what also warrants notice is that Foucault himself linked each of these foci to Nietzsche. In fact, in his own interpretations of the evolution of his thought, Foucault consistently inscribed his thinking in a space opened by Nietzsche's philosophical labors, especially as they concerned the attention to language and discourse, the will to truth and knowledge, the will to power, and the *Übermensch*. Therefore, Nietzsche's recurring appearance in the text of Foucault also serves to challenge the orthodox division in his thinking. At the same time, Foucault's constant appeal to Nietzsche suggests the privileged place Nietzsche occupies in the establishment of that analytic grid that will make possible a genealogy of the present.

For example, while Nietzsche appears in *The Order of Things* at the crucial moment where Foucault marks the first attempt at the uprooting of anthropology and the dissolution of man,[11] Nietzsche figures at an even deeper level in the construction of Foucault's archaeological project, a project that he acknowledged "owes more to the Nietzschean genealogy than to structuralism properly called."[12] Insofar as Nietzsche was "the first to connect the philosophical task with a radical reflection upon language," his work opened the philosophical-philological space of the twentieth century, a space dominated as it has been by language's appearance as "an enigmatic multiplicity that must be mastered."[13]

Similarly, Foucault cites Nietzsche as the first to address a certain kind of question to "truth," a question that no longer restricted truth to the domain of epistemic inquiry nor took the value of "truth" as a given. By posing moral and political questions to "truth," Nietzsche saw "truth" as an ensemble of discursive rules "linked in a circular relation with systems of power which produce and sustain it, and to effects of power which it induces and which extend it."[14] When Nietzsche claimed, in *On the Genealogy of Morals*, that philosophy must for the first time confront the question of the *value* of truth (*GM*, III, 24), he was the first to recognize "truth" no longer as something given in the order of things. That is to say, he was the first to recognize "truth" as something produced within a complex socio-political institutional *regime*:

> The problem is not changing people's consciousnesses—or what's in their heads—but the political, economic, institutional regime of the production of truth.
>
> It's not a matter of emancipating truth from every system of power (which would be a chimera, for truth is already power) but of detaching the power of truth from the forms of hegemony, social, economic and cultural, within which it operates at the present time.
>
> The political question, to sum up, is not error, illusion, alienated consciousness or ideology; it is truth itself. Hence the importance of Nietzsche.[15]

The inscription of Nietzschean thought throughout Foucault's career suggests that it may be a mistake to see Foucault's evolving project as a series of "corrections" of his earlier works. Similarly, it may be a mistake to conclude that power is accorded once and for all some methodological privilege over language, or that the subject is definitively privileged over power. Instead, the nature of the interaction among the three moments (the archaeological, the genealogical, and the ethical) can be clarified in terms of one of the many Nietzschean dimensions of Foucault's thinking. I refer here to Nietzsche's blurring the borders among epistemology, psychology and politics—between truth and power, between language and knowledge, between the self-constructing and the self-constructed. In so doing, Nietzsche indicates his refusal to constrain concepts and fields of inquiry within their traditional borders, a refusal that makes it difficult to determine where Nietzsche's epistemology ends and his psychology or politics begins.

Foucault also refused to frame his analyses within the traditional categories of philosophy or the history of ideas. While he often spoke about his work in terms of a tripartite schema, like Nietzsche the overlap between the diverse components of his analytic framework makes problematic any neat division between them. In fact, it would be more accurate to see the three moments working together in Foucault's later work. For example, in response to a question concerning the structure of his "genealogy project," Foucault remarked:

> Three domains of genealogy are possible. First, a historical ontology of our-selves in relation to truth through which we constitute ourselves as subjects of knowledge; second, a historical ontology of ourselves in relation to a field of power through which we constitute ourselves as subjects acting on others; third, a historical ontology in relation to ethics through which we constitute ourselves as moral agents.[16]

Foucault goes on to add that while all three domains "were present, albeit in a somewhat confused fashion, in *Madness and Civilization*," in later works, particular domains were emphasized: "The truth axis was studied in *The Birth of the Clinic* and *The Order of Things*. The power axis was studied in *Discipline and Punish*, and the ethical axis in *The History of Sexuality*."[17] But emphasizing one particular domain should not be regarded as a repu-diation of the previously studied axes. Instead, as Foucault makes clear, each axis brings an analytic dimension that is *added* to the prior studies, and all three axes will play a role in the genealogical project as a "critical ontology of ourselves... conceived as an attitude, an ethos, a philosophical life in which the critique of what we are is at one and the same time the historical analysis of the limits that are imposed on us and an experiment with the possibility of going beyond them."[18]

Questioning Power as a Sovereign Possession

Nietzsche's inscription within Foucault's oeuvre goes much deeper than their shared desire to break the traditional borders between domains of inquiry. In particular, Foucault took from Nietzsche a number of insights concerning how to think about power and power relations. Throughout his career, Foucault drew inspiration from Nietzsche's linkage between power, truth, and knowledge, a linkage that was both explicit in such Nietzschean remarks as "Knowledge functions as an *instrument* of power" (*KSA*, 13: 14[122]; *WP*, 480), and implicit in the fluidity of Nietzsche's movement between "will," "will to truth," "will to knowledge," and "will to power." Nietzsche's rhetoric of will to power drew attention away from substances, subjects, and things, and focused that attention instead on the *relations between* these substantives. According to Nietzsche, these relations were relations of forces: forces of attraction and repulsion, domination and subordination, imposition and reception. Similarly, Foucault argued that power should not be construed as a substantive:

> Power in the substantive sense, *"le" pouvoir*, doesn't exist.... The idea that there is either located at—or emanating from—a given point something which is a "power" seems to me to be based on a misguided analysis, one which at all events fails to account for a considerable number of phenomena. In reality power means relations, a more-or-less organized, hierarchical, co-ordinated cluster of relations.[19]

Foucault thus engaged in a highly sophisticated analysis of power that followed Nietzsche's example and focused not on the subjects of power but on power *relations*, the relations of force that operate within social practices and social systems. Where Nietzsche saw a continuum of will to power and sought to incite a becoming-stronger of will to power to rival the progressive becoming-weaker he associated with modernity, Foucault saw power relations operating along a continuum of repression and production, and he sought to draw attention to the becoming-productive of power that accompanies the increasingly repressive power of that normalizing, disciplinary, carceral society we call "modern."

This is the reason Foucault speaks of an "analytics" of power rather than a "theory" of power. Theories bring with them an implied ontology, a metaphysic of substances, and all theories of power have assumed that power is some *thing* that is univocal in all its manifestations, some *thing* that remains constant regardless of whether one possesses or lacks it. Following the direction indicated by Nietzsche when he put forward will to power as having "existence... (not as a 'being,' but as a *process*, a *becoming*) as an affect" (*KSA*, 12: 2[151]; *WP*, 556), Foucault's analytic draws our attention away from the substantive notion of power and directs that attention instead to the multifarious ways that power operates through the social order.

To paraphrase one of Jean-François Lyotard's characterizations of the postmodern, Foucault moves from this Nietzschean perspective to initiate what we might regard as the discursive practices of *postmodern* political thought by putting forward his analytics of power as a presentation of the unpresentable.[20] "Power," Foucault writes, "is tolerable only on condition that it mask a substantial part of itself. Its success is proportional to its ability to hide its own mechanisms."[21] As a consequence, analysis must avoid looking only at those places where power announces itself. Instead, Foucault advises us to attend to the diverse ways that power is exercised, for it is at least as important to understand *how* power is exercised as it is to identify *who* exercises it. And to begin an analysis with the question "how?", Foucault writes, "is to suggest that power as such does not exist,"[22] that power is its own simulacrum.[23]

As a result, when he speaks of social relations and the forms of rationality that rule and regulate them, Foucault does not refer "to Power—with a capital P—dominating and imposing its rationality upon the totality of the social body."[24] By presenting "power" not as a substance or essence, but as a network of relations that works through the order of things, Foucault presents "power" as conditioning what is to count as "knowledge" and "truth." And insofar as "power" functions differently at different nodes along this social network, a complex grid of analysis is necessary in order to understand the different appearances of power relations.

As Deleuze has noted, one of the basic points of connection between Foucault and Nietzsche is their shared conception of force—they each view power (*pouvoir* in Foucault's case, *puissance* in Nietzsche's) not as a force in relation to a being or an object (i.e., not as "violence") but as "the relation of force with other forces that it affects or that affect it."[25] Because power acts not on things or persons but on other forces, Foucault argues that we must free the analysis of power relations from the traditional assumptions that have guided political thought. Therefore, the first step in analyzing contemporary power relations will be to extricate "power" from what Foucault calls the juridico-discursive framework where it is represented substantively in terms of law, sovereignty, and the thematics of repression. If one assumes the form of law and the sovereignty of the state, one sets up at the origin of power what in fact are products of power, terminal forms that power takes. Whether conceived according to a legal model that asks "What legitimates power?" or conceived along the lines of an institutional model that questions "What is the state?" the juridico-discursive framework of power already accepts that power is some *thing* that is possessed— whether by the state, the sovereign, or the law—something that is centralized, and something that functions in essentially repressive ways. These juridico-discursive assumptions are symptoms of traditional ways of conceiving power and, as such, are precisely what Foucault's power analytic seeks to re-think.

According to Foucault, the representation of power as a thing inhibits our understanding how power operates in a contemporary world that has been marked by the passage from a monarchical version of the state to an institutionalized governmental apparatus.[26] This is to say, power is no longer isolated in the person of the sovereign but is disseminated throughout an institutional network and is exercised in decentralized ways throughout the social body.[27] As a consequence, the modern governmentalized state is more stable, both in the sense of permanence and resistance to change, because it is much more difficult to locate the points at which resistance to the current regime should intervene in order to change that regime. In 1789, it was sufficient to cut off a few heads to change the government. Today, there are no such heads, so where can resistance cut?[28]

For this reason, Foucault argues that future analyses must understand power as operating outside the traditional binary of ruler and ruled, coming from below as well as above, being intentional but at the same time non-subjective, and always accompanied by points of resistance.[29] By analyzing power in this way, Foucault's position develops as an analogue to Nietzsche's "monism" of will to power: for the Nietzschean interpretive framework in which everything is evaluated as a manifestation of healthy or decadent will to power, Foucault substitutes an analytic grid that transforms the traditional disjunctions concerning conceptions of power—as something possessed by some and imposed upon others—into a continuum of power-knowledge which views "power" as omnipresent in the body politic.[30] Power, in other words, is produced and operates in every relation. Moreover, relations of power are not exterior to other relations, whether economic, emotional, sexual, or epistemological; rather, power is immanent to these relations. As we will see in more detail in what follows, it is this analogy to Nietzsche's will to power that makes possible the most Nietzschean dimension of Foucault's power-analytic—the emphasis on the *productivity* of power. Contrary to the "repressive hypothesis" which functions as one of the privileged myths of modernity, Foucault claims that power relations are not pre-eminently repressive. Power relations do not manifest themselves only in laws that say "no"; they are also productive, traversing and producing things, inducing pleasures, constructing knowledge, forming discourses, and creating truths.[31]

Many readers of Foucault, like readers of Nietzsche, overlook the fundamental ambivalence that characterizes their respective accounts of power. For Nietzsche, what is frequently overlooked is his judgment concerning the harmful consequences of those manifestations of will to power whose source is genealogically located in reactive forces. While, for example, Dionysus or Goethe exhibit will to power as *affirmative* force, Socrates, Wagner, or St. Paul exhibit will to power also, but in their cases, the will to power is the *nihilistic* product of *reactive* forces. As his arguments in *On the Genealogy of Morals* and *The Antichrist* make clear, Nietzsche genealogically discriminates between healthy and decadent forms of will to power and his affirmation of will to power does not thereby entail an affirmation of all manifestations of it.

Let me clarify this point, whose importance extends beyond the question of a minor issue in Nietzsche scholarship. A distinction needs to be made between Nietzsche's affirmation *in principle* of *all* manifestations of will to power and his retention of a criterion in terms of health or life-enhancement that allows him to affirm—*qua manifestation of will to power*—an action or creation that he at the same time criticizes on genealogical grounds insofar as the action or creation manifests decadent or reactive or life-negating will to power. It is only by making a distinction like this that we can make sense, for example, of Nietzsche's admiration—in *On the Genealogy of Morals*—of the creative power of the ascetic priests while he at the same time criticizes their creations for being decadent or life-negating. Deleuze's distinction between the quantitative and qualitative dimension of Nietzsche's account of forces is helpful here: *quantitatively*, Nietzsche affirms all manifestations of power or force. But *qualitatively*, he affirms only active or affirmative force while criticizing those forces that he determines to be qualitatively *reactive* .[32]

Foucault's attack on the repressive hypothesis likewise demonstrates a certain ambivalence regarding the appearance of relations of power. Even the body—the "object" of the microphysics of power analyzed in *Discipline and Punish*—can be regarded as a useful force *only* if, while becoming a subjected body, it remains a *productive* body.[33] Foucault's analytic grid of power reminds us not to lose sight of the fact that the exercise of power, even repressive power, always produces resistances and these resistances can be and often are positively productive. This productivity can be quite individually localized, as in the case, for example, of the production of the "autonomous self" of the adolescent in response to the "repressive" power exercised by parental authority; or it can be productive of more global possibilities, as is the case in the productivities of various counter-knowledges—gay and lesbian studies, post-colonial studies, women's studies, African-

American studies—all of which would not have evolved as they have had there not been a repressive majoritarian exercise of power in the construction of the Western "canon." Similarly, we must remember that the same laws that were supposed to inhibit sexual expression gave rise to a proliferation of "discourse" about sex whose end we have not yet seen or that the laws restricting sexuality to "normal" expressions produce those "transgressive" sexual behaviors that Foucault chronicled.

The fundamental ambivalence between repression and production that characterizes the exercise of power leads Foucault to suggest that we should not look at power simply in terms of who has it and who is deprived of it, nor should we view power-knowledge relations as static forms of binary distribution between parties with competing agendas and interests. For example, we should not view relations of power in terms of fixed oppositions like doctor vs. patient, parent vs. child, or bourgeois vs. proletarian. We should instead examine the fluctuations and modifications of these power relations while remembering that resistance is *internal* to power as a permanent possibility.[34] As Foucault writes, "we must not imagine a world of discourse divided between accepted discourse and excluded discourse, or between the dominant discourse and the dominated one." Instead, we must view power-knowledge relations as matrices of transformation, "as a multiplicity of discursive elements that can come into play in various strategies" that permit discourses to transmit and produce power, to reinforce it, but also to undermine and expose it, render it fragile, and make it possible to thwart it.[35]

Questioning the Subject: Foucault's Nietzschean Trajectory

The force of his narratives in *Discipline and Punish* and the first volume of *The History of Sexuality* has tended to seduce Foucault's readers into dispensing altogether with any notion of agency as one comes to view human beings merely as nodes through which institutionalized power relations are transmitted. When analyzing concrete political situations, however, we must take care to avoid overreacting to and overcompensating for the juridico-discursive focus on power as a sovereign possession. To move too quickly toward dispensing with everything that pertains to the individual human subject fails to attend to the last development in Foucault's thought, where he suggests several ways we might reconfigure our understanding of the relationships between power and subjects. In the previous chapter, we looked briefly at Nietzsche's deconstruction of his own authorial subjectivity in the context of Derrida's discussion of the "ends" of "man." In that context, we had occasion to mention Foucault's linking the death of God with the end of the last man, an end punctuated by the laughter of the *Übermensch* that closes *The Order of Things*.[36] Now we must return to this issue in order to examine whether Foucault's reconfiguration of the subject within his analytic of power ever exceeded the Nietzschean trajectory that he cited in the closing sentence of his 1960 *thèse complémentaire* "Introduction à l'*Anthropologie* de Kant," where he wrote: "The trajectory of the question '*Was ist der Mensch?*' in the field of philosophy culminates in the challenging and disarming response: '*der Übermensch*'."[37]

In *The Order of Things*, Foucault raises the question of the subject in terms of what he refers to as the Nietzschean question, "who is speaking?"[38] This question appears in the context of Foucault's crediting Nietzsche for opening up language as "an enigmatic multiplicity that must be mastered." Foucault writes:

> For Nietzsche, it was not a matter of knowing what good and evil were in themselves, but of who was being designated, or rather *who was speaking* when one said *Agathos* to designate oneself or *Deilos* to designate others. For it is there, in the *holder* of the discourse and, more profoundly still, in the *possessor* of the word, that language is gathered together in its entirety.[39]

Here we see the effects of Nietzschean genealogy, alluded to in a remark cited earlier, operating at the center of Foucault's thinking. Nietzsche traced the genealogical developments that led him to distinguish the noble's "good," operating as it does within the couplet "good-bad," from the slave's "good," which functions within the very different couplet "good-evil." In drawing this genealogical distinction, Nietzsche was perhaps the first to notice that words had "ceased to intersect with representations and to provide a spontaneous grid for the knowledge of things."[40] His recognition that the faith in the representational accuracy of language had been eclipsed led Nietzsche to shift the focus of his critical attention away from *what* was said, turning this attention instead toward a genealogical critique of *who* said what was said, and what the *reasons* were which had given rise to what was said.

Foucault had already made this point in the underappreciated essay "Nietzsche, Freud, Marx," his contribution to the 1964 Colloquium on Nietzsche held at Royaumont. In his concluding remarks on the obligation of interpretation to interpret itself to infinity, he noted that interpretation will be henceforth always interpretation by the "who?": one does not interpret what there is in the signified, but one interprets, fundamentally, *who* has posed the interpretation. The origin [*principe*] of interpretation is nothing other than the interpreter, and this is perhaps the sense that Nietzsche gave to the word "psychology".[41]

To ask "*who* interprets?" or "*who* speaks?", however, does not produce an answer taking the form of a subject's name, as Foucault indicated when he inscribed the question "who?" within "psychology," understood by Nietzsche in *Beyond Good and Evil* as "morphology and *the doctrine of the development of the will to power*" (*BGE*, 23). "'The subject' itself," Nietzsche writes, is an interpretation, "something created," a "simplification with the object of defining the *force* that posits, invents, thinks" (*KSA*, 12: 2[152]; *WP*, 556). And for this reason, Nietzsche concludes that it is the will to power that speaks and interprets, not a subject, as we can see when we look at his own answer to the question concerning "who speaks?": "Now suppose that belief in God has vanished: the question presents itself anew: 'who speaks?' —My answer, taken not from metaphysics but from animal physiology: *the herd instinct speaks*. It *wants* to be master: hence its 'thou shalt!'" (*KSA*, 12: 7[6]; *WP*, 275). Elsewhere, Nietzsche is even more explicit: "The will to power *interprets*" (*KSA*, 12: 2[148]; *WP*, 643), and, as a consequence "one may not ask '*who* then interprets' for the interpretation itself is a form of will to power" (*KSA*, 12: 2[151]; *WP*, 556). From these remarks, it appears that rather than eliciting the name of a subject, the question "who?" calls for a genealogical inquiry into the type of will to power (life-affirming or life-negating) that manifests itself in speech or interpretation.

When Foucault turned, in his work of the sixties, to the Nietzschean question "who speaks?" he gave two answers. In *The Order of Things*, Nietzsche's question was followed by a response drawn from Mallarmé:

> what is speaking is, in its solitude, in its fragile vibration, in its nothingness, the word itself—not the meaning of the word, but its enigmatic and precarious being.... Mallarmé was constantly effacing himself from his own language, to the point of not wishing to figure in it except as an executant in a pure ceremony of the Book in which the discourse would compose itself.[42]

And when he returned to the question in "What Is an Author?" Foucault now responded with Beckett's indifference to the question "Who speaks?": "What does it matter who is speaking?"[43] Within these two answers, we locate Foucault's earliest position on the question of the subject—the subject appears as an ideological product, a functional principle of discourse rather than its privileged origin. This is not to say that the subject is to be entirely abandoned, however, as Foucault's transformation of the author in "What Is an Author?" from a "natural subject" to a constructed "author-function" makes clear. Instead, it is for Foucault a matter of depriving the subject of its role as originator and analyzing the subject as a variable and complex function of discourse and power. To do so means that we must give up the traditional questions: "How can a free subject penetrate the substance of things and give it meaning? How can it activate the rules of a language from within and thus give rise to the designs which are properly its own?" replacing them, instead, with the following questions: "How, under what conditions, and in what forms can something like a subject appear in the order of discourse? What place can it occupy in each type of discourse, what functions can it assume, and by obeying what rules?"[44]

This was not to be Foucault's final position on this matter, however. Nor was it to mark his final appeal to Nietzsche in grounding this issue. In displacing the question of the "free subject's" endowing things with meaning, it is clear that Foucault was distancing himself from the phenomenological-existential and, in particular, the Sartrean subject.[45] By returning to a Nietzschean account of the subject, Foucault replaces the Sartrean project of an authentic self with the Nietzschean project of creatively constructing oneself.[46] In so doing, he both displaces the valorized, free, existential subject and retrieves a more ambivalent subject whose constitution takes place within the constraints of institutional forces that exceed its grasp and even at times its recognition.

This is the subject whose genealogy Nietzsche traced in *On the Genealogy of Morals* (*GM*, I, 13). In an analysis that exhibits the traits Foucault himself noted in his crucial early essay "Nietzsche, Genealogy, History," Nietzsche focuses not on the valorization of origins (*Ursprung*) but on a critical analysis of the conditions of emergence (*Entstehung*) and descent (*Herkunft*).[47] Pursuing the task of "history as a curative science" (*WS*, 188), Nietzsche locates the subject not as a metaphysical given but as a historical construct, and a construct whose conditions of emergence are far from innocent. The "subject" is not only a superfluous postulation of a "'being' behind doing," a "doer" fictionally added to the deed. In addition, the belief in this postulate is exploited by "vengefulness and hatred" to convince the strong that they are *free* to be weak and, therefore, are to be held accountable for their failure to be weak. Prompted by the instinct for self-preservation and self-affirmation which sanctifies self-serving lies, Nietzsche writes:

> the subject (or, to use a more popular expression, the *soul*) has perhaps been believed in hitherto more firmly than anything else on earth because it makes possible to the majority of mortals, the weak and oppressed of every kind, the sublime self-deception that interprets weakness as freedom, and their being thus-and-thus as a *merit*. (*GM*, I, 13)

In this remark, we see that it is not simply the subject's ignoble origin that comes under genealogical scrutiny. In addition, Nietzsche directs his genealogical gaze to the life-negating uses to which the idea of the subject has been put in a further effort to challenge the subject's privileged status. Foucault comments that a genealogy of *Herkunft* "is not the erecting of foundations: on the contrary, it disturbs what was previously considered immobile; it fragments what was thought unified; it shows the heterogeneity of what was imagined consistent with itself."[48] This is precisely what Nietzsche does as his genealogy of the subject demonstrates the oppressive use made of the principle of subjectivity as a principle of domination in the service of a "hangman's metaphysics" that invents the concept of the responsible subject in order to hold it accountable and judge it guilty (see *TI*, "The Four Great Errors," 7).[49] And it is this account of the subject that leads Foucault to link the modern form of power with subjects and subjection:

> It is a form of power that makes individuals subjects. There are two meanings of the word *subject:* subject to someone else by control and dependence, and tied to his own identity by a conscience or self-knowledge. Both meanings suggest a form of power which subjugates and makes subject to.[50]

Reconfigurations of the Subject as Relation (to Itself)

This linkage sets the stage for the final turn in Foucault's thinking, namely, his return to ethics as the inquiry into the self's relationship to itself: "For let us not deceive ourselves; if we speak of the structures or the mechanisms of power, it is only insofar as we suppose that certain *persons* exercise power over others."[51] From the publication of the first volume of *The*

History of Sexuality in 1976 until the end of his life, Foucault focused his attention on the ways in which "techniques of power" are exercised and resisted *and* the link between contemporary power relations and the construction of the modern subject.

While his turn toward the subject is associated with the *History of Sexuality*, and especially the second and third volumes, we can already see indications of Foucault moving in this direction in *Discipline and Punish*. In this, his most Nietzschean text, Foucault notes the link between power and the subject while arguing that the history of the micro-physics of punitive power would be an element in the genealogy of the modern "soul."[52] Foucault addresses this soul most explicitly in the discussion of the construction of the delinquent as a responsible subject, arguing that there is a subtle transformation in the exercise of power when punishment no longer is directed at the delinquent's *actions*, but at his very person, his "being" as (a) delinquent. While acknowledging the innovative productivity of power at work in the construction of "deviant" subjectivities like the delinquent, Foucault's attention in *Discipline and Punish* remained focused not on the subject constructed but on the power-knowledge relations that made possible this construction and, in so doing, gave rise to the science of criminology. Because power and knowledge directly implicate one another, power-knowledge relations

> are to be analyzed, therefore, not on the basis of a subject of knowledge who is or is not free in relation to the power system, but, on the contrary, the subject who knows, the objects to be known and the modalities of knowledge must be regarded as so many effects of these fundamental implications of power-knowledge and their historical transformations. In short, it is not the activity of the subject of knowledge that produces a corpus of knowledge, useful or resistant to power, but power-knowledge, the processes and struggles that traverse it and of which it is made up, that determines the forms and possible domains of knowledge.[53]

Insofar as Foucault's discussion here does not go much further than linking the genealogy of the modern, disciplined subject with the genealogy of the carceral system, I think we might accept Dreyfus and Rabinow's suggestion that the move from *Discipline and Punish* to the first volume of the *History of Sexuality* is a move from a genealogy of the modern individual as *object* to a genealogy of the modern individual as *subject*.[54] But to accept their characterization is not to accept that Foucault has returned to a philosophy of the subject. Rather, as Deleuze correctly notes, "Foucault does not use the word subject as person or as form of identity, but the words 'subjectivation' as process and 'Self' as relation (relation to itself [*relation à soi*])."[55]

When Foucault attends to the problematics of the subject, he is not rediscovering a principle of subjectivity that marks a rupture with his earlier reflections on the "end of man." Instead, he remains insistent in his belief

> that there is no sovereign, founding subject, a universal form of subject to be found everywhere. I am very sceptical of this view of the subject and very hostile to it. I believe, on the contrary, that the subject is constituted through practices of subjection, or, in a more autonomous way, through practices of liberation, of liberty, as in Antiquity, on the basis, of course, of a number of rules, styles, inventions to be found in the cultural environment.[56]

It is by retrieving the subject in the form of questions concerning the process of subjectivation that Foucault adds the third axis of his genealogical project. In the introduction to the second volume of the *History of Sexuality* and elsewhere in interviews in the 1980s, Foucault speaks of his "new" project as operating now along three axes: an archaeological axis that will analyze forms of knowledge, a genealogical axis that will focus on systems of normativity, and an ethical axis that will examine forms of subjectivation. Projecting these three axes onto the experience of "sexuality" produces an analysis that will be constituted in terms of "(1) the formation of sciences (*savoirs*) that refer to [sexuality], (2) the systems of power that regulate its practice, (3) the forms within which individuals are able, are obliged, to recognize themselves as subjects of this sexuality." [57]

In another context, Foucault makes this same point as he discusses his project in terms of the four types of techniques or technologies at work in the human sciences: technologies of production, of signification, of domination, and of the self. While acknowledging that the technologies of domination were his fundamental focus prior to his analysis of sexuality, he does not introduce the technologies of the self in order to exclude the other technologies. Instead, a "genealogy of the subject" will have to "take into account the interaction" of all these technologies and, in particular, the interaction of the techniques of domination and of the self "where the technologies of domination of individuals over one another have recourse to processes by which the individual acts upon himself. And conversely, he has to take into account the points where the techniques of the self are integrated into structures of coercion or domination."[58] The contact point between these technologies is what Foucault calls "government" and his emphasis on the care and cultivation of the self is a tacit admission that his earlier genealogies of the subject had placed too great an emphasis on domination by others as the sole form of governing.[59]

This being the case, it nevertheless bears repeating that each subsequent analytic dimension explored by Foucault does not appear as a dialectical supercession of the previous analyses. Returning to a point made earlier concerning the *continuity* in Foucault's thinking, it is important to note that the introduction of a third ethical axis or a fourth technique of the self does not take the place of an earlier analytic level. Rather, the care of the self is *added* on as a *supplément* in the Derridean sense of that term, deepening the analysis by adding a dimension—the self's relations to itself (in terms including but not limited to relations of power and knowledge)—that had been insufficiently attended to in the earlier analyses. In other words, the move from one axis or technique to the next has a *cumulative* effect, as they work together toward establishing the analytic grids that make possible genealogical critique.

Drawing attention to the ethical dimension that he calls the care of the self was momentous insofar as it marked the first time in nearly twenty-five years that the concept of the subject or self had appeared in French discourse as a concept worth recuperating. It was momentous also for Foucault's project, as he could no longer finish the initial plan for the *History of Sexuality*, opting instead to begin again with a history of the construction of the self as a sexual subject from Greek antiquity through early Christianity. Like Nietzsche before him, in one final tragic analogue between their respective careers, Foucault's final project was never completed, cut short not by madness but by Foucault's untimely death. And what Foucault left to us were several thoughts on the self or subject in terms of an aesthetics of existence that resist easy integration into the power analytics of his earlier works, a self that at times appears autonomous and able to extricate itself from the normalizing practices that work to construct disciplined and docile subjects.

The Discourse Continues

Foucault left to us the task of thinking a notion of a subject that is both autonomous and disciplined, both actively self-forming and passively self-constructed, as he left us to think about the emergence of a modern state whose exercising of pastoral power both totalizes and individualizes.[60] By way of concluding this chapter, I would like to explore several directions for future thinking about the subject and power that follow the general itinerary indicated by Foucault. In his analysis of the French academy, Pierre Bourdieu makes an interesting and important conceptual distinction between "empirical individuals" and "epistemic individuals."[61] For Bourdieu, the former are historical singularities while the latter are sociological constructs that exist in the epistemic space framed by the variables relevant to a particular analysis. Drawing upon this distinction in the context of my discussion here, we may say that we can distinguish between empirical individuals as real, flesh and blood historical people, and epistemic individuals as human functionaries within an institutional setting that they occupy but do not and cannot control.[62] Empirical individuals are historical agents who act within both the public and private spheres; they fall in love, have children and parents, work, vote, feel pain, anger, sympathy, and so on. Epistemic individuals, on the other hand, act in terms of their place in an institutional matrix,[63] making the "tough decisions" that "have to be made" whether or not they "like it." A major problem in understanding contemporary power relations is the conflation of these two concepts and the failure to strategically anticipate how an epistemic individual's actions may differ from those expected of the empirical individual with whom we thought we were dealing.[64] As we see perhaps most clearly in the domain of academic politics, decision-making is not only a question of personalities but of institutional connections among various nodes through which pass pedagogical, curricular, financial, libidinal, and ideological relations of power. And every time that someone we think we know makes a decision in an administrative capacity that, given the sort of person with whom we thought we were dealing, surprises us, I would suggest that their decision is likely to be understood in terms of what I am here calling their epistemic individuality. As we are all no doubt aware, what "power" is depends on the specificity of the local relation we are considering, and in all of these relations we can locate forces of repression *and* forces of production. Similarly, we must see the agents exercising power both as persons and institutionalized markers through whom power moves.

While Foucault's own suggestions as to how we should set up our initial analytic grid seem to me to be a fruitful place to begin our local projects of resistance, they are only a beginning. Deleuze, in his remarks at the 1988 Colloquium on Foucault organized by the newly formed Centre

Michel Foucault in Paris, noted that Foucault's analyses of apparatuses (*dispositifs*) are comprised of two lines: "the lines of the recent past and those of the near future: that which belongs to the archive and that which belongs to the present; that which belongs to history and that which belongs to the process of becoming; *that which belongs to the analytic and that which belongs to the diagnostic.*"[65] Deleuze goes on to claim that in his books, Foucault addresses his attention primarily to the first of these lines as he specifies the archives he analyzes with great precision. But for whatever reason (Deleuze suggests "confidence in his readers"[66]), Foucault does not formulate the other line, the one that addresses the present. And here we find our task: we need to develop Foucault's suggestions and explore the interlaced technologies of subjects and power, recognizing, as Foucault reminds us, "not that everything is bad, but that everything is dangerous"[67] as we work toward identifying the "main dangers" and organizing the forces of production to resist them.

Relations of power are inevitable, but we need not accept as inevitable the particular forms in which those relations have emerged. There is, in other words, an emancipatory dimension of Foucault's analytic insofar as the understanding of how power relations function in the local arenas in which we act can aid us in diagnosing and resisting the more repressive exercises of these relations. The omnipresence of relations of power, therefore, does not lead to a resigned acceptance of the fact of domination, as a nihilistic reading of Foucault often concludes. To the contrary, in one of his final interviews, Foucault remarks that when he rejects as utopian Habermas's idea that "there could be a state of communication which would be such that the games of truth could circulate freely, without obstacles, without constraint and without coercion," his alternative is not a dystopian vision of inevitable oppression:

> relations of power are not something bad in themselves, from which one must free one's self. I don't believe there can be a society without relations of power, if you understand them as means by which individuals try to conduct, to determine the behavior of others. The problem is not of trying to dissolve them in the utopia of a perfectly transparent communication, but to give one's self the rules of law, the techniques of management, and also the ethics, the *ethos,* the practice of self, which would allow these games of power to be played with a minimum of domination.[68]

In this remark, Foucault makes clear that it is a mistake to regard his power-analytic as leading to a quietist acceptance of the inevitability of oppression. Far from producing a neo-conservative acceptance of the status quo, we see the potential usefulness of the Foucaultian analytic for a strategy of liberation in two recent works that have justifiably attracted a great deal of attention. Judith Butler's *Gender Trouble: Feminism and the Subversion of Identity* offers one of the most sophisticated, thought-provoking, and potentially valuable accounts of the "subject" to have appeared following the structuralist "death" and post-structuralist "decentering" of "subjectivity." And while her account of the subject as a performative is far more than an "application" of the Foucaultian analytic, it remains nevertheless a profoundly Foucaultian enterprise. In fact, she acknowledges at the start of her text the political import of Foucault's emphasis on the productive power of law for a subversion of identity.[69] She also acknowledges, albeit less frequently, the import of Nietzsche for a critical project that seeks to rethink gender (and) identity insofar as Nietzsche's challenge to a metaphysics of substance opens the possibility for a performative account of identity. Drawing upon Foucault and Nietzsche both, Butler challenges the language of interiority or internalization, offering in its stead the language of performativity in which "the gendered body [as] performative suggests that it has no ontological status apart from the various acts which constitute its reality."[70]

While critical of some of Foucault's positions on sexual difference and the body, the political dimension of Butler's conclusions that identity is a practice and gender a performative remains profoundly Foucaultian as it articulates the alternative gender possibilities produced within the repressive and constraining practices of our compulsory heterosexist culture. Arguing that "all signification takes place within the orbit of the compulsion to repeat," Butler locates "'agency'… within the possibility of a variation on that repetition."[71] In order to be intelligible, cultural forces compel certain repetitions, but at the same time, these forces *produce* possibilities of alternative performances. The task for a subversion of identity, therefore, "is not whether to repeat, but how to repeat or, indeed, to repeat and, through a radical proliferation of gender, *to displace* the very gender norms that enable the repetition itself."[72] By keeping in view the Nietzschean-Foucaultian dimension of her thinking on the question of the subject, one can thus avoid the precipitous misreading of "performative" as "performance," an all too common misreading producing the view that Butler in *Gender Trouble* articulates a voluntaristic notion of a subject who willfully decides one day to adopt one gender position, with the implication that it could just as willfully adopt a different gender position the next day.

This point bears repeating, for the Nietzschean dimension of Butler's position here is rarely noted, and it is precisely in terms of this dimension that she avoids the voluntaristic position she is mistakenly accused of holding. In *Gender Trouble*, when arguing for a nonsubstantive notion of gender, Butler quotes Nietzsche's remark, cited above, from *On the Genealogy of Morals* (*GM*, I, 13): "there is no 'being' behind doing, effecting, becoming; 'the doer' is merely a fiction added to the deed—the deed is everything."[73] While this remark is not cited in her latest work—*Bodies That Matter*—I would argue that insofar as for Nietzsche there is no 'being,' his "metaphysics of the subject" offers neither a metaphysics as traditionally understood nor a position that allows for a substantive subject. And for just this reason, Nietzsche's "metaphysics of the subject" continues to serve as a resource for Butler's performative account of gender identity, as we see in the following remark from the concluding pages of *Bodies That Matter*:

> One might be tempted to say that identity categories are insufficient because every subject position is the site of converging relations of power that are not univocal. But such a formulation underestimates the radical challenge to the subject that such converging relations imply. For there is no self-identical subject who houses or bears these relations, no site at which such relations converge. This converging and interarticulation *is* the contemporary fate of the subject. In other words, the subject as a self-identical identity is no more.[74]

While it would take us too far afield to demonstrate in detail the Nietzschean character of Butler's position, I would like here simply to note that one could easily show that Nietzsche's account of a non-substantive self as a convergence of relations of will to power confronts a traditional metaphysics of the subject with the same radical challenge.

Before leaving Butler, it is worth noting that in her recent work, she develops her position through the Derridean notion of iterability; what she earlier discussed in terms of performative repetition, she now recasts as a subversive reiteration which reembodies subjectivating norms while at the same time redirecting the normativity of those norms.[75] Even in this Derridean incarnation, however, her position remains, it seems to me, more congenial to a Foucaultian than a Derridean politics, a fact Butler herself seems to acknowledge as she reiterates her Foucaultian sympathies in a recent comment on the work of Drucilla Cornell and Ernesto Laclau. She concludes her discussion of "Poststructuralism and Postmarxism" by posing a Foucaultian alternative to "the Derridean approach pursued, for the most part, by both Laclau and Cornell."[76] And for those who are willing to see, one must also note that this Foucaultian alternative is itself couched in the language of Nietzschean genealogy, language which calls for a shift in the focus of critical inquiry. Leaving the question "what kinds of political practices are opened up now that Emancipation and the Good have proven their unrealizability," Butler suggests we move "to the more Nietzschean query: 'how is it that the unrealizability of the Good and/or Emancipation has produced a paralyzed or limited sense of political efficacy, and how, more generally, might the fabrication of more local ideals enhance the sense of politically practicable possibilities?'"[77] In so doing, she displays her continued affinity for operating out of a Foucaultian grid, framed within the ambivalence of production and repression, an affinity she recalls in the concluding chapter of *Bodies That Matter*:

> The question for thinking discourse and power in terms of the future has several paths to follow: how to think power as resignification together with power as the convergence or interarticulation of relations of regulation, domination, constitution? How to know what might qualify as an affirmative resignification—with all the weight and difficulty of that labor—and how to run the risk of reinstalling the abject at the site of its opposition? But how, also, to rethink the terms that establish and sustain bodies that matter?[78]

While Butler in *Gender Trouble* develops a Foucaultian position that primarily addresses politics at the level of individual agents enacting their gender while subjected to various cultural constraints,[79] Ernesto Laclau and Chantal Mouffe in *Hegemony and Socialist Strategy* have argued for a radical democratic politics that is dependent in part upon reconfiguring subjectivity in terms of a multiplicity of subject positions. While Laclau and Mouffe make a strong case for the necessity of reconfiguring subjectivity, they fail to see how Foucault's turn toward the subject in his last works can serve as a resource that will help facilitate a radical and plural democratic leftist politics. That is to say, Foucault showed how the discursive practices of modernity served to construct the modern docile and disciplined subject. In so doing, he demonstrated the historically contingent character of the subject's construction while showing as well the possibility of alternative constructions. This is the sense in which Foucault's works can be regarded as a "critical ontology of the present": insofar as the subject position delivered to us by modernity is not an ontological necessity, other subject positions will be historically possible in terms of the contingencies of the present moment.

Acknowledging the multiple positions that "subjects" occupy helps to explain both the current resistance to enduring political allegiances and the attractiveness of a model of coalition politics that will allow temporary alliances among various groups in response to contingent developments that call for these groups to mobilize collectively. Foucault's genealogy of the subject provides a theoretical articulation of this account of a multiple subject positioning insofar as it frames the subject not as a substance but as a form, a form, moreover, that is not always identical to itself.

> You do not have towards yourself the same kind of relationships when you constitute yourself as a political subject who goes and votes or speaks up in a meeting, and when you try to fulfill your desires in a sexual relationship. There are no doubt some relationships and some interferences between these different kinds of subject but we are not in the presence of the same kind of subject. In each case, we play, we establish with one's self some different relationship. And it is precisely the historical constitution of these different forms of subject relating to games of truth that interest me.[80]

Like Foucault, Laclau and Mouffe advocate a dispersion of a fixed and unified subjectivity, but they also claim that the moment of dispersion cannot exist in theoretical isolation. Instead, a second analytic moment is required, as "it is necessary to show the relations of overdetermination and totalization that are established among these [moments of dispersion]."[81] It is precisely this second moment that Foucault's last works, in which he began his "hermeneutic of the self," sought to articulate. For Laclau and Mouffe, the hegemonic relations established among the discursively dispersed subject positions are what provide the conditions for their notion of a *radical and plural democracy.*[82] While they do acknowledge Foucault's importance in terms of his concept of "discursive formation,"[83] they fail to acknowledge the profoundly Foucaultian character of their own identity politics. That is to say, democracy requires a fluid, transformative, and historically contingent notion of identity:

For there to be a 'democratic equivalence' something else is necessary: the construction of a new 'common sense' which changes the identity of the different groups, in such a way that the demands of each group are articulated equivalentially with those of the others—in Marx's words, 'that the free development of each should be the condition for the free development of all.' That is, equivalence is always hegemonic insofar as it does not simply establish an 'alliance' between given interests, but modifies the very identity of the forces engaging in that alliance.[84]

For this reason, there can be no foundational, unified discourse. Instead, "discursive *discontinuity*" becomes for Laclau and Mouffe "primary and constitutive"[85] inasmuch as the social sphere of radical and plural democracy is, by design, precarious and incomplete. And in such a society, characterized essentially by tension and openness, the "identity" of the democratic subject will likewise always be *in process*, a work in progress and never finished, producing itself in response to and being produced by the contingent antagonisms and alliances that constitute the social.

In Laclau and Mouffe's call for discursive discontinuity and the multiplicity of subject positions, as in Butler's bringing to the fore the productive resistances called forth by the repressive constraints of contemporary gender/identity politics, we see the evolution of a series of positions whose genealogies can be traced to Foucault. As these positions, and others with which they share philosophical assumptions and political affiliations, develop in response to changing political contingencies, the attentive reader will continue to be able to hear clearly the echoes of Foucault. Which is to say, returning to the image with which this chapter opened, that although Foucault himself may have been "erased, like a face drawn in sand at the edge of the sea,"[86] the discursivity founded by his analytics of power has established possibilities whose end we are far from reaching.

Deleuze: Putting Nietzsche to Work: Genealogy, Will to Power, and Other Desiring Machines

➤

A new species of philosophers is coming up: I venture to baptize them with a name that is not free of danger. As I unriddle them, insofar as they allow themselves to be unriddled—for it belongs to their nature to *want* to remain riddles at some point—these philosophers of the future may have a right— it might also be a wrong—to be called *experimenters* [*Versucher*]. The name itself is in the end a mere experiment [*Versuch*] and, if you will, a temptation [*Versuchung*].

—NIETZSCHE, *Beyond Good and Evil*

Reading a text is never a scholarly exercise in search of what is signified, still less a highly textual exercise in search of a signifier. Rather, it is a productive use of the literary machine, a montage of desiring machines, a schizoid exercise that extracts from the text its literary force.

—DELEUZE AND GUATTARI, *Anti-Oedipus*

WHEN ENCOUNTERING THE WRITINGS OF GILLES DELEUZE, ONE IS reminded of the signs that flash warnings to Harry in Hesse's *Steppenwolf:* "Magic Theater," "Entrance Not for Everyone," "For Madmen Only," "Price of Admittance Your Mind." Entering Deleuze's texts is for many people a frightening, indeed, even an overwhelming experience. To help find one's way, it is often useful to bring along something familiar, some appropriate baggage or some useful tool to help one to make one's way. If, as Deleuze remarked in a 1972 conversation with Michel Foucault, a "theory is exactly like a box of tools,"[1] then even a cursory examination of Deleuze's theoretical productions reveals the writings of Friedrich Nietzsche to be a central tool in the Deleuzian toolbox. With this in mind, I would like to suggest that we can use "Nietzsche" as a portal into the Deleuzian matrix. By departing from Nietzsche and following the transformation of his thought as it becomes Deleuze's, we can gain access to the Deleuzian project. If we are successful, what will result will not be a systematic treatment of Deleuze or a totalizing interpretation of his relation to Nietzsche. Instead, by making use of some Deleuzian and Nietzschean ideas and showing how they intersect and cross-fertilize one another, we will highlight several ways that Nietzsche's philosophy has been put to work in the thought of Deleuze.

Textual Practices

If we follow the trajectory of Deleuze's thought on Nietzsche, we see it move from a more or less traditional philosophical exegesis of Nietzsche, in *Nietzsche and Philosophy,*[2] to a self-conscious utilization of Nietzsche for purposes other than the philosophical *explication de texte*. *Nietzsche and Philosophy* appeared in 1962, early in Deleuze's career, during the period when he was primarily engaged in fairly straightforward and traditional philosophical analyses of more or less canonical figures within the history of philosophy. In addition to his text on Nietzsche, during the fifties and early sixties Deleuze wrote works addressing Lucretius, Hume, Kant, Bergson, and Spinoza.[3]

His text on Nietzsche is an excellent study that was instrumental in developing French interest in Nietzsche's thought during the sixties and seventies. In this text, Deleuze directs himself against what he regards as a misguided attempt to strike a compromise between the Hegelian dialectic and Nietzsche's genealogy, and his desire to offer an interpretation of Nietzsche's philosophy is matched by a desire to show the impropriety of reading Nietzsche as a neo-Hegelian dialectician.[4] Where Hegel's thinking is always guided by the movement toward some unifying synthesis, Nietzsche, in contrast, is seen to affirm multiplicity and rejoice in diversity.[5] In fact, Deleuze comes to view the entirety of Nietzsche's corpus as a polemical response to the Hegelian dialectic, one that opposes its own discovery—"the negativity of the positive"—to the famous Hegelian discovery of the "positivity of the negative."[6]

Focusing on the *qualitative* difference in Nietzsche between active and reactive forces, Deleuze argues that the mastery of the *Übermensch* derives from her or his ability *actively* to negate the slave's reactive forces, even though the slave's reactive forces may exceed quantitatively the active forces of the master. In other words, whereas the slave moves from the negative premise ("you are other and evil") to the positive judgment ("therefore I am good"), the master works from the positive differentiation of self ("I am good") to the negative corollary ("you are other and bad"). There is, according to Deleuze, a qualitative difference at the origin of force, and it is the genealogist's task to attend to this differential and genetic element of force that Nietzsche calls "will to power."[7] Thus, whereas in the Hegelian dialectic of master and slave, the reactive negation of the other has as its consequence the positive affirmation of self, Nietzsche reverses this situation: the master's active positing of self is accompanied by and results in a negation of the slave's reactive force.[8]

Offering the first major French alternative to Heidegger's monumental 1,200-page interpretation of Nietzsche,[9] *Nietzsche and Philosophy* occupies an important place in the development both of French Nietzsche studies and of poststructural French philosophy in general.[10] While much can be learned reading *Nietzsche and Philosophy*, this text remains content to express Nietzsche's thought more or less within the discursive practices of traditional ontology. For this reason, it is not the most interesting place to locate what one might call the ongoing Nietzsche-effect within Deleuze's writings. In fact, we can allow Deleuze himself to speak, albeit obliquely, against his early work on Nietzsche. The history of philosophy, he writes, is "philosophy's own Oedipus," and although Deleuze confesses to being a member of "a generation, one of the last generations, who were more or less ruined by the history of philosophy," he acknowledges that he was "pulled out of all of this" by Nietzsche.[11] In a remark that recalls Foucault's account of the normalizing power of the disciplinary rules that govern institutionalized discourses,[12] Deleuze writes that the history of philosophy has always played the repressor's role as the agent of power in philosophy.

[H]ow can you think without having read Plato, Descartes, Kant and Heidegger, and so-and-so's book about them? A formidable school of intimidation which manufactures specialists in thought—but which also makes those who stay outside conform all the more to this specialism they despise. An image of thought called philosophy has been formed historically and it effectively stops people from thinking.[13]

Deleuze goes on to claim that he prefers philosophers who appear to be part of the history of philosophy but who escape from that "bureaucracy of pure reason" in one respect or altogether.[14] Deleuze's text on Nietzsche comes close to escaping the bounds of traditional philosophical discourse insofar as it develops Nietzsche's affirmation of difference as an alternative to the Hegelian paradigm for resolving opposition, the *Aufhebung*. It is in his later texts, however, where Deleuze moves from an interpretation *of* Nietzsche to an experimentation *with* Nietzsche, that we see him begin to operate outside of the "official language" of philosophy, outside of those organizing rules that govern what can and cannot be said within philosophy, and outside as well of the typical power plays that operate within philosophy insofar as these later texts acknowledge the political and libidinal dimensions inscribed in every philosophical gesture.

Like Foucault, but unlike Derrida, Deleuze is not particularly comfortable with the language games of textuality. In his later works, several of which are written together with radical psychoanalyst Félix Guattari,[15] he comes to reject the entire project of "interpretation," opting instead for a process of *experimentation* whose explicit intention is to promote or incite political change. Since the signifier was invented, Deleuze writes, things have not yet sorted themselves out, as the obsession with interpreting sends readers off in all directions looking for hidden, secret meanings. Significance and "interpretosis"—the obsessive-compulsive deciphering of hidden signification—are the "two diseases of the earth, the pair of despot and priest." As an antidote, Deleuze prescribes: "Experiment, never interpret."[16] In contrast to the hermeneutic project of interpretation that aims to recover "sense" and the structuralist project that tracks the play of signifiers, Deleuze and Guattari place their emphasis on codes, decoding, and recoding. The processes of codification, whether legal, contractual, or institutional, constitute for Deleuze the very being of politics, and it is for this reason that Deleuze and Guattari regard every act of interpretation as a political act. To read and write politically is thus to experiment with codes—writing politically encodes certain relations (ultimately, relations of *power*) and reading politically confronts codes from a more or less antagonistic position, decoding certain power relations in order to recode them in new and less restrictive ways.

Nietzsche, for his part, occupies a privileged place in the project of political reading and writing insofar as his writings confound all codes. Nietzsche's originality, Deleuze claims, lies in part in his having written a new kind of book, one that defies codification insofar as his aphorisms transmit forces rather than signify meanings.[17] In other words, and following Blanchot's earlier demonstration,[18] Nietzsche's aphorisms are in relation to the outside, the exterior: incapable of codification, his aphorisms make the nomad's response—they demand to be elsewhere. As a consequence, Nietzsche's texts exhibit the deterritorializing politics to which all texts should aspire by presenting themselves as tools to be used rather than privileged objects to be understood. While Derrida offered as a motto the now infamous "*Il n'y a pas de hors-texte*,"[19] Deleuze seeks instead to exit the text: insofar as reading is a political act, the task is not to remain within the textual network but to execute lines of escape into extra-textual practice (not to interpret the world, Marx would say, but to change it!). In this regard, Deleuze's response to a question posed to him following his presentation of the paper "Pensée nomade" at the Cerisy Colloquium on Nietzsche in 1973 is significant. When queried on the relation between his thought and "deconstruction," Deleuze responded:

> If I understand you, you say that there is some suspicion on my part of the Heideggerian point of view. I'm delighted. With regard to the method of deconstruction of texts, I see well what it is, I admire it greatly, but I don't see it having anything to do with my own. I never present myself as a commentator on texts. A text, for me, is only a little wheel in an extra-textual practice. It is not a question of commenting on the text by a method of deconstruction, or by a method of textual practice, or by any other method; it is a question of seeing what use a text is in the extra-textual practice that prolongs the text. You ask me if I believe in the nomad's response. Yes, I believe it.[20]

While not directed in response to Derridean deconstruction per se, this remark points out an important difference between Deleuze's and Derrida's positions with respect to Nietzsche—the difference between "use" and "method."[21] Bearing this distinction in mind, one notes that Derrida methodically reiterates the proper name "Nietzsche" at significant points in his commentaries on several of the privileged texts and canonical thinkers in the history of philosophy. As suggested in chapter one, "Nietzsche" in fact comes to function as a metonymy for the possibility of thinking otherwise than logocentrically. This should not be taken to imply that the iteration of the name "Nietzsche" lacks political implications, however, either within or outside the academy. In fact, I would claim just the opposite, offering the two Derridean texts "on" Nietzsche that followed *Spurs*—"Interpreting Signatures (Nietzsche/Heidegger)" and *Otobiographies: The Teaching of Nietzsche and the Politics of the Proper Name*[22] —as evidence of his attempt to address issues concerning academic/intellectual and world politics respectively. But acknowledging the political dimension of Derrida's writings should not obscure the fact that this dimension is textually contextualized; that is, it appears in the context of a methodological intervention into the practices of reading and interpretation. Derrida himself acknowledges this in "Force of Law: The 'Mystical Foundation of Authority,'" when he distinguishes between the two ways or styles in which deconstruction is generally practiced: "One takes on the demonstrative and apparently ahistorical allure of logico-formal paradoxes. The other, more historical or more anamnesic, seems to proceed through readings of texts, meticulous interpretations and genealogies."[23] Although Derrida holds that these two styles are often grafted together, to both sympathetic and critical readers of deconstruction alike, it is often the latter style that seems to predominate.

For Deleuze, on the other hand, the question is never one of method. Where Derrida claimed that "*Il n'y a pas de hors-texte*," Deleuze and Guattari mark their departure from the traditional problematics of reading in another way. The book, they write, is not an image of the world, nor an organic totality, nor a unity of sense. "In a book, there is nothing to understand, but much to make use of. Nothing to interpret or signify, but much to experiment with. The book must form a machine with something; it must be a small tool operating on an exterior. The combinations, permutations, utilizations are never internal to the book, but depend on connections with a particular outside."[24] Against the contemporary hermeneutic fetish with meaning and interpretation, Deleuze and Guattari suggest an alternative model—the book as assemblage (*agencement*). "A book," they write, "exists only through the outside and on the outside." As an assemblage, a book exists in connection with other assemblages; it exists in terms of what it can be conjoined with, what it can be made to function with. The book does not stand as an object to be understood, and the question to ask, therefore, is not "what a book means, as signified or signifier?" Instead, Deleuze and Guattari suggest that we confront the books we read with the following questions: "what does it function with, in connection with what other things does it or does it not transmit intensities, in which other multiplicities are its own inserted and metamorphosed, with what other bodies without organs does it makes its own converge?"[25]

We can see this notion of assemblage exemplified in the creative conjunction Deleuze constructs between Nietzsche and Orson Welles in
Cinema 2: The Time–Image, as he connects Nietzsche's "will to power,"
which "substitutes the power of the false for the form of the true," with
Welles's notion of "character," not as a function of truth but as the power to
affect and be affected.[26] That Welles was or was not conscious of his affinity with Nietzsche is, of course, not the issue for Deleuze, and his
Nietzsche-Welles assemblage does not pretend to disclose the meanings
hidden within Nietzsche's text or Welles's cinema. Instead, this assemblage
demonstrates that writing for Deleuze has more to do with surveying or
mapping than with signifying—writing does not represent or reproduce the
world; it creates connections, "forms rhizomes with the world."[27]

In order to develop further the difference between use and method—
and develop further the contrast between Deleuze's textual practices and
Derridean deconstruction—we must now examine some of the other
assemblages Deleuze constructs with Nietzsche's texts, some of the other
connections he makes between Nietzsche's texts and extra-textual practices;
in other words, some of Deleuze's other Nietzsche-experiments.

Willing, Power, Desire

Nietzsche announced, in the remark that would become the closing
entry in the non-book published as *The Will to Power*, that the solution to
the riddle of his Dionysian world was that "*This world is will to power—and
nothing besides!* And you yourselves are also will to power—and nothing
besides!"(*KSA*, 11: 38[12]; *WP*, 1067). In so doing, he issued a challenge
to all future dualisms: it would no longer be possible for understanding to
proceed according to a model that operated in terms of a simple binary
logic. Opting instead for a polyvalent monism that distinguishes between
both degrees and kinds of will to power, Nietzsche's announcement stands
as a challenge to all subsequent dualistic attempts to divide and hierarchize
the world neatly into dichotomous groups: good or evil, minds or bodies,
truths or errors, us or them. The world is much more complicated than
such dualistic thinking acknowledges, and Nietzsche's announcement that
everything is will to power suggests the radically contextual and contingent
nature of all conceptual distinctions while making suspect any appeal to a
rigidly hierarchized metanarrative of binary opposition.

But while Nietzsche acknowledged that "the typical prejudice" and
"fundamental faith" of all metaphysicians "is the faith in opposite

values" (*BGE*, 2), he nevertheless continued to utilize such oppositional pairs as master morality and slave morality, Apollonian and Dionysian, life-enhancement and life-negation, etc. And as a consequence, his texts present us with the recurring problem of how to understand his use of dualistic concepts in a non-oppositional way. To pose this problem as starkly as possible, alongside the monistic final note, quoted above, from Nietzsche's most (in)famous unpublished work, that "this world is will to power—and nothing besides," we need only set the final remark of his final (albeit posthumously) *published* work, a remark that appears to pose the ultimate binary choice: "Have I been understood?—*Dionysus versus the Crucified*" (*EH*, IV, 9).

Nietzsche's semiotically condensed formula has its analog in what Deleuze and Guattari call their "magic formula … PLURALISM = MONISM."[28] Like Nietzsche, Deleuze and Guattari collapse the distinction between monism and pluralism, and they likewise follow Nietzsche in their willingness to utilize binary concepts *strategically*. This willingness to adopt a binary format marks one of the most obvious points at which Deleuze and Guattari differentiate themselves from Derrida and other recent French thinkers as well as from the Hegelian tradition. While the Hegelian *Aufhebung* resolves dualistic opposition in a higher synthesis, Derrida traces binary opposition to a more primordial transcendental "non-concept," for example, "*archi-trace*" as condition for the possibility of the opposition between writing and speech, or "*différance*" as what makes possible both the presentation or absence of the being-present.[29]

In contrast, even a brief survey of some of their basic analytic categories—paranoia and schizophrenia, molar and molecular, arborescent and rhizomatic, state apparatus and nomad war machine, smooth and striated—shows Deleuze and Guattari to be content to work within the framework of a certain kind of binarism, one which seeks not to dissolve but to multiply dualistic concepts. While Nietzsche leaves unthematized the problem of utilizing dualistic concepts in non-oppositional ways, Deleuze and Guattari confront this issue directly in the introduction to *A Thousand Plateaus*, where they admit to using dualisms but only in order to challenge other dualisms. When binary concepts are employed, they write, "mental correctives are necessary" to undo those dualisms that one does not "wish to construct but through which [one must] pass" as one moves beyond dualisms to the realization of a pluralist monism.[30] One can use dualistic concepts, indeed their use may be necessary; but one must take care to avoid privileging and reifying these dualisms as absolute. And, at the same time, one must take care as well to remember both that these dualisms mark *differences* rather than oppositions and that their use is always strategic and provisional.

Arriving at the perspective of a pluralist or polyvalent monism that can acknowledge differences without falling victim to conceiving these differences as marking inherently opposed subjects is one of the central points of contact between the projects of Nietzsche and Deleuze. As we saw in the previous chapter, when he claims that everything is will to power, Nietzsche draws our attention away from substances and subjects and refocuses that attention on the *relations between* these substantives. Such relations, according to Nietzsche, were relations of forces: forces of attraction and repulsion, domination and subordination, imposition and reception, and so on. If there is a metaphysic in Nietzsche—and I'm not at all sure that there is or that it is particularly helpful to view Nietzsche in these terms (as Heidegger did)—then this metaphysic will be a dynamic, "process" metaphysic and not a substance-metaphysic, a metaphysic of becomings and not of beings. These processes, these becomings, will be processes of forces: becomings-stronger or becomings-weaker, enhancement or impoverishment. There is, for Nietzsche, no escaping these becomings other than death. The goal he advocates, therefore, is not to seek Being but to strive for the balance-sheet of one's life to include more becomings-stronger than -weaker, more overcomings than goings-under.

When we look to Deleuze's work, we can see him making double use of Nietzsche's will to power. Deleuze engages in a project that reformulates traditional binary disjunctions between given alternatives in terms of a pluralistic continuum in which choices are always local and relative rather than global and absolute. When, for example, he speaks with Guattari of a continuum of desiring production, the model they appeal to takes the form of Nietzsche's "monism" of the will to power, a monism understood as the differential of forces rather than in the Heideggerian sense of will to power as Nietzsche's foundational answer to the metaphysical question of the Being of beings.[31] This is to say, where Heidegger, himself the consummate metaphysician, understood will to power in terms of a logic of Being, an onto-logic, Deleuze situates will to power within a differential logic of affirmation and negation that facilitates the interpretation and evaluation of active and reactive forces. Will to power thus operates at the genealogical and not the ontological level, at the level of the qualitative and quantitative differences between forces and the different values bestowed upon those forces rather than at the level of Being and beings.[32] In going beyond good and evil, beyond truth and error to the claim that all is will to power, Nietzsche attempted to think relationality without substantives, relations without relata, difference without exclusion. And in so doing, his thought serves as a model for Deleuze's desiring assemblages conceived in terms of a logic of events.

In addition to using Nietzsche's formal structure as a model, Deleuze seizes upon what we might call the "content" of Nietzsche's will to power and he offers expanded accounts of the two component poles: will and power. While French thought in general has worked for the past thirty years under the aegis of the three so-called "masters of suspicion" Nietzsche, Freud, and Marx, we can understand Deleuze privileging Nietzsche over Marx and Freud on precisely this point. Marx operates primarily with the register of power and Freud operates primarily within the register of desire. Yet each appears blind to the overlapping of these two registers, and when they do relate them, one is clearly subordinate to the other. Nietzsche's will to power, on the other hand, makes impossible any privileging of one over the other, and his thinking functions in terms of an inclusive conjunction of desire and power. That is to say, for Nietzsche, "will to power" is redundant insofar as will wills power and power manifests itself only through will. In privileging Nietzsche over Marx or Freud, Deleuze recognizes the complicity between the poles of will and power and, as a consequence, he can focus on one of the poles without diminishing the importance of the other pole or excluding it altogether from his analyses.

In his own studies and especially in his work with Guattari, Deleuze has focused on the *willing* of power, that is to say, desire. Like Foucault, he refrains from subjectifying desire while recognizing the intimate and multiple couplings of desire and power. In *Nietzsche and Philosophy*, Deleuze first linked the notion of desire with will to power, and the insight that desire is productive follows from his reflection on will to power in terms of the productivity of both active and reactive forces. In *Anti-Oedipus*, he and Guattari introduce the desiring machine as a machinic, functionalist translation of Nietzschean will to power. A desiring machine is a functional assemblage of a desiring will and the object desired. Deleuze's goal, I think, is to place desire into a functionalist vocabulary, a machinic index, so as to avoid the personification or subjectivation of desire in a substantive will, ego, unconscious, or self. By avoiding the organicist connotations of a discrete subject characterized by a realm of interiority within which desire is located, Deleuze can avoid the paradox Nietzsche sometimes faced when speaking of will to power without a subject doing the willing or implying that will to power was both the producing "agent" and the "object" produced.

Insofar as the machinic language of assemblages connotes exteriority—connections to the outside are always already being made—to speak of desire as part of an assemblage, to refuse to reify or personify desire at the subject pole, recognizes that desire and the object desired arise together. Deleuze rejects the account of desire as lack—a view shared by Freud, Lacan, Sartre, and many others that has dominated the Western philosophical and psychological tradition since Plato's *Symposium*.[33] "Who, except priests," Deleuze remarks, "would want to call [desire] 'lack'? Nietzsche called it 'Will to Power'. There are other names for it. For example, 'grace'. Desiring is not at all easy, but this is precisely because it gives, instead of lacks, 'virtue which gives'. Those who link desire to lack, the long column of crooners of castration, clearly indicate a long resentment, like an interminable bad conscience…. Lack refers to a positivity of desire, and not the desire to a negativity of lack."[34]

To view desire as lack assumes that desire is derivative, arising in response to the perceived lack of the object desired or as a state produced in the subject by the lack of the object. For Deleuze, on the other hand, desire is a part of the perceptual infrastructure:[35] it is constitutive of the objects desired as well as the social field in which they appear.[36] It is, in other words, what first introduces the affective connections that make it possible to navigate through the social world. Which is to say that desire, again like Nietzsche's will to power, is productive—it is always already at work within the social field, preceding and "producing" objects as desirable. And as Nietzsche sought to keep will to power multiple so that it might appear in multiple forms, at once producer and product, a monism and a pluralism, so too Deleuze wants desire to be multiple, polyvocal, operating in multiple ways and capable of multiple and multiplying productions.[37] Nietzsche encouraged the maximizing of strong, healthy will to power while acknowledging the necessity, indeed, the inevitability of weak, decadent will to power. Deleuze advocates that desire be productive while recognizing that desire will sometimes be destructive and will sometimes have to be repressed, while at other times it will seek and produce its own repression. Analyzing this phenomenon of desire seeking its own repression is one of the goals of Deleuze and Guattari's schizoanalysis, and we should not fail to notice the structural similarity between desire desiring its own repression and Nietzsche's "discovery" in *On the Genealogy of Morals* that the will would rather will nothingness than not will (*GM*, III, 1 and 28).

To speak very generally, then, we can say that as Deleuze appropriates Nietzsche, will to power is transformed into a desiring-machine: Nietzsche's biologism becomes Deleuze's machinism; Nietzsche's "everything is will to power" becomes Deleuze's "everything is desire"; Nietzsche's affirmation of healthy will to power becomes Deleuze's affirmation of desiring-production. Now, what is to be gained, one might ask, through this transformation? By way of answering this question, I will undertake two textual experiments. In the first, moving from Deleuze to Nietzsche, I will show how one could use a Deleuzian approach to offer a novel interpretation of one of Nietzsche's central themes: the *Übermensch*. In the second experiment, I will reverse the direction and show how attending to Nietzsche's genealogical critique of Christian morality highlights a number of features in Deleuze and Guattari's critique of psychoanalysis.

Becoming-Übermensch

One of the themes frequenting Deleuze's later work is the process he calls "becoming." He distinguishes becoming from several other transformative processes with which it can be confused, most notably evolution. The central feature distinguishing becoming is the absence of fixed terms: "What is real is the becoming itself, the block of becoming, not the supposedly fixed terms through which that which becomes passes.... Becoming produces nothing other than itself.... [A] becoming lacks a subject distinct from itself.... Becoming is a verb with a consistency all its own; it does not reduce to, or lead back to, 'appearing,' 'being,' 'equaling,' or 'producing.'"[38] What Deleuze finds missing in all of these apparent synonyms for "becoming" is the focus on process itself. Whereas evolutionary language focuses our attention on the beginning and endpoint of a process in a way that obscures the passage between them, the language of compound becoming draws our attention to what happens *between* these ever-receding endpoints. Becomings take place *between* poles; they are the in-betweens that pass only and always along a middle without origin or destination.[39]

The experimental value of these movements of becoming are displayed, for example, in Deleuze and Guattari's reading of Kafka, especially in terms of Kafka's use of metamorphosis to counter metaphor. Whereas metaphor recalls relations of resemblance and imitation, metamorphosis inscribes processes of becoming. They read "The Metamorphosis" not as an allegory of an individual who considers himself to be as insignificant as an insect, a reading that would interpret the insect as a metaphor or symbol of dehumanized humanity. It is, instead, the becoming-insect of Gregor that is the "subject" of the story: Gregor's becoming-insect deterritorializes the politics of the family, while the story concludes with Gregor's being re-territorialized by his family, as his refusal to give up the picture of his sister leads to the throwing of the apple which eventually results in Gregor's becoming-dead. Likewise, the becoming-machine of the officer in "The Penal Colony" or the becoming-human of the ape in "Report to an Academy" is at issue in Kafka's short stories. This attention to becoming allows Deleuze and Guattari, and their readers, to experiment with alternative notions of subjectivity as a process of multiplicity in which Kafka's characters are freed radically to transform themselves while becoming-other. This is to say, Kafka's characters are freed from the constraints imposed upon them by the more traditional psychoanalytic or existential interpretations, which overdetermine these characters as fixed and fully formed, albeit Oedipally crippled or intersubjectively alienated. In Deleuze and Guattari's reading, on the other hand, anything is possible—the subject is a process of multiple becoming in which anything can be connected to anything else; humanity becomes insect becomes ape becomes killing machine becomes humanity, *da capo*.

An attention to becoming can also be put to use in terms of experimenting with Nietzsche's *Übermensch*, and many of the interpretive paradoxes concerning the *Übermensch* can be avoided if one refrains from interpreting *Übermensch* as Nietzsche's model of the ideal subject or perfect human being. Unfortunately, many of Nietzsche's most influential interpreters, including, among others, Heidegger and Kaufmann, have viewed the *Übermensch* in just this way. Caricaturish images from the Left and Right thus portray Nietzsche's *Übermensch* alternatively as a model of the Maslowian self-actualized individual or a fascist moral monster. We thus find, on the one hand, Arthur Danto writing:

> The *Übermensch*, accordingly, is not the blond giant dominating his lesser fellows. He is merely a joyous, guiltless, free human being, in possession of instinctual drives which do not overpower him. He is the master and not the slave of his drives, and so he is in a position to make something of himself rather than being the product of instinctual discharge and external obstacle.[40]

And on the other hand, we have the example of J. P. Stern:

> [Nietzsche] seems unaware that he is giving us nothing to distinguish the
> fanaticism that goes with bad faith from his own belief in the unconditioned
> value of self-realization and self-becoming—that is, from his own belief in
> the Superman. We for our part are bound to look askance at this questionable
> doctrine. We can hardly forget that the solemn avowal of this reduplicated
> self—the pathos of personal authenticity—was the chief tenet of fascism and
> national socialism. No man came closer to the full realization of self-created
> "values" than A. Hitler.[41]

Nietzsche himself warned against interpreting the word *Übermensch* either
as "a higher kind of man" or in a Darwinistic, evolutionary fashion. "The last
thing *I* should promise," he writes in the preface to *Ecce Homo*, "would be
to 'improve' mankind. No new idols are erected by me" (*EH*, Pr2). Later in
Ecce Homo, he takes note of the fact that "The word '*Übermensch*,' as the des-
ignation of a type of supreme achievement... has been understood almost
everywhere with the utmost innocence in the sense of those very values whose
opposite Zarathustra was meant to represent—that is, as an 'idealistic' type
of a higher kind of man, half 'saint,' half 'genius.' Other scholarly oxen have
suspected me of Darwinism on that account" (*EH*, III, 1).[42] Remarks like
these make clear that it is a mistake to read Nietzsche as a philosopher of the
Superman or as someone who seeks to exalt Man as that being who will serve
as God's replacement in terms of some new anthropo-theology following the
death of God. As Deleuze himself notes in the appendix to his book on
Foucault, it is not Nietzsche but Feuerbach who is the thinker of the death of
God and who seeks to install Man in the space vacated by God's absence.[43]
For Nietzsche, on the other hand, God's death is an old story, of interest only
to the last Pope (see *Z*, "Retired"), a story told in several ways, more often as
comedy than tragedy.[44]

Rather than trying to understand what Nietzsche means by *Übermensch*
in terms of some model of ideal humanity, a Deleuzian approach would experiment with how the *Übermensch* functions in the Nietzschean text. One notes
immediately that we are told very little about what an *Übermensch* is like, and
nowhere does Nietzsche give us as detailed a picture of the *Übermensch* as we
have of the last man, the higher men, the free spirit, or the slave and master
moralists. As Deleuze remarks, "we have to content ourselves with very ten-
tative indications if we are not to descend to the level of cartoons."[45]

Unfortunately, too often the discourse descends to this level as Nietzsche's commentators seek to provide an answer to the question "Who is Nietzsche's *Übermensch*?" If we look to how " *Übermensch*" functions in the Nietzschean text, however, we find it functioning not as the name of a particular being or type of being. " *Übermensch*" is, rather, the name given to an idealized conglomeration of forces which Nietzsche refers to as an "achievement" (*EH*, III, 1). Nietzsche does not provide, in *Thus Spoke Zarathustra* or anywhere else, a philosophical guidebook for *Übermenschen*; he provides instead suggestions for steps to take in order to become-*Übermensch*. Following Deleuze, I would suggest we construe becoming-*Übermensch* with a hyphen as a compound verb marking a compound assemblage. In so doing, we draw attention to the active process of assembling rather than hypostatizing, re- or deifying the endpoint to be assembled. We can only speak of the becoming-*Übermensch* of human beings, of the process of accumulating strength and exerting mastery outside the limits of external authoritarian impositions. Nietzsche called this process of becoming-*Übermensch* "life-enhancement," and he indicated by this a process of self-overcoming and increasing of will to power rather than an ideal form of subjectivity.

Nietzsche's failure—or more accurately, his refusal in *Thus Spoke Zarathustra*—to present an *Übermensch* in any form other than as a vision or a riddle thus leads to the conclusion that the answer to the question "Is S an *Übermensch*?" will always be "No" insofar as " *Übermensch*" does not designate an ontological state or way of being that a subject could instantiate.[46] By experimenting with the different possibilities of becoming-*Übermensch*, we can read *Thus Spoke Zarathustra* not as providing the blueprint for constructing a centered super-subject called "Overman," as was tragically the case in several readings of Nietzsche offered earlier this century. Instead, an experimental approach attends to Zarathustra's own experimentalism, noting as he does that one must find one's own way, "for *the* way—that does not exist!" (*Z*, "On the Spirit of Gravity," 2). This approach will emphasize not a way of Being but the affirmation of self-overcoming and transvaluation that makes possible the infinite processes of becoming that I am here suggesting we call becoming-*Übermensch*.

And the outcome of this approach will be to reformulate the notion of the subject itself, not as a fixed and full substance or completed project, but always as a work in progress. I do not want to make too much of this aesthetic analogy however, for the important idea here is not to create one's life as a work of *art*. Rather, the central idea is that as a work *in progress*, one's life is never complete. One is always on the way, and the emphasis is always on the process of going rather than the destination reached. This, I would suggest, is the central issue in the discussion, at the opening of the second essay of *On the Genealogy of Morals*, of the active forgetting of the "*sovereign individual*" who has earned the right to make promises: it is only in the case of this "emancipated individual," this "master of a *free* will" (*GM*, II, 2), who is capable of *becoming other than he was* by forgetting what he was, that promising appears as the praiseworthy act of a responsible agent. And this idea animates as well the "great health" that Nietzsche alludes to at the conclusion of the *Genealogy's* second essay, that health which knows that growth requires destruction, which knows that to become requires that we in some sense destroy what we presently are (*GM*, II, 24). What we find, in other words, is the idea of the "subject" as a process of becoming-other residing at the very heart of Nietzsche's genealogical project.

Anti-Oedipus, or the Genealogy of Psychoanalysis

As we turn now to the second experiment, I must admit that the details of Deleuze and Guattari's critique of psychoanalytic theory and practice and the relations between psychoanalysis and capitalism are far too complex to be addressed here in great detail. What I would like to suggest instead is that the outlines of their critique can be sketched in terms of the ways this critique follows an analytic pattern elaborated nearly a century earlier by Nietzsche in *On the Genealogy of Morals*.[47] While no one would challenge the general claim that the author of the *Anti-Christ* influenced the development of the argument by the authors of the *Anti-Oedipus*, I want to bring clearly into view several of the specific ways Deleuze and Guattari draw upon Nietzsche's genealogical account of church practices as they analyze the practices of psychoanalysis.

It will be helpful at this point to rehearse very quickly some of the central issues in Nietzsche's analysis of the origins of bad conscience and the alliance between the church and the state that appear in the *Genealogy*, a work Deleuze and Guattari cite as "*the* great book of modern ethnology."[48] In the first essay, Nietzsche chronicles "the birth of Christianity out of the spirit of *ressentiment*" (*EH*, III, GM). The inability to respond actively leads to the invention of a concept that will legitimate and justify this inability— the concept "subject." By the invention of the subject, the slave creates a substratum (ultimately the soul) that underlies and supports activity and that is conceived as *free not to act*. The slave is now in a position to demand of strength that it should not express itself as strength, that it should not desire to overcome nor desire to be master. Slave morality thus draws the moral implication that the strong don't have to be evil; they could have chosen, like the weak, to be "good," to not act. Like a lamb who regards itself as a bird of prey that *chooses* to refrain from action, the slavish type's invention of the subject/soul as a fiction that separates force from what it can do allows it to interpret itself as good, to interpret its essential lack of strength as a voluntary, meritorious achievement; in other words, the invention of the subject allows the slaves to interpret their weakness as freedom.

The second essay opens with Nietzsche's assertion that promising is the essential problem of man insofar as there exists, at the foundation of promising, an opposition that makes morality possible. This is the opposition between active forgetfulness as a preserver of psychic order and repose, and memory as what makes possible the right to make promises and the ability to anticipate and make plans for the future. Having posited this opposition, Nietzsche traces the cruel history of disciplinary mnemotechnics involved in breeding the powers of memory in human beings, the powers that make possible guilt, bad conscience, punishment, and responsibility—i.e., morality.

Pain, Nietzsche notes, is the most powerful aid to mnemonics: if something is to remain in memory it must be burned in, it must hurt.[49] To explain the mechanics of this mnemonic breeding, Nietzsche turns first to the origins of guilt and bad conscience, and he offers a materialist account that reveals the origins of these apparently moral concepts to lie in the economic relation of creditor and debtor. The moral concept "guilt"—*Schuld*—conceived as a debt (*Schuld*) that is essentially unredeemable, has its origin in the economic, legal notion of debt as essentially repayable. We see this double meaning of *Schuld* (guilt/debt) at work in Nietzsche's genealogy of the origin of punishment, which as retribution emerges from the inability to repay the debt. *Schuld*, debt/guilt, is part of the strange logic of compensation that seeks to establish equivalences between creditors and debtors: because everything has its price and all things can be paid for, the debtors, having made a promise to repay, would offer a substitute payment of something they possessed: their body, their spouse, their freedom, even their life. Here we see the primitive intertwining of guilt and suffering: suffering will balance debts to the extent that the creditors get pleasure from making suffer. There is, for Nietzsche, a basic joy in the exercising of mastery, and by making suffer, the creditors thus participate in the pleasures of the masters. For Nietzsche, the degree to which cruelty constituted a pleasure for primitive people is evidenced by their turning this suffering into a festival play for themselves and the gods.

When he turns to modern cultures, Nietzsche observes a spiritualization and deification of cruelty. Whereas the primitives were cheerful, modern man is ashamed of his instincts for cruelty. Modern man has to invent free will to justify suffering: punishment now appears as deserved because one could have done otherwise, which is to say, punishment now appears no longer as the result of the human desire for pleasure and mastery but instead as the consequence of God's judgment. The "moral" function of punishment is thus to awaken the feeling of guilt, and it is supposed to function as an instrument to create bad conscience.

To this account, Nietzsche offers his own account of the origin of bad conscience as a serious illness contracted when human beings entered into communities. Anticipating both the general Freudian model of tension-reduction and the specific account of the functioning of the superego that Freud offers in Chapter VII of *Civilization and its Discontents*, Nietzsche claims that upon entering into a community, the prohibition against discharging one's instincts externally led to these instincts being turned inward. This "internalization [*Verinnerlichung*] of man" (*GM*, II, 16), Nietzsche argues, is the origin of "bad conscience," as the instinct for hostility, cruelty, joy in prosecuting and attacking, the desire for change and destruction are inhibited from being discharged and are turned instead against the possessor of these instincts. Bad conscience, that uncanniest of illnesses, Nietzsche thus concludes, is man's suffering of himself.

In an analytic move that clearly inspires Deleuze and Guattari's materialist psychiatry, Nietzsche links this psychological account of bad conscience to the origin of the state as he offers an account of the establishment of society from out of the "state of nature," a tale that echoes the one told by Hobbes much more than the myth told by Locke or Rousseau. Bad conscience does not originate gradually or voluntarily, but all at once. This change is initiated by an act of violence: the institution of the state. The state is a violent, tyrannical, oppressive machine, created by those unconscious, involuntary artists and beasts of prey—the conquerors and masters who impose form on nomadic, formless masses (*GM*, II, 17). Although the masters themselves lack bad conscience, it originates through their making latent in others the instinct for freedom. When repressed and incarcerated, this instinct for freedom—the will to power as autonomous imposition of form—can only be turned against itself. In other words, while masters and artists are able to vent their will to power on others, the weak can only vent their will to power on themselves and they can experience the joy in making suffer only by making themselves suffer.

While its origin resides in the institution of the primeval state, bad conscience plays a central role in the evolution of the state's modern form. Bad conscience, Nietzsche tells us, is an illness as pregnancy is an illness (*GM*, II, 19), and he concludes the Second Essay by exposing this illness's progeny to be Christian morality and the church. As society evolved, the creditor/debtor relation took the form of a relation between the present generation and its ancestors: we pay back our ancestors by obeying their customs. Our debt to our ancestors increases to the extent that the power of the community increases. Ultimately, our ancestors are transfigured into gods and, in successive generations, this unpaid debt to our ancestors is inherited with interest. As the power of the community increases, as the community advances toward a universal empire, the divinity of the ancestors also increases. With Christianity, Nietzsche sees a "stroke of genius" in the eventual moralization of debt/guilt and duty, as the Christian God, "the maximum God attained so far," is accompanied by maximum indebtedness. Christianity's stroke of genius was to have God sacrifice himself for the guilt of humanity. By sacrificing himself for the debtor, the creditor both removed the debt and made the debt eternal and ultimately unredeemable. The origin of the Christian God is this mad will to guilt and punishment, this will to a punishment incapable of becoming equal to the guilt. This new guilt before God results in the complete deification of God as holy judge and hangman, at once man's infinite antithesis and the ultimate instrument of his self-torture (*GM*, II, 22).

Nietzsche's *On the Genealogy of Morals* shows the ways in which the ascetic priests, in the form of the founders of Christianity and the ideologues of science, have constructed an interpretation of the modern world in which they are made to appear essential (see *A*, 26). Deleuze and Guattari argue that the psychoanalyst is the "most recent figure of the priest"[50] and throughout *Anti-Oedipus* their analyses of the practices of psychoanalysis parallel the practices of Christianity as analyzed by Nietzsche. Like the early priests, psychoanalysts have reinterpreted the world in a way that makes themselves indispensable. The whole psychoanalytic edifice is constructed on the basis of the Oedipal drama, and the primary task of psychoanalysis is to successfully Oedipalize its public: "Oedipus is the disease," the psychoanalysts announce, "and we have the cure!" Nietzsche showed how much of

Christianity's practice requires convincing its adherents of their guilt and sin in order to make tenable Christianity's own claim of redemptive power. Deleuze and Guattari take a similar approach, developing at length the ways in which the psychological liberation promised by psychoanalysis requires first that it imprison libidinal economy within the confines of the family. To Nietzsche's "internalization of man," they add man's Oedipalization: Oedipus repeats the split movement of Nietzschean bad conscience—projecting onto the other while turning back against oneself—as the unsatisfied desire to eliminate and replace the father is accompanied by guilt for having such desire. They view psychoanalytic interpretive practices as no less reductive than the interpretations of Nietzsche's ascetic priests. Just as Nietzsche's priests reduce all events to a moment within the logic of divine reward and punishment, Deleuze and Guattari's psychoanalysts reduce all desire to a form of familial fixation. Like Nietzsche's ascetic priests, psychoanalysts have created for themselves a mask of health that has the power to tyrannize the healthy by poisoning their conscience. Where Nietzsche notes the *irony* of the Christian God sacrificing himself for humanity "out of *love*"(*GM*, II, 21), Deleuze and Guattari ironically chronicle the various expressions of the psychoanalysts' concern for their Oedipally crippled patients. The ultimate outcomes of these ironic twists also parallel one another: where Christianity's self-sacrificing God makes infinite its adherents,'guilt and debt, psychoanalysis creates its own infinite debt in the form of inexhaustible transference and interminable analysis.[51]

What is, I think, the most interesting transformation of Nietzsche's analysis is the way Deleuze and Guattari adapt Nietzsche's link between the rise of Christianity and the rise of the state to their discussion of libidinal and political economy. They want to introduce desire into the social field at all levels and this prompts their entire critique of psychoanalysis. Freud could only view libidinal social investments as subliminal and, as a result, he interpreted all social relations as desexualized representations of unconscious desire. Likewise, when sexual relations do appear in the social field, they are interpreted by Freud as symbolic representations of the Oedipal family. Deleuze and Guattari want to liberate desire from its enslavement within the theater of representation, and they reject the reductive familialism that sees the family everywhere while it obscures all relations of wealth, class, gender, race—i.e., all social relations outside the family. They criticize Freud for failing to acknowledge the sexual dimension of economic dependence, a failure exemplified in his consistent reduction of women of subordinate social standing ("maids," "peasant girls," etc.) to substitutes for incest with the mother or sister (e.g., in the case of the "Rat Man" or the "Wolf Man").[52] For Deleuze and Guattari, on the other hand, every investment, libidinal or otherwise, is social.[53] "One can put it best by saying that social investments are themselves erotic and, inversely, that the most erotic of desires brings about a fully political and social investment, engages with an entire social field."[54] Insofar as social production is libidinal and libidinal production is social, they claim it is a mistake to desexualize the social field.

> The truth is that sexuality is everywhere: in the way that a bureaucrat fondles his records, a judge administers justice, a businessman causes money to circulate; in the way the bourgeoisie fucks the proletariat; and so on. And there is no need to resort to metaphors, any more than for the libido to go by way of metamorphoses. Hitler got the fascists sexually aroused. Flags, nations, armies, banks get a lot of people aroused.[55]

Revising both Marx and Freud, Deleuze and Guattari conclude that insofar as desire is constitutive of the social field, "social production is desiringproduction itself *under determinate conditions.*"[56]

In linking desire to production in this way, Deleuze and Guattari "replace the theatrical or familial model of the unconscious with a more political model: the factory instead of the theater."[57] The question of desire is, *pace* Freud, a question not of dramatic familial representation but of material production, which is to say, a political question, a question of experimentation, power and justice. As Nietzsche earlier accused Plato of cowardice before his own ideas (see *TI*, "What I Owe the Ancients," 2), Deleuze and Guattari imply that Freud did not have the courage to confront what his investigations of the unconscious disclosed to him: "It is as if Freud had drawn back from this world of wild production and explosive desire, wanting at all costs to restore a little order there, an order made classical owing to the ancient Greek theater."[58] In his retreat, the productive potency of desire was "reduced to mere fantasy production.... The unconscious ceases to be what it is—a factory, a workshop—to become a theater, a scene and its staging. And not even an avant-garde theater, such as existed in Freud's day (Wedekind), but the classical theater, the classical order of representation. The psychoanalyst becomes a director for a private theater" in which the dramas of familial romance are staged.[59]

This point cannot be emphasized too strongly: according to Deleuze and Guattari, the great discovery of psychoanalysis was the discovery of "the production of desire, of the productions of the unconscious." But as soon as psychoanalysis turns to *Oedipus Rex*, Oedipus wrecks: with the introduction of Oedipus, desire was restricted to the production of fantasy, representation was substituted for production, units of expression replaced units of production, "and an unconscious that was capable of nothing but expressing itself—in myth, tragedy, dreams—was substituted for the productive unconscious."[60]

This link between desire and material production is central to Deleuze and Guattari's analysis in *Anti-Oedipus*, which we must recall is the first volume of *Capitalism and Schizophrenia*. Associating Oedipus with idealism and showing how psychoanalysis restricts the productivity of the unconscious to fantasy production is crucial to their critique. Equally crucial is their development of the real, material libidinal productivity that is made possible by reversing the relation between desire and lack. That is to say, desire is not the effect of lack, but rather the reverse: "lack is a countereffect of desire.... Desire is not bolstered by needs...; needs are derived from desire: they are counterproducts within the real that desire produces."[61]

Deleuze and Guattari here follow a line of argumentation that is clearly Marxist in its orientation: lack is a social product; it is "created, planned, and organized" in accordance with the interests of the dominant class. Never primary,[62] lack is a deliberate creation that functions within a market economy that "involves deliberately organizing wants and needs amid an abundance of production; making all of desire teeter and fall victim to the great fear of not having one's needs satisfied."[63] Deleuze and Guattari name this production of organized lack "antiproduction," and they regard it as one of the defining characteristics of capitalist economies operating at the heart of capitalist production itself.[64] The reason why they privilege the schizo as a threat to capitalism is that for capitalism to function, it must be able to control (i.e., code, decode, recode) desire, to construct and insinuate need and lack at the center of abundance. But the schizo's desire cannot be controlled, as Freud himself was forced to concede. It is because the schizo's desire productively exceeds the limits of capitalist and psychoanalytic control alike that the schizo provides a "line of flight" that Deleuze and Guattari pursue through the pages of *Anti-Oedipus*.

What psychoanalysis failed to recognize was that the successful Oedipalization of its public depends upon the phenomenon of desire desiring its own repression. For Deleuze and Guattari, the discovery of this phe-nomenon is associated first and foremost with Wilhelm Reich,[65] who refused to explain fascism in terms of the false consciousness of the masses. Instead, Reich formulated an explanation that takes the desires of the mass-es into account: they *wanted* fascism, and it is this perverse manifestation of desire that must be explained. For Reich, the explanation comes in terms of the pleasures of exercising authority that are vicariously experienced by the "little man's" identification with the "Führer."[66] Deleuze and Guattari's account of this desire, along with their fascination with the relation of the officer to the machine in Kafka's "Penal Colony" and their analyses of psy-choanalysis, leads them to Nietzsche's *Genealogy of Morals*. Here, in Nietzsche's account of the will to nothingness as preferable to not willing and in bad conscience choosing to make itself suffer rather than relinquish the pleasure in making suffer, they locate their answer to Reich's question of the link between psychic repression and social repression in the libidinal economy of fascism. Where Reich saw desire activated through a passive identification of the masses with their fascist master(s), Nietzsche saw the ascetic desire to make itself suffer as perverse but fundamentally *active* and ultimately *positive* because through this perverse desire, "*the will itself was saved*" (*GM*, III, 28).

On the basis of their experimentations with Reich and Nietzsche, Deleuze and Guattari draw the following conclusion: desire is productive, it must be productive, and it will be productive. If a social field does not allow for desire to be productive in non-repressive forms, then it will produce in whatever forms are available to it, even those that it recognizes to be socially or psychi-cally repressive. Like Nietzsche in his analyses of will to power, Deleuze and Guattari conclude that desire can only be analyzed locally, relative to the social field in which it operates. There can be no global, universal or totalizing judg-ment concerning desire. As Nietzsche's Third Essay of *On the Genealogy of Morals* analyzed the concrete practices of the ascetic priests in terms of the enhancement and impoverishment of will to power, Deleuze and Guattari continued this critique, questioning political and psychoanalytic practices in terms of productive and repressive libidinal capacities, microproductivities and microfascisms. The question that must ultimately be placed to their work, a question first articulated by Nietzsche with regard to truth which Deleuze and Guattari themselves articulate in terms of the challenges posed by desire, is not "what does it mean?" or "is it true?" but "how does it work?"[67] In the preceding pages, we have seen some of the ways that it does.

CHAPTER FOUR

Cixous: On the Gift-Giving
Virtue as Feminine Economy

➤

...a gift-giving virtue is the highest virtue.

—NIETZSCHE, *Thus Spoke Zarathustra*

Desire knows nothing of exchange, *it knows only theft and gift.*

—DELEUZE AND GUATTARI, *Anti-Oedipus*

Who could ever think of the gift as a gift-that-takes? Who else but man, precisely the one who would like to take everything?

—CIXOUS, "The Laugh of the Medusa"

IT HAS LONG BEEN RECOGNIZED THAT NIETZSCHE, WHOSE PERSPECTIVES CAN at times mimic the worst of nineteenth-century prejudices, is also able to give voice to insights that a century later are still at the forefront of critical reflection. With this in mind, I would like to explore a possible linkage between Nietzsche's thinking and the work of French feminist writer Hélène Cixous.

In "The Laugh of the Medusa," upon introducing "the whole deceptive problematic of the gift," Cixous suggests in a footnote that the reader "reread Derrida's text, 'Le Style de la femme.'"[1] In that essay, originally presented at the 1972 Colloquium on Nietzsche at Cerisy and eventually reappearing in revised form as *Spurs: Nietzsche's Styles*, Cixous is particularly interested in Derrida's identifying the gift, in Nietzsche, as "the essential predicate of woman."[2] Taking this interest as our point of departure, in this chapter I would like to examine several of Cixous's comments on giving, property, appropriation, generosity, exchange—what I will call the logic of the gift. And following Cixous's own oblique suggestion, I would like to begin by rereading several of Nietzsche's reflections on economy, exchange, and the giving of gifts in an effort to show how Cixous's reflections on the logic of the gift can be located as part of Nietzsche's French legacy.

Joining Nietzsche and Cixous in this way will no doubt strike many readers as an odd union, and a word or two of explanation is called for at the outset. While not as closely associated with Nietzsche as is the work of Derrida, Foucault, or Deleuze, Cixous's work provides further evidence of the extent to which Nietzsche's thinking serves as a resource for the critical projects undertaken within recent French philosophy. However, I should make it clear that my goal in this chapter is not to demonstrate that Cixous is a Nietzschean—she is not! Nor is it my goal to show Nietzsche to be a feminist—he is not! In what follows, then, I will not discuss directly Nietzsche's various comments about women, "woman," or the "feminine." That one can use Nietzsche's words to paint a picture of him as a misogynist is clear. And it is equally clear that one can construct an interpretation that explains, or explains away, many of the most offensive of Nietzsche's remarks about women.[3] In the present discussion, however, I am interested neither in condemning Nietzsche's misogyny nor apologizing for it. Such efforts, both of the condemnatory and apologetic variety, when done well, can be useful and important in terms of understanding Nietzsche's thinking and in terms of understanding the depth to which misogyny characterizes the Western philosophical tradition. My interest, however, lies elsewhere.

Rather than examining Nietzsche's remarks on women per se, I want instead to explore a possible distinction between what one might call a masculine and a feminine economy in Nietzsche's work, and the locus of this distinction is centered around the logic of the gift. Although not specifically connected to gender in Nietzsche's texts, setting Nietzsche's discussion of gifts and gift-giving alongside Cixous's will highlight what one might regard as an unacknowledged "feminine" side of Nietzsche's economic discourse. Bringing Nietzsche and Cixous into dialogue on gifts and gift-giving, we will see that they each articulate an account of the gift that challenges the hegemonic assumption that gifts are circulated within a context always already governed by an economics of reciprocal exchange. And by listening for echoes of Zarathustra's laughter in the laugh of the Medusa, we can examine the exchange model and the definition of subjectivity in terms of the acquisition of property that accompanies this model. In so doing, we will experiment with another model, one based on an economy of excess that in different ways is suggested by both Nietzsche and Cixous, and we may glimpse what intersubjective relations might look like if grounded in an economy of excess rather than the reciprocal exchange of private property that is itself grounded on the economic assumption of scarcity.

Nietzschean Economics: From Revenge to Expenditure

> Nietzsche is on the side of *those who give*, and his thought cannot be isolated from the movement that tried to promote a resumption of life in the moment, in opposition to the bourgeoisie, which accumulates.... Nietzsche's gift is the gift that nothing limits; it is the sovereign gift, that of subjectivity.
>
> —GEORGES BATAILLE, *The Accursed Share*, Vol. III

We noted in the previous chapter that Deleuze and Guattari regard "The great book of modern ethnology [to be] not so much Mauss's *The Gift* as Nietzsche's *On the Genealogy of Morals*."[4] As we saw in our discussion of Deleuze, in the second essay of the *Genealogy*, Nietzsche turns to the origins of guilt and bad conscience and offers us a mythological ethnology that rivals Rousseau's myth of human beings' departure from the "state of nature" through the forging of a social contract. Nietzsche's myth traces the genealogy of guilt and bad conscience back to their economic roots in "The oldest and most primitive personal relationship, that between buyer and seller, creditor and debtor" (*GM*, II, 8). The moral concept "guilt," conceived as a debt that is essentially unredeemable, is shown to have its origin in the economic-legal notion of a debt as something that can and should be repaid. This for Nietzsche explains the earliest account of punishment, which as retribution emerges from the inability to repay the debt. Because "everything has its price [and] *all* things can be paid for" (*GM*, II, 8), the debtors, having made a promise to repay that they now cannot keep, are obliged to offer as payment something else they possess: their body, their spouse, their freedom, their life. *Schuld*, which translates both debt and guilt, was thus revealed to operate within a strange logic of compensation that establishes equivalences between the creditor and the debtor.

Like guilt, obligation, and punishment, Nietzsche also sees the origin of *justice* residing in the relationship between creditor and debtor. This primitive contractual relationship made possible comparative evaluations of relative worth, and it allowed primitive society to arrive at "the oldest and naïvest moral canon of *justice* [*Gerechtigkeit*], the beginning of all 'goodnaturedness,' all 'fairness,' all 'good will,' all 'objectivity' on earth" (*GM*, II, 8)—by which Nietzsche means the *jus talionis:* "an eye for an eye." In the preface to the *Genealogy*, Nietzsche refers us to several passages in his earlier works where he treats topics to which he here returns. One of these, entitled "*Origin of Justice* [*Ursprung der Gerechtigkeit*]," offers a succinct summary of Nietzsche's view of the egoistic and economic origin of justice:

> Justice (fairness) originates between parties of approximately *equal power:*... where there is no clearly recognizable superiority of force and a contest would result in mutual injury producing no decisive outcome the idea arises of coming to an understanding and negotiating over one another's demands: the characteristic of *exchange* is the original characteristic of justice. Each satisfies the other, inasmuch as each acquires what he values more than the other does. One gives to the other what he wants to have, to be henceforth his own, and in return receives what one oneself desires. Justice is thus requital and exchange under the presupposition of an approximately equal power position: revenge therefore belongs originally within the domain of justice, it is an exchange. Gratitude likewise. (*HH*, 92)

The Hobbesian character of Nietzsche's view of the origin of justice is clear: assuming equality of power, it is in the interests of all parties not to take from one another more than what each is willing to return. Based on economic principles of universal exchange and equivalency, this initial canon of justice thus gave rise to communities that operated on the assumption that equal settlements between individuals were always possible and socially, if not morally, obligatory.

The evolution of society saw the creditor-debtor relationship extended from a social/moral guideline among individuals to the standard that dictated the relationship between individuals and the community itself. The community now stood in relation to its members as a creditor to its debtors (*GM*, II, 9). To break the laws of the community would now necessitate future payment of a debt (punishment understood as "a debt paid to society"). In primitive, insecure, and unstable societies, Nietzsche claims, debts had to be repaid in accordance with the primitive canon of justice, the *jus talionis*. But as a community gained in strength, Nietzsche locates the emergence of a new notion of justice. The creditor, now confident of its wealth/strength, might measure this strength precisely in terms of how much injury it could endure *without* suffering and feeling the compulsion to respond. The self-overcoming of the old model of justice that demanded equal payment for debts incurred has "given itself a beautiful name—*mercy* [*Gnade*]."

> It is not unthinkable that a society might attain such a *consciousness of power* that it could allow itself the noblest luxury possible to it—letting those who harm it go *unpunished*. "What are my parasites to me?" it might say. "May they live and prosper: I am strong enough for that!" The justice which began with "everything is dischargeable, everything must be discharged," ends by winking and letting those incapable of discharging their debts go free,— it ends, as does every good thing on earth, by *overcoming itself* [*sich selbst aufhebend*]. (*GM*, II, 10)

This image of strength as the ability to actively forget and forgive the debts one is owed, to endure petty injury without reacting, to withhold punishment, recurs throughout Nietzsche's texts. Earlier in the *Genealogy*, it is offered as a fundamental contrast to *ressentiment*. The men of *ressentiment* react negatively to external conditions; but lacking the strength to act, they are forced to take refuge in the imagination. Unable to act, and unable to forget the "harm" done to them by the outside, *ressentiment* festers in the weak and poisons their thinking. When they are finally prompted to create, these men of *ressentiment* can only create a system of diseased values that reflects their decadent desires. On the other hand, when *ressentiment* does appear in noble and strong individuals, and it does on rare occasions, its harmfulness is mitigated by their ability to act directly. But what is more likely the case with noble individuals is that *ressentiment* does not appear at all because they have the strength to actively forget what displeases them: "To be incapable of taking one's enemies, one's accidents, even one's misdeeds seriously for very long—that is the sign of strong, full natures in whom there is an excess of power to form, to mold, to recuperate and to forget" (*GM*, I, 10).[5]

This strength to forget will promote the "deliverance from revenge" which Zarathustra teaches is "the bridge to the highest hope." Where the preachers of equality proclaim the necessity of revenge, Zarathustra teaches that "to *me*, justice speaks thus: 'Men are not equal.' Nor shall they become equal! What would my love of the *Übermensch* be if I spoke otherwise?" (*Z*, "On the Tarantulas"). In *Daybreak*, Nietzsche envisions a time when revenge and the law of equal return will no longer be the principle of justice to which society appeals:

> At present, to be sure, he who has been injured, irrespective of how this injury is to be made good, will still desire his *revenge* and will turn for it to the courts—and for the time being the courts continue to maintain our detestable criminal codes, with their shopkeeper's scales and the *desire to counterbalance guilt with punishment*: but can we not get beyond this? (*D*, 202)

To overcome the old instinct for revenge, and with it to get rid of the concepts of sin and punishment, will be for Nietzsche a sign of the health of a community. A healthy community will be characterized not by revenge but by generosity which will be evaluated "according to how many parasites it can endure" (*D*, 202). Nietzsche develops this line of thinking in a way that, had he chosen to pursue it, might have led to an interesting encounter with the thought of Marx: noting that not only has no thinker yet evaluated society or individuals in terms of how many parasites it could support, he concludes that there has not "yet been a founder of a state who has wielded the ploughshare in the spirit of that generous and mild-hearted dictum: 'if thou wouldst cultivate the land, cultivate it with the plough: then the bird and the wolf who follow behind the plough shall rejoice in thee—*all creatures shall rejoice in thee*'" (*D*, 202).[6]

To summarize the preceding discussion, we find Nietzsche isolating two types of economy that give rise to two types of justice. The lower, baser, slave economy is grounded on the law of equal return: justice demands that all debts be paid in kind; the creditor is not capable of forgetting the debt, and the debtor is obliged to return some equivalent form of payment. This notion of justice, exhibited in the *jus talionis*, operates in those societies whose economies depend on rules of exchange and, we might note, it serves as an axiom of primitive capitalist economies. Nietzsche's theorizing of slave economics here anticipates the account provided by Marcel Mauss's *Essai sur le don*:[7] a "genuine," "free," "unencumbered" gift is not possible. Instead, gifts are given in a social context whose "rules" obligate the receiver to return the gift in kind, that is, to offer in return a counter-gift. This account does not, of course, conflate gift-giving with barter, however, for the former has an essential diachronic dimension (the passage of some determinate

amount of time) which the latter lacks. Nevertheless, the principle of reciprocal, equivalent exchange underlies and makes possible the transactions in
either a barter or a gift-giving relationship as understood by Mauss. And,
as Nietzsche makes clear, the assumption and expectation of a reciprocal
return is what gives rise to the vengeful economic logic that characterizes
slave morality.

The higher, nobler economy that Nietzsche sketches is based on a fundamentally different principle, one closer to what Georges Bataille called a
"general economy" of "expenditure" than to a simple, restricted exchange
economy.[8] Nietzsche's higher economy is one grounded in excess strength
sufficient to squander its resources if it so chooses. In the foreground of
this noble economy "is the feeling of fullness, of power that seeks to overflow, the happiness of high tension, the consciousness of wealth that would
give [*schenken*] and bestow [*abgeben*]: the noble human being, too, helps the
unfortunate, but not, or almost not, from pity, but prompted more by an
urge begotten by excess of power [*Überfluss von Macht*]" (*BGE*, 260).[9] In
this economy, gifts can be given without expectation of return and debts
can be forgiven without penalty or shame.[10] Justice here can, but need not,
demand repayment; tempered with mercy, it is motivated not by revenge
but is empowered to forgive and *actively* forget what it is due.[11] We see this
higher, nobler justice and "general economy" most clearly at two points in
Nietzsche's texts: in the relationships between Zarathustra and those to
whom he offers his teachings, and in the relationship between Nietzsche
and the readers to whom he offers his texts.

A General Economy of Gift-Giving

It has rarely been noticed that *Thus Spoke Zarathustra* opens with a
reflection upon gifts and the necessity of giving.[12] When Zarathustra first
goes down from his cave to rejoin humanity, like the bee that has gathered
too much honey or the cup that wants to overflow, he is overfull and needs
to locate those to whom he can bring the gift of his teaching (see *Z*,
Prologue, 1–3). Initially, as the hermit who meets him along the way pre-
dicted, Zarathustra encounters only those who are suspicious of the gifts
he brings. Soon enough the situation changes, however. Zarathustra quickly comes to stand in relation to his followers as a giver of gifts, and his followers are only too eager to receive his teachings as gifts from on high. But
unlike his followers, Zarathustra knows the dangers involved in gift-giving;
he knows that the gift is a *pharmakon*,[13] for those who benefit from receiv-

ing the gifts often feel beholden to the one who gave to them. Zarathustra thus cautions:

> Great indebtedness does not make men grateful, but vengeful; and if a little charity is not forgotten, it turns into a gnawing worm.
>
> "Be reserved in accepting! Distinguish by accepting!" Thus I advise those who have nothing to give.
>
> But I am a giver of gifts; I like to give, as a friend to friends. Strangers, however, and the poor may themselves pluck the fruit from my tree: that will cause them less shame. (Z, "On the Pitying")

To be able to give gifts rightly is an "*art* [*Kunst*]" (see Z, "The Voluntary Beggar"), and great care and skill is required in order to prevent feelings of indebtedness in the recipients of one's generosity. One repays one's teacher badly if one remains only a student, Zarathustra tells his followers at the end of Part One, as he urges them to lose him and find themselves (Z, "On the Gift-Giving Virtue"). To remain a student is to return the teacher's gifts in kind, either by simple obedience to the teacher's lessons or by presenting the teacher with a comparable counter-gift in return. Neither response takes the gift freely and with forgetfulness of its origin, neither receives the gift with compassion (*Erbarmen*). For Zarathustra, overfull with wisdom, giving is a necessity (*Nothdurft*) (see Z, "On the Great Longing"), and while his followers will return eternally to the words of their teacher, the return on Zarathustra's gifts will not return to him, who confesses not to know the happiness of those who receive. This, says Zarathustra, is his poverty, that his hand never rests from giving (see Z, "The Night Song"). His gifts, to be sure, are investments, but investments in a future that he will not share nor one from which he will derive profit.

We see a similar relationship exhibited with respect to the "presents" Nietzsche gives to his readers in the form of his texts. With *Thus Spoke Zarathustra*, Nietzsche "has given humanity the greatest present [*das grösste Geschenk*] that has ever been made to it so far" (*EH*, Pr4). In the frontispiece to *Ecce Homo*, Nietzsche refers to his texts of the last quarter of 1888 (*The Antichrist, Twilight of the Idols, Dionysus Dithyrambs*) as "presents" (*Geschenke*), and *Ecce Homo* itself is a present Nietzsche makes to himself on the occasion of his forty-fourth birthday. What is to be done with these presents? Are they to be returned to their author in the same condition that he delivered them? Or are they to be used, not to be returned but to be put into circulation in order to produce other gifts? For Nietzsche, the writer's task is to stimulate, not to be consumed: "We honor the great artists of the past less through that unfruitful awe which allows every word, every note, to lie where it has been put than we do through active endeavors to help them to come repeatedly to life again" (*AOM*, 126). Good philosophical writing should inspire one to action and, Nietzsche writes, "I consider every word behind which there does not stand such a challenge to action to have been written in vain" (*SE*, p. 184). Nietzsche does not so much want to be understood as to incite: his writings are incendiary devices, he speaks "no longer with words but with lightning bolts" (*EH*, III, UM3). He seeks readers who will not be mere consumers of his texts but experimenters, *Versucher*, "monster[s] of courage and curiosity; moreover, supple, cunning, cautious; born adventurer[s] and discoverer[s]" (*EH*, III, 3). He seeks, in other words, to free his readers from the constraints of a textual economy that demands that they occupy a place as passive beneficiary or consumer of the text rather than as its active co-producer. Which is to say, as Bataille noted, "Nietzsche is on the side of *those who give*;"[14] he seeks to write as an act of generosity within a textual economy that does not guarantee the author any return on his or her gift as it circulates through an intertextual field and escapes this textual field into extratextual practice.[15]

Engendering Economics

To write, and live, within a textual/libidinal/political economy[16] freed from the constraints of the law of return is also part of Hélène Cixous's vision of a post-patriarchal future. Approaching Cixous's comments from a Nietzschean perspective brings to the fore a "feminine" side of Nietzsche's economic reflections, a side, moreover, that is obscured within Georges Bataille's better-known incarnation of Nietzschean economics as the tension between an emasculated, restricted economy and a potent, general economy. Where Bataille affirms an economic account based on excess and waste to counter the utilitarian assumptions that all expenditures must be productive and compensated, Cixous frames the issue in a decidedly different manner.

Like Bataille, however, Cixous suggests we distinguish between two kinds of economies, which she links to two kinds of writing, two kinds of spending, two kinds of giving. The one, grounded on the law of return, finds its philosophical justification in Locke's definition of property in chapter five of the *Second Treatise of Government*: one possesses and has a right to as one's private property whatever "he removes out of the state that nature hath provided and left it in [and] he hath mixed his labor with." This account of property and the practices that it underwrites find themselves instantiated throughout what has counted as "History."

The other set of practices, only recently voiced, also has a long history, but one that has until recently not been acknowledged "publicly" because it concerned only "women." We must hasten to add that Nietzsche too does not acknowledge the practices of this other economy as feminine. In fact, on those few occasions when he does engender his economic reflections, more often than not and in the most traditional of ways, he associates giving with the feminine and possession with the masculine, as for example when he writes that man has a "lust for possession" and man's "love consists of wanting to *have* and not of renunciation and giving away," while "woman gives herself away" and "wants to be taken and accepted as a possession" (*GS*, 363).[17] Nevertheless, insofar as Cixous does obliquely connect her remarks to Nietzsche's through the mediating effect not of Bataille but of Jacques Derrida, we will need to experiment with the connections that can be forged between their thinking as we try to ascertain whether Nietzsche's thought can be moved from the closed economy suggested by passages like that in *The Gay Science* 363.

According to Cixous, current economic realities operate within what she calls "*L'Empire du Propre*," the "Empire of the Selfsame/Proper."[18] She identifies the philosophical underpinnings of this empire with Hegel, who in the *Phenomenology of Spirit* framed the fundamental relationship between self and other in terms of the acquisition of property: the subject goes "out into the other *in order to come back* to itself."[19] The phallocentric desire that animates the Hegelian dialectic of self and other is a desire for appropriation: one confronts the other as different and unequal and one seeks to make the other one's own. The desire to possess, to receive a return on one's investments, animates an economy that Cixous suggests we call "masculine," in part because it "is erected from a fear that, in fact, is typically masculine"—the fear of castration—"the fear of expropriation, of separation, of losing the attribute."[20] Cixous summarizes her point succinctly in the following remark quoted at length:

Etymologically, the "proper" is "property," that which is not separable from me. Property is proximity, nearness: we must love our neighbors, those close to us, as ourselves: we must draw close to the other so that we may love him/her, because we love ourselves most of all. The realm of the proper, culture, functions by the appropriation articulated, set into play, by man's classic fear of seeing himself expropriated, seeing himself deprived... by his refusal to be deprived, in a state of separation, by his fear of losing the prerogative, fear whose response is all of History. Everything must return to the masculine. "Return": the economy is founded on a system of returns. If a man spends and is spent, it's on condition that his power returns. If a man should go out, if he should go out to the other, it's always done according to the Hegelian model, the model of the master-slave dialectic.[21]

In other words, economies of the *propre*, proper economies, economies based on the possession of private property, are driven not so much by the desire to appropriate; they are structured instead around the fear of loss, the fear of losing what is already possessed, a fear of being expropriated that Cixous designates with the qualifier "masculine."

Sensitive to the dangers of linking economy with biology in some essentialist way, Cixous warns that "Words like 'masculine' and 'feminine' that circulate everywhere and that are completely distorted in everyday usage—words which refer, of course, to a classical vision of sexual opposition between men and women—are our burden, that is what burdens us." Her work, she continues, "aims at getting rid of words like 'feminine' and 'masculine,' 'femininity' and 'masculinity,' even 'man' and 'woman,' which designate that which cannot be classified inside of a signifier except by force and violence and which goes beyond it in any case."[22] To avoid the burdens of the classical vision, Cixous sometimes speaks of "the *so-called feminine economy*," acknowledging that "one can find [both masculine and feminine] economies in no matter which individual."[23] And for this reason, Cixous herself prefers the language of bisexuality, "that is to say, the location within oneself of the presence of both sexes, evident and insistent in different ways according to the individual, the nonexclusion of difference or of a sex."[24]

Although she prefers the language of bisexuality and she frequently cautions against the dangers of resorting to the classical binaries of "feminine"/"masculine" or "femininity"/"masculinity," Cixous nevertheless continues to use the qualifiers "masculine" and "feminine" in reference to economies because

The (political) economy of the masculine and the feminine is organized by different demands and constraints, which, as they become socialized and metaphorized, produce signs, relations of power, relationships of production and reproduction, a whole huge system of cultural inscription that is legible as masculine or feminine.[25]

Guided by the prime directive to appropriate, a masculine economy is not truly capable of giving. Inscribed under the law of return, the masculine gift expects, nay demands, a return, as Mauss's *Essai sur le don* demonstrated and as Derrida reiterates in his recent articulation of the impossibility of the gift.[26] Rephrasing the insights of Mauss, Derrida, and Nietzsche in terms of a gendered unconscious, Cixous notes the lack of ease with which a masculine economy confronts generosity: "Giving: there you have a basic problem, which is that masculinity is always associated—in the unconscious, which is after all what makes the whole economy function—with debt."[27] Freud showed the debilitating effects that this debt has on the child, who must confront the obligation to repay his parents for their gift of his life.[28] And Nietzsche showed the equally crippling effects of indebtedness in his genealogical account of modern society's obligations to uphold the values of tradition. If you are a man, Cixous observes, nothing is more dangerous than to be obligated to another's generosity: "for the moment you receive something you are effectively 'open' to the other, and if you are a man you have only one wish": to return the gift as quickly as possible.[29]

Escaping from the openness to the other has driven masculine exchange practices that, grounded on opposition, hierarchy, and a Hegelian struggle for mastery, "can end only in at least one death (one master—one slave, or two nonmasters = two dead)." Although these practices arose in a time "governed by phallocentric values," Cixous argues that another system of exchange is possible. The fact that the period of phallocentric values

> extends into the present doesn't prevent woman from starting the history of life somewhere else. Elsewhere, she gives. She doesn't "know" what she's giving, she doesn't measure it; she gives, though, neither a counterfeit impression nor something she hasn't got. She gives more, with no assurance that she'll get back even some unexpected profit from what she puts out. She gives that there may be life, thought, transformation. This is an "economy" that can no longer be put in economic terms.[30]

A "feminine" "economy," one no longer understandable in classical "exchangist" economic terms, allows for the possibility of giving without expectation of return, for giving that is truly generous: it gives without trying to "recover its expenses.... If there is a *propre* to woman, paradoxically it is her capacity to de-propriate herself without self-interest."[31] Although brought up in a social space framed by debt, "one can ask oneself about the possibility of a real gift, a pure gift, a gift that would not be annulled by what one could call a countergift."[32] Cixous is quick to point out, however, that "there is no 'free' gift. You never give something for nothing. But all the difference lies in the why and how of the gift, in the values that the gesture of giving affirms, causes to circulate; in the type of profit the giver draws from the gift and the use to which he or she puts it."[33]

Where masculine economies can make only *quid pro quo* exchanges by means of which a direct profit is to be recouped, feminine economies transact their business differently. They are not constrained to giving as a means of deferred exchange in order to obligate a countergift in return; instead, they encourage giving as an affirmation of generosity in which the gift is not "actively forgotten" but is, instead, remembered otherwise.[34] A feminine libidinal economy, she writes, "is an economy which has a more supple relation to property, which can stand separation and detachment, which signifies that it can also stand freedom—for instance, the other's freedom."[35] It is an economy, in other words, in which profit can be deferred, perhaps infinitely, in exchange for the continued circulation of giving.

The distinction Cixous draws between masculine and feminine economies can be supported by the work of anthropologist C. A. Gregory, who distinguishes between an economy based on the exchange of *gifts* and an economy based on the exchange of *commodities*. According to Gregory, "commodity exchange establishes objective quantitative relationships between the objects transacted, while gift exchange establishes personal qualitative relationships between the subjects transacting."[36] Where commodity exchange is focused on a transfer in which objects of equivalent exchange-value are reciprocally transacted, gift exchange seeks to establish a relationship between subjects in which the actual objects transferred are incidental to the value of the relationship established. Commodity exchange thus exhibits the values that, for example, Carol Gilligan associates with an ethic of rights based on abstract principles of reciprocity while gift exchange exhibits the forming of and focus on relationships which she associates with an ethic of care based on interpersonal needs and responsibilities, an ethic that speaks in a voice different from the one that has heretofore dominated the moral tradition.[37] And so, returning to Gregory's distinction, we might say that while both commodity and gift exchange are potentially profitable, the nature of their respective profits differ dramatically. Where commodity exchange produces surplus value in the form of capital—creating material wealth where none was before—gift exchange produces a surplus value in the form of relationships, creating connections between people where no connection existed prior to the circulation of the gift.

Here it may be worthwhile to distinguish Cixous's formulation from Bataille's (and Nietzsche's). Where Nietzsche focuses on the excessive quality of the gift (which can be squandered by the overpowerful), Bataille focuses almost exclusively on the destructive aspect of this expenditure. In other words, the expenditure that characterizes a general economy distinguishes itself from a restrictive economy precisely in terms of its non-productive, non-utilitarian properties.[38] For Cixous, on the other hand, the giving of feminine economy is equally excessive, but unlike Bataille, it avoids the constraints of an economy of return without being either unproductive or destructive. In fact, the reverse is more nearly the case: Cixous's feminine economy *produces* relations out of the continuing transmission and circulation of the excess.

In other words, because of its "more supple relation to property," Cixous herself highlights the difference between feminine and masculine economies insofar as the former promotes the establishment of interactive relations through the giving of gifts. In particular, she draws our attention to maternal gifts as ones that escape the logic of appropriation that structures the commodity economy she labels "masculine." Mother and child do not stand in a relationship of self vs. other, opposing parties with competing interests, and the gift to the child of a mother's love or a mother's breast is not comprehensible in terms of quantifiable exchange-values or the law of return that governs an economy based on the exchange of commodities. Nor are these maternal gifts understandable in terms of the fear of expropriation or the destructive expenditure of a potlatch, for the mother is willing to expend these gifts without reserve or expectation of return. In fact, like Nietzsche, Cixous emphasizes and affirms the positive value of plenitude, but unlike Nietzsche, she wants to gender this positive value "feminine": insofar as the mother can supply as much love or as much milk as the child might demand, Cixous articulates a set of economic principles that refuses to accept the modern assumption of the givenness of conditions of scarcity.

Cixous encourages us to understand this ability to give that animates feminine (libidinal) economy in terms of maternity and the specificity of women's bodies: insofar as women have the potential to give birth/life to another, they have an anatomically grounded relationship that makes possible their experiencing "the not-me within me."[39] While Cixous tethers this relationship to pregnancy, lactation, and childbearing, at the same time she wants to link it to the possibility of writing. "Woman is body more than man is... more body, hence more writing."[40]

> It is not only a question of the feminine body's extra resource, this specific power to produce something living of which her flesh is the locus, not only a question of a transformation of rhythms, exchanges, of relationship to space, of the whole perceptive system, but also of the irreplaceable experience of those moments of stress, of the body's crises, of that work that goes on peacefully for a long time only to burst out in that surpassing moment, the time of childbirth. In which she lives as if she were larger or stronger than herself. It is also the experience of a "bond" with the other, all that comes through in the metaphor of bringing into the world. How could the woman, who has experienced the not-me within me, not have a particular relationship to the written? To writing as giving itself away (cutting itself off) from the source?[41]

To put the issue this way comes dangerously close to the sort of "essentialist ideological interpretation" that Cixous acknowledges is "a story made to order for male privilege."[42] Yet she is willing to run this risk, as she frequently appeals to highly romanticized maternal and anatomical images and metaphors when expressing the implications of feminine economies and *écriture féminine*. Whether or not Cixous herself sometimes falls victim to essentialist thinking when she focuses on the anatomical specificity of women's bodies in terms of the possibilities of pregnancy and childbirth,[43] one could, however, less problematically ground the practices of feminine economies and writing in terms of a history of socially constructed and therefore contingent practices rather than in the determinist-essentialist terms of anatomy or biology. To do so would focus attention on those maternal practices discussed by Cixous as *exemplary* of different intersubjective relations that warrant further generalization, while avoiding the problems raised by either the culturally constraining aspects of maternity or the appeal to anatomical specificity.

Cixous herself appears to move in this direction when she replaces "*écriture féminine*" ("feminine writing") with "*écriture dite féminine*" ("writing said to be feminine"):

It is not anatomical sex that determines anything here. It is, on the contrary, history from which one never escapes, individual and collective history, the cultural schema and the way the individual negotiates with these schema, with these data, adapts to them and reproduces them, or else gets round them, overcomes them, goes beyond them, gets through them.[44]

To speak of a feminine economy, Cixous writes, "does not refer to women, but perhaps to a trait that comes back to women more often."[45] Insofar as women have been prohibited throughout history from possessing things for themselves, they have come to understand and appreciate property differently in terms of an economy based not on the law of return but on generosity. Likewise, insofar as women have at times been positioned socioeconomically *as* gifts, it is not at all surprising, nor should it be taken as a function of anatomy or biology, that women's perspectives *on* gifts and giving might differ from men's.[46] By virtue of certain social necessities, Cixous writes in "The Laugh of the Medusa," women constitute themselves as "'person[s]' capable of losing a part of [themselves] without losing [their] integrity."[47] They are able to exist in a "relationship to the other in which the gift doesn't calculate its influence."[48] And they can negotiate within an economy "that tolerates the movements of the other."[49]

They have learned, to use a distinction made by Pierre Bourdieu in his critique of Lévi-Strauss's analysis of gift exchange, to distinguish "giving" from "swapping" or "lending." This distinction, central to Bourdieu's critique of objectivist anthropological accounts of gift exchange, points to the fact that by reducing the exchange of gift and counter-gift to a straightforward transfer of commodities of relatively equal worth, the objectivist account conflates gift exchange with "*swapping*, which... telescopes gift and counter-gift into the same instant, and... *lending*, in which the return of the loan is explicitly guaranteed by a juridical act and is thus *already accomplished* at the very moment of the drawing up of a contract capable of ensuring that the acts it prescribes are predictable and calculable."[50] According to Bourdieu, on the other hand, the reality of the gift-exchange presupposes both the necessity of a deferred and different counter-gift *and* the "(individual and collective) misrecognition (*méconnaissance*) of the reality of the objective 'mechanism' of the exchange."[51]

Unlike Bourdieu, Cixous is not content to describe gift-giving practices in terms of a misrecognition of what is in reality reciprocal exchange. Instead, she wants to retrieve gift-giving from the economic necessities

imposed upon it within an exchangist economy and to reframe the practices of giving in an account that does not imprison transactions within private proprietary relationships in which loans and loans paid back masquer-
ade as the bestowal of gifts. In so doing, she allows certain heretofore
unrealized opportunities to emerge. In Cixous's idiom, women have
learned how to exceed the limits of themselves and enter into the between
of self and other without losing themselves in the process. Escaping the proprietary constraints on subjectivity is itself part of the project of *écriture
féminine.* "The question a woman's text asks," Cixous writes, "is the question of giving—'What does this writing give?' 'How does it give?'" To these
questions, she answers that *écriture féminine* "'gives a send-off' (*donne le
départ*).... giving a send-off is generally giving the *signal* to depart,... making a *gift* of, departure, allowing departure, allowing breaks, 'parts,' partings,
separations." And by allowing for separation, by giving the freedom to
depart, "we break with the return-to-self, with the specular relations ruling
the coherence, the identification, of the individual."[52]

Écriture féminine thus transgresses the central assumptions of a mod-
ernist subjectivity grounded on notions of autonomous and isolated individuality and the personal possession of privatized property. And it does so
by reflexively situating itself *as* a relation between self and (both internal-
ized and externalized) other:

> Writing is working; being worked; questioning (in) the between (letting one-
> self be questioned) of same *and of* other without which nothing lives; undo-
> ing death's work by willing the togetherness of one—another, infinitely
> charged with a ceaseless exchange of one with another—not knowing one
> another and beginning again only from what is most distant, from self, from
> other, from the other within. A course that multiplies transformations by the
> thousands.[53]

A writing that puts the isolated, autonomous self at risk, questioning and
being questioned in the between of self and other, goes to the roots of our his-
torical-cultural gender constructions. In response to such radical questioning
of the well-defined boundaries between self and other, Cixous suggests that

> "femininity" and "masculinity" would inscribe quite differently their effects
> of difference, their economy, their relationship to expenditure, to lack, to the
> gift. What today appears to be "feminine" or "masculine" would no longer

amount to the same thing. No longer would the common logic of difference be organized with the opposition that remains dominant. Difference would be a bunch of new differences.[54]

And with gender difference reformulated as a range of multivalent differential relations would come a reformulation of the very notion of identity itself. That is to say, no longer would the oppositional logic of "self vs. all others" allow for the self-construction of isolated and atomistic subjectivities. Instead, having reconfigured difference as a "bunch of new differences," self-construction will take place in the tensional between of the full range of intersubjective and differential relations that one is.

Teaching Nietzsche a Lesson in Reception

What has so far been the greatest sin on earth? Was it not the word of him who said, "Woe unto those who laugh here?" Did he himself find no reasons on earth for laughing? Then he searched very badly.

—NIETZSCHE, *Thus Spoke Zarathustra*

You only have to look at the Medusa straight on to see her. And she's not deadly. She's beautiful and she's laughing.

—CIXOUS, "The Laugh of the Medusa"

"We are forgetting how to give presents," Adorno wrote in *Minima Moralia*.[55] Cixous, wondering whether we ever really knew how to give presents, seeks a place "where it was not impossible or pathetic to be generous."[56] Nietzsche envisions a society with a level of power sufficient to allow it to be merciful, that is, sufficient for it to allow its debts to go unpaid. To be sure, Nietzsche did not identify this society with the feminine, nor did he associate the generosity of overfullness with the feminine. In fact, the reverse is more nearly the case: the degree of strength necessary for such generosity was almost always put forward in masculine images of mastery, virility, productivity, and activity. But need this have been the case? I think not. When Nietzsche addresses issues of gender, his thinking remains constrained within the human, all-too-human prejudices that he, as a transvaluer of values, must be faulted for not having gone beyond. By setting Nietzsche's discussion of plenitude and generosity together with Cixous's discussion of feminine libidinal economies and the giving of gifts, the affinities between their respective accounts emerge in a way that shows how Nietzsche might have gone beyond his misogynistic prejudices.

In fact, what this comparison reveals is that Nietzsche is prevented from fully realizing the potential of his economic reflections on the gift because he fails to recognize that the logic of the gift involves both giving *and receiving*.[57] That is to say, how the gift functions will be determined both by the attitude of the donor and the attitude of the recipient. As Nietzsche notes, for the gift to be an act of generosity requires that it originate out of overfullness. But what he fails to note is that for the gift to be received *as* a gift requires that its recipient not feel obligated to offer a counter-gift in return. While acknowledging the interpretive dangers of identifying Zarathustra's speeches straightforwardly with Nietzsche's thoughts, nevertheless do we not hear a Nietzschean confession in Zarathustra's admission that he does "not know the happiness of those who receive" (*Z*, "The Night Song")? Like Zarathustra, Nietzsche can imagine an economy of givers; but also like Zarathustra, Nietzsche seems uncomfortable with any notion of reception insofar as he is unable to understand reception in a way that can avoid entailing some indebtedness on the part of the recipient to the donor. And the reason for his lack of comfort, of course, is his association of reception and indebtedness with need and weakness.[58]

Cixous's feminine economy escapes the constraints imposed by framing reception as a sign of weakness, but as I have tried to suggest, her project remains situated within a field of thought opened by Nietzsche. In *Ecce Homo*, when discussing the dithyramb as the language the Dionysian speaks to itself, Nietzsche cites in its entirety "Night Song"—Zarathustra's melancholic lament at being condemned to overfullness—where Zarathustra admits to having often dreamt "that even stealing must be more blessed than receiving" (*EH*, III, Z7). The answer to this dithyramb of suffering and solitude, he notes in the next section (*EH*, III, Z8), would be Ariadne. Is Cixous perhaps making the response of Ariadne when she locates *voler*, *theft/flight*, as an other/the other side of giving?

> To fly/steal [*voler*] is woman's gesture, to steal into language to make it fly. We have all learned flight/theft, the art with many techniques, for all the centuries we have only had access to having by stealing/flying; we have lived in a flight/theft, stealing/flying, finding the close, concealed ways-through of desire. It's not just luck if the word "voler" volleys between the "vol" of theft and the "vol" of flight, pleasuring in each and routing the sense police.[59]

When she supplements "theft" with "flight," noting that woman's gesture is always both at once, Cixous makes it clear, however, that her "Ariadnean" answer is not just for Dionysus, but for herself as well. And I would argue that in so doing, Cixous shows herself to be the sort of reader Nietzsche was seeking, one who would pay him back not by repeating his text, but by taking that text and making it her own, putting it to use as *she* sees fit.

This is precisely what Cixous does when she provides an account of generosity that does not require *übermenschliche* strength to enact, when she substitutes maternal compassion for the masterly indifference to one's parasites affirmed by Nietzsche. By recasting the economic insights of Nietzsche, Mauss, and Bataille in terms of sexual difference, and by making it possible to see the gendered dimension of gift-giving that Nietzsche too quickly discarded, Cixous articulates more clearly an alternative logic of the gift, one with several advantages over more classical exchangist logics that imprison gift-giving within the constraints of the economic assumptions of commodity trading. Cixous shows generosity and non-proprietary relations of cooperative ownership to have always been options of which, for complex social and historical reasons, men have not sufficiently availed themselves. She also articulates a notion of self freed from the constraints of atomistic individuality, a notion of self that can go out to the other which was and still is itself, which is to say, a notion of an intersubjective self that is fully at home in the between of self and other. In so doing, we still hear the faint echo of the laughter Zarathustra tried to teach the higher men (*Z*, "On the Higher Man," 20) in the laughter of the Medusa, but we must also hear that Medusa is laughing her own laugh, a laughter that was no *übermenschliche* laughter.[60]

CHAPTER FIVE

Why the French
Are No Longer Nietzscheans

➤

Nietzsche, offering this future to us as both promise and task, marks the threshold beyond which contemporary philosophy can begin thinking again; and he will no doubt continue for a long while to dominate its advance. If the discovery of the Return is indeed the end of philosophy, then the end of man, for its part, is the return of the beginning of philosophy.

—FOUCAULT, *The Order of Things*

Nietzsche, in whose light and shadow everyone today thinks and reflects with his "for him" or "against him."
—MARTIN HEIDEGGER, *The Question of Being*

I know my fate. One day my name will be associated with the memory of something tremendous—a crisis without equal on earth, the most profound collision of conscience, a decision that was conjured up *against* everything that had been believed, demanded, hallowed so far. I am no man, I am dynamite.—Yet for all that, there is nothing in me of a founder of a religion— ... —I *want* no "believers."
—NIETZSCHE, *Ecce Homo*

As THE TWENTIETH CENTURY DRAWS TO A CLOSE, ONE NOTES THAT THE PAGE has been turned on French Nietzscheanism. Foucault is dead. Deleuze has retired. Derrida and many of the deconstructionists, like Cixous and many of the feminists, have, for various and different reasons, turned away from Nietzsche. This is not to say that there are no longer books written in France on Nietzsche, as the two recent *Explosions* of Sarah Kofman attest.[1]

But it is to say that the status and stature of "Nietzsche" in French philosophy has decidedly changed as he now appears to be simply one more figure
in the history of philosophy. After almost three decades at the vanguard, his
name, and his works, no longer function as the signifier for a philosophical
position's being *au courant*, as was the case in the 1960s and 1970s.

The turn away from Nietzsche is marked by more than the passing of
those philosophers discussed in the previous chapters, however. In fact, the
new generation of French philosophers who have followed in the wake of the
"philosophers of the sixties" have made a conscious choice not only to turn
away from the philosophical perspectives of their teachers, but they appear
to have made an equally conscious choice to turn away from Nietzsche.
Moreover, in a gesture that is all too common in twentieth-century philosophical polemics, they have set "Nietzsche" up as one of the primary sites
where they locate their reasons for turning away from the philosophical
views of those philosophers that in the English-speaking philosophical community have come to be called "poststructuralists."[2]

These reasons have much to do with what each generation saw to be the
task of philosophy. But they have to do as well with the new generation's turn
away from what they have come to regard as the excessive and irresponsible
political stances of their philosophical predecessors. Seeing the need both for
a rejuvenated notion of the subject and for a notion of community grounded
in liberal-democratic principles, they refuse to overlook the incommensura-
bility of many of the assumptions and conclusions of French Nietzscheanism
with this or any other notion of community. As a consequence, many of the
philosophers who "came of age" as students in the 1960s have taken their
stand on Nietzschean ground against the "philosophers of the sixties."

This is certainly the case in two of the better known works to have been
written by this new generation of French thinkers: Vincent Descombes's *Le
même et l'autre: Quarante-cinq ans de philosophie française (1933–1978)* [3]
and Luc Ferry and Alain Renaut's *La pensée 68: Essai sur l'anti-humanisme
contemporain*.[4] If these works left any doubt concerning the role their
authors thought Nietzsche played in the evolution of the French Left avant-
garde in the 1960s, their position on the Nietzschean tradition in France
was made explicit in a work on which they, and several others, collaborated,
a work whose polemical title states the matter clearly: *Pourquoi nous ne
sommes pas nietzschéens*.[5]

In this collection, the authors put forward their objections both to
Nietzsche and to those "master thinkers" of the sixties—Foucault, Deleuze,

Derrida, Althusser, Lacan—who taught them that the ideal of the Enlightenment was only a "bad farce, a somber mystification" and who introduced them to "the masters of suspicion: Marx, Freud, Heidegger, of course, but above all, Nietzsche, the inventor of that 'genealogy' in whose name one had to treat all discourse as symptoms."[6] Arguing against the basic precepts of poststructuralism, they call for a return to a rationality that the "relativism of the thinking of difference" made too easy to renounce. And in so doing, they make clear that while "thinking with Nietzsche," they will also think against him—against his resistance to argumentation, against his repudiation of truth, against his objections to democracy and equality.

Although the authors of the essays collected in this volume admit a certain indebtedness to Nietzsche, they refuse to follow the philosophical itinerary marked by the *Nietzscheanism* of the generation of thinkers in France who immediately preceded them. In fact, in many of the essays, it is the Nietzschean*ism* of their predecessors, rather than Nietzsche's ideas themselves, that becomes the focus of critique. Because the French Nietzscheans are seen to be valorizing Nietzsche's immoralism, elitism, and hierarchisation—positions that, while perhaps philosophically interesting, they argue, must be challenged on *realpolitikal* grounds—they are in turn criticized for overlooking all that is politically problematic in Nietzsche's thinking. And for this reason, the French Nietzscheans are collectively rejected by this new generation on grounds of political irresponsibility.

To conclude this discussion of Nietzsche's French legacy, therefore, it seems appropriate to examine this latest development in recent French philosophy. And to do this, I look at the work of a couple of the leading representatives of this development: Vincent Descombes, and Luc Ferry and Alain Renaut. But before I do so, I would like first to examine the recent work of someone who, while himself one of the leading members of the "generation of sixties philosophy," has nevertheless also made the turn away from Nietzsche: Jean-François Lyotard.

Lyotard's Turn from Nietzsche to Kant and Levinas

It is only fitting that we begin this chapter with a discussion of one of the French Nietzscheans who, as it were, has turned in his card. Although never as closely associated with Nietzsche as were Deleuze, Foucault, or even Derrida, Jean-François Lyotard was a participant in the 1972 conference at Cerisy that some have cited as the initial moment of contemporary French Nietzscheanism.[7] And although his works of the 1960s and 1970s do not show the constant references to Nietzsche that one finds, for example, in Derrida or Deleuze, they do nevertheless display many of the Nietzschean characteristics that were in the air in Paris during those years. In fact, while I discussed in chapter three the emergence of Nietzsche as the voice through which Deleuze and Guattari's *Anti-Oedipus* responds to Parisian Freudo-Marxism, one could address many of the same issues in relation to one of Lyotard's works, *Économie libidinale*,[8] a work about which one of Lyotard's better informed and more sympathetic critics, Peter Dews, has remarked that it "illustrates—perhaps more clearly than any other post-structuralist text—the fundamental dynamic of the shift towards Nietzsche during the 1970s."[9]

Throughout his career, Lyotard's writings have never strayed far from the realms of aesthetics and politics. Moreover, since his emergence as one of, if not *the*, leading French figure in the discussions of postmodernity, his thought has increasingly blurred the lines that separate these two realms. In addition, and perhaps as a consequence of his early association with and commitment to the far-left political group *Socialisme ou Barbarie*,[10] Lyotard has emerged as the leading poststructuralist French philosopher most sensitive to the political implications of his philosophizing. With these two features of Lyotard's career in mind, I would like to suggest that while his attempt to provide an aesthetic solution to the question of how to make ethical and political decisions from within a postmodern perspective first led him from Kant to Nietzsche, the inability to ground a politics in a Nietzschean aesthetic ultimately led Lyotard beyond Nietzsche and, in a peculiar irony, back to Kant.

Specifically, one finds this movement from Kant to Nietzsche and back again in the evolution of Lyotard's position on "justice" from *Just Gaming* to *The Differend*. Stated most simply, the question that *Just Gaming* poses is this: How can we make ethical judgments without appealing to absolute moral principles or a moral law? For Lyotard, the question is put this way: if "one is without criteria, yet one must decide," from where does one derive the ability to judge? He proceeds to offer a Nietzschean answer to this Kantian question, as this ability "bears a name in a certain philosophical tradition, namely Nietzsche's: the will to power."[11]

For Lyotard, Nietzsche's will to power provides an answer analogous to that provided for aesthetic judgment by Kant in the third *Critique*, but Nietzsche extends this answer beyond aesthetics to all judgment: "The ability to judge does not hang upon the observance of criteria. The form that it will take in the last *Critique* is that of the imagination. An imagination that is constitutive. It is not only an ability to judge; it is a power to invent criteria."[12] Where Kant located within aesthetic judgment the ability to judge in the absence of a rule, Nietzsche's philosophical viewpoint subsumes *all* judgment—political, metaphysical, epistemological, ethical, and aesthetic—under these conditions. There are no universally given rules, no absolutely privileged criteria in any of these realms; it is our task to invent these criteria and make our judgments accordingly.

This ability to invent criteria without appeal to any universal rule or rules of judgment operates at the heart of Nietzsche's genealogical analyses. By making its judgments on the basis of the criteria invented (masterly or slavish, life-affirming or life-negating) rather than the specific choices made, Nietzschean genealogy was able to distinguish critically between the worth of apparently similar actions or judgments. We see this exemplified in Nietzsche's noting the qualitative difference—based on the type of will to power at work—between creation out of need or out of excess (see *GS*, Pr2, 370) or between those judgments concerning what is good that emerge from the good-evil in contradistinction to the good-bad criteria (*GM*, I). In making these differential determinations, Nietzsche thereby provides a model that Lyotard puts to work in his pagan project of conceiving judgment other than as the application of a valid and validating general rule to a particular case.

This Nietzschean moment in Lyotard's thought has been overlooked by most of Lyotard's commentators. For example, Peter Dews sees in *Just Gaming* "a crucial break with the Nietzscheanism of the 1970s."[13] Dews draws this conclusion because, like Heidegger, he identifies "will to power" with a "philosophy of the will." He thus concludes that insofar as Lyotard in *Just Gaming* criticizes the philosophy of the will,[14] he has turned away from the commitment to a libidinal politics that underlies *Économie libidinale*. But as we saw in our discussion of Deleuze in chapter three, unlike Heidegger, the French generally do not take Nietzsche's notion of will to power to articulate a "philosophy of the will." Lyotard makes clear the French refusal to follow Heidegger in interpreting "will to power" as a new voluntarism precisely in *Just Gaming*, where he continues to appeal to Nietzsche's will to power even as he distances himself from any "philosophy of the will." And it is precisely this appeal to Nietzsche's will to power as the power of the constitutive imagination to invent criteria for judgment that allows Lyotard to extend the Kantian answer to the question of the ability to judge beyond the confines of aesthetic judgment as articulated in Kant's third *Critique*.

Lyotard goes on to develop his Nietzschean solution to the Kantian question of judgment with the help of the Wittgensteinian language game of language games: there is no universal criterion to justify or legitimate the translation from the language games of description to those of prescription. Because there is no higher order rule of judgment to which those hetero-geneous language games could both appeal, the criterion will always remain in dispute, incapable of proof, a *differend*. When he suggests that post-modernity's "criterion" is "the absence of criteria,"[15] or when he offers "the end of great narratives" as postmodernity's "great narrative,"[16] Lyotard appears to openly affirm the self-referentiality that plagues Nietzsche's perspectival view that there are no "truths," only "interpreta-tions." Nietzsche certainly acknowledged that the absence of truth left open the possibility of infinite interpretations (see *GS*, 374), and Lyotard is will-ing to follow Nietzsche on this path. When Lyotard writes that "one can never reach the just by a conclusion," or that "prescriptives, taken serious-ly, are never grounded,"[17] he makes the ultimate Nietzschean gesture and accepts that the non-resolution of oppositions, the affirmation of differ-ences and dissensus, and the acceptability of multiple and discordant voices are the inevitable consequences of refusing to sanction the move to a meta-narrative in the ethical and political as well as aesthetic and metaphysical domains.

In the laughter that closes the conversation with Jean-Loup Thébaud that is *Just Gaming*, however, Lyotard appears to acknowledge the untenability of his position. That is to say, if one follows the argument as it develops over the course of the "Seventh Day" of their conversation, one finds Lyotard boxed into an untenable and self-contradictory position. The conversation begins with a critique of Kant's grounding the regulative idea of justice in either unity, the unity of humanity in the political domain, or totality, the totality of reasonable beings in the moral domain.[18] To this, Lyotard responds that any society, in order to function, will require a multiplicity of language games and by that very fact, the idea of multiplicity or diversity—marking "an absence of unity, an absence of totality"[19]—will necessarily be a part of justice as a regulative ideal. What results is a Nietzschean reformula-tion of the categorical imperative that appears precisely as the negation of the Kantian original: "Always act in such a way that the maxim of your will may... *not* be erected... into a principle of universal legislation."[20]

But the problem with this reformulation is recognized immediately, as both Lyotard and Thébaud note that this very formulation operates within the horizon of both unity and totality.[21] And this problem becomes acute in the final exchange within their dialogue as Lyotard distinguishes between the "multiplicity of justices" and the "justice of multiplicity." The former, which is in conformity with Lyotard's paganism, notes that justice is to be defined locally "in relation to the rules specific to each game" and, as in all games, "justice here does not consist merely in the observance of the rules;... it consists in working at the limits of what the rules permit, in order to invent new moves, perhaps new rules and therefore new games." The latter, "justice of multiplicity," presents a problem for the pagan, however, insofar as it is prescribed *globally* as a universal value that "prescribes the observance of the singular justice of each game such as it has just been situated: formalism of the rules and imagination in the moves."[22] This universal proclamation of the justice of multiplicity is, however, difficult to maintain from within a Nietzschean perspective, as both Lyotard and Thébaud realize when they laugh in response to Thébaud's closing observation that Lyotard here "is talking like the great prescriber himself."[23]

Samuel Weber puts the point succinctly in his afterword to *Just Gaming*: "By prescribing that no game, especially not that of prescription, should dominate the others, one is doing exactly what it is simultaneously claimed is being avoided: one is dominating the other games in order to protect them from domination."[24] What this shows, and what Lyotard came to realize as he reframed these issues in his next major work—*The Differend*— is that it is not so easy to keep language games pure, that the descriptive language games with their rules governing criteria, and the prescriptive language games with their rules concerning justice, are subject to multiple linkages that, if one is to foreclose the worst sorts of political injustice, will require conceptual safeguards beyond those he finds in Nietzsche's texts.

Whether or not Lyotard is correct in seeing a limitation in Nietzsche's position here is, however, subject to question. If I am understanding Lyotard correctly on this point, then I think that he has misunderstood Nietzsche here. For while Lyotard's position may be difficult to maintain from within a Nietzschean framework, it is not an impossible position to maintain from Nietzsche's perspective. That is to say, Nietzsche *can* justify just the sort of move that Lyotard looks to make in terms of a universal, formalistic prescription that can accommodate an infinite number of creative responses. In fact, this is precisely what Nietzsche does when he puts forward "will to power" as a "formal" principle that states something like "all things act so as to increase their power." Having offered this "universal principle" as an overarching framework, Nietzsche has not, thereby, specified a norm or rule that will prescribe any particular being's actions; and this point—allowing the greatest multiplicity of possible responses—seems to be exactly what Lyotard hopes to preserve when he calls for "imagination in the moves."

Lyotard chose, however, to move in a different direction. While "will to power" may be a concept useful for characterizing the imaginative, inventive capacity needed for the postulation of criteria for judgment, he finds that a finer distinction must be drawn if one is to clarify the concept of "justice" in a way that will allow this concept to function "after the death of God." To put this another way, what Lyotard came to realize is that a sharp separation needs to be drawn between ethics and politics and such a separation could not be drawn in terms of the will to power. The search for this finer distinction leads Lyotard to the linguistic framework of phrases (*phrases, Sätze*), phrase regimens, phrase universes, and genres of discourse that one finds in *The Differend*. And it is in terms of this framework that Lyotard is able to restrict "justice" to the phrase universe of politics governed by "norms," while "obligation" dominates the phrase universe of ethics governed by "laws."

In so doing, Lyotard leaves Nietzsche behind, replacing him as philosophical resource with Levinas in the ethical phrase universe and Kant in the political phrase universe. Following Levinas, Lyotard argues that the ethical phrase operates in a universe in which there is no symmetry between I and you: the addressee of the prescription (the I) receives the prescription as a law that obligates the I.[25] And the source of this prescription, the source of the ethical law, the addressor whose address obligates the addressee, is an Absolute Other whose authority can never be legitimated and whose place must remain empty.[26] Like Kierkegaard's Abraham, the addressee accepts the obligation of the law as an act of faith whose legitimation could only take place in the cognitive and not the ethical phrase universe. Kierkegaard's Abraham had to accept God's prescription in silence, because to speak would involve leaving the religious realm of faith;[27] Lyotard-Levinas's ethical addressee is obligated prima facie by the law, and to seek to justify, legitimate, or explain the law would be for the addressee (the I) to usurp the empty place of the addressor (the you) and, thereby, would be to annihilate the ethical phrase qua ethical.[28]

What distinguishes the ethical and political phrase universes is precisely the question of the symmetry of addressor and addressee, and it is the possibility of this symmetry that for Lyotard makes a political community—the *we*—possible. Where an ethical law prescribes "it is obligatory for *x* to carry out act *a*," the corresponding political norm would be formulated this way: "it is a norm decreed by *y* that it is obligatory for *x* to carry out act *a*." Here we see the difference between ethics and politics, for while *x* can never be the source of obligation in the ethical phrase, the political phrase derives its authority from the fact that *x* (the addressee) can occupy the place of *y* (the addressor). This is, according to Lyotard, the Kantian principle of autonomy: when any *x* so obligated by the norm can occupy the place of the norm's legislator *y*, the political norm can be reformulated in terms that authorize the formation and formulation of a political community: "*we* decree as a norm that it is an obligation for *us* to carry out act *a*."[29]

Although Kant himself tried to account for this community *ethically* in terms of the transcendental Idea of humanity (the community of ethical, reasonable beings),[30] he did so by effacing the differend between the ethical phrase ("You ought to") and the cognitive phrase ("ought implies can"). That is to say, Lyotard argues that when Kant claims that the action that follows a prescriptive must be possible, he introduces the notion of consequences which, "by definition, cannot be ethical."[31] Instead, these consequences function within a cognitive phrase and bring with them a cognitive linkage (implication) rather than an ethical linkage (judgment). This shows not so much a flaw in the Kantian ethical position but what we might call an ontological limitation in the phrase universe of ethics.

> As a sign, the ethical phrase is without sequel, and thus final. But as there is no final phrase, another phrase must link onto it. And, as this linkage cannot be the linkage of an ethical implication—which is an impossibility—this implication, if it is still an implication (a series of consequences), then is not ethical, but cognitive. The "possibility" required by Kant that pure obligation give rise to a phenomenon ascertainable in reality and explicable according to the rules of cognition, in other words, that it give rise to a referent, signifies that the you of the obligation should always be able to be taken as the referent of a subsequent cognitive phrase. We don't really see what would prohibit a linkage of this sort. We do see, however, that this linkage prohibits the making of a world (in the Kantian sense) with ethical phrases. Either implication, or obligation. There is no ethical community.[32]

But while there may be no ethical community, there is political community, a community made possible by the symmetry between addressor and addressee at the level of norms and made actual by the recognition that any linkage between phrases could give rise to a differend.[33] This symmetry makes the prescriptive *common* and thereby removes it from the ethical as it constitutes the addressees of the prescriptive into a community whose members, "qua addressees of the normative, are advised that they are, if not necessarily equal before the law, at least all subject to the law."[34] This commonality of the prescriptive is, of course, what Nietzsche could never accept insofar as he seems unwilling to understand what is common in any way other than as an attribute of the herd (cf. *GS*, 354), an unwillingness that is in part responsible for the ultimate insufficiency of Nietzsche's own positive account of society. And while Lyotard's continued commitment to dissensus and heterogeneity could be articulated in Nietzschean terms, as it was by, among others, Foucault and Deleuze, it is clear that his effort to think the political could not be. That is to say, Lyotard's desire to think the political in a way that will accommodate differends in a shared social space where norms work to minimize evil (rather than maximize good), and where evil is itself defined in terms of the continued interdiction of possible phrases,[35] requires him to go beyond the conceptual resources that he is able to locate in Nietzsche's texts.

The New French Anti-Nietzscheans: Ferry, Renaut, Descombes

While Lyotard has turned away from Nietzsche, his turn is not replicated in the works of the new generation of French anti-Nietzscheans. In fact, while they might applaud Lyotard's motivation—to raise anew the question of justice—they clearly fault him for maintaining what this new generation sees to be the major flaws in the philosophizing of their predecessors: the stylistic excess that leads them to "absurd" conclusions and the continued anti-humanism that accompanies their failure to account for a politically and socially acceptable notion of the subject.[36] That is to say, even as Lyotard seeks to account for a notion of political community, he does so by means of a *hyper*-linguisticism that appears to call for eliminating any notion of the subject.[37] It is precisely this hyperbolic, excessive style and the elimination of the subject that emerge as the focus of much of the criticism that writers like Vincent Descombes and Luc Ferry and Alain Renaut have directed at the philosophers of the sixties.

Turning first to Ferry and Renaut, the outline of their argument was put forward initially in *La pensée 68*, and they have repeated the same basic line of argumentation in several other forums.[38] In *La pensée 68*, Ferry and Renaut chart in quick and somewhat loose fashion, how Foucault, Lacan, Bourdieu, and Derrida each function as a radicalized, hyperbolic and anti-humanistic repetition of the thinking of a previous, *German* master— Nietzsche, Freud, Marx, and Heidegger, respectively. But already in their introductory sketch of what they call the "ideal type" of "Sixties Philosophy," the profoundly Nietzschean character of "Sixties Philosophy" emerges. This ideal type is circumscribed in terms of four basic characteristics: "the Theme of the End of Philosophy," "the Paradigm of Genealogy," "the Disintegration of the Idea of Truth," and "the Historicizing of Categories and the End to Any Reference to the Universal." While each of these characteristics can appear in a Marxian or Heideggerian form, Ferry and Renaut's discussion reveals them each as an essentially Nietzschean thematic.

From these four characteristics, according to Ferry and Renaut, two objectionable effects emerge. The first involves the transformation of philosophical style, both in the sense of the style of writing philosophically and the style of a philosophical life. As regards the former, Ferry and Renaut criticize the philosophers of the sixties for cultivating paradox, demanding complexity, and rejecting clarity. Taking Derrida's *Glas* as the "no doubt quintessential 'sixties' discourse," they conclude that the "taste for provocation through absurdity is a widely shared propensity" among the sixties philosophers.[39] And as concerns the latter, they find in the preceding generation a "*pathos* of 'victimization'"[40] that actively seeks out the margins only to subsequently lament having been marginalized.

The second effect, which brings Ferry and Renaut to the central focus of their own critique, is the radical critique of subjectivity. Ferry and Renaut do not want to discount entirely Nietzsche's critique of the subject. But the problem with the Nietzsch*eans*, according to Ferry and Renaut, is that, having made legitimate criticisms of metaphysical and bourgeois notions of the subject, they leap to the extreme, and ultimately untenable, position of calling for the complete elimination of all notions of subjectivity. They see the problems with this position to be twofold, one philosophical and one political. The philosophical problem with the elimination of the subject is that if successful, it leaves no room for recuperating any positive notion of agency. In other words, it is impossible to take a position that calls for the complete elimination of all notions of agency without self-contradiction, for some notion of agency must be assumed if one—the always presupposed agent—is to be able to adopt any position whatsoever.

And the political problem, while not self-contradictory, is no less troubling, for eliminating subjectivity leaves open the possibility of the real elimination of subjects, that is, it leaves little ground for defending notions of human rights. Ferry and Renaut have little sympathy for the cavalier way in which the French Nietzscheans were willing to give up all notion of human rights grounded upon some concept of the autonomous subject. To turn one's back on human rights, to turn one's back on the republican ideal, runs the risk of barbarism insofar as "when only exaggerated individual differences survive, then everyone's other becomes 'wholly other,' the 'barbarian'."[41] Such barbarism, they think, is inevitable when one tries to adopt a politics grounded upon Nietzschean principles.[42] That is to say, a Nietzschean politics will be vitalist, not humanist; it will be based upon the principle of life and not on principles of human rights. And, insofar as for Nietzsche life is will to power, they find it difficult to imagine how a Nietzschean politics can avoid devolving into a situation in which all questions of justice are determined on the basis of the will of the strongest.

This will be, they argue, the inevitable result of an analysis that denounces all notions of subjectivity and all humanism while regarding society to be an arena of competing forces. And whether or not the Nietzscheans actually believed in their denunciations, Ferry and Renaut conclude that some version of "might makes right" is precisely the political outcome that one can expect to follow from a politics grounded upon the principles of French Nietzscheanism. In its stead, Ferry and Renaut advocate that we not follow the human sciences' critique of the subject with a naive and total denunciation of that subject, but assume the task of rethinking the subject anew in a way that can accommodate a notion of human rights while taking into account the critiques of the metaphysical and bourgeois subject that have emerged in the "French philosophy of the Sixties."[43] For without some minimal account of the subject and the assumption that, at least in principle, the establishment of some communication among subjects is possible, there can be no meaningful notion of universal human rights. And without some such reference and appeal to "the rights of humanity (which, think of them as we will, do imply a minimum of universality and subjectivity)," Ferry and Renaut conclude that, "perhaps without wishing to, one thus opens another door: that of barbarism."[44]

Of course, the validity of much of Ferry and Renaut's critique depends on whether or not any of the Nietzscheans do, in fact, want to *completely elim-inate* any positive notion of the subject. There is ample textual evidence to support an alternative reading, however. In fact, Ferry and Renaut may here be guilty of the same sort of excessive hyperbole of which they accuse the Nietzscheans. As we saw in chapter two, rather than eliminating the sub-ject, Foucault's entire corpus can be read in terms of an attempt to recon-figure our understanding of how we become subjects. And Derrida has con-sistently defended himself against this sort of a reading. For example, in 1966, in the discussion following his presentation of "Structure, Sign, and Play in the Discourse of the Human Sciences," Derrida responds directly to this point: "The subject is absolutely indispensable. I don't destroy the subject; I situate it. That is to say, I believe that at a certain level both of experience and of philosophical and scientific discourse one cannot get along without the notion of the subject. It is a question of knowing where it comes from and how it functions."[45]

More recently, Derrida has addressed this issue in an interview with Jean-Luc Nancy prompted by the question "Who comes *after* the subject?" Derrida begins, in fact, by challenging those who seek a "return of or to the subject" following the previous generation's "liquidation" of the subject. He comments, in what we can take as, in part, a response to the accusations of Ferry and Renaut:

> If over the last twenty-five years in France the most notorious of strategies have in fact led to a kind of discussion around "the question of the subject," none of them has sought to "liquidate" anything.... Did Lacan "liquidate" the subject? No. The decentered "subject" of which he speaks certainly doesn't have the traits of the classical subject (though even here, we'd have to take a closer look...), though it remains indispensable to the economy of the Lacanian the-ory.... As for Foucault's discourse, there would be different things to say according to the stages of its development. In his case, we would appear to have a history of subjectivity that, in spite of certain massive declarations about the effacement of the figure of man, certainly never consisted in "liquidating" the Subject. And in his last phase, there again, a return of morality and a certain ethical subject. For these three discourses (Lacan, Althusser, Foucault) and for some of the thinkers they privilege (Freud, Marx, Nietzsche), the subject can be re-interpreted, restored, re-inscribed, it certainly isn't "liquidated." The ques-tion "who," notably in Nietzsche, strongly reinforces this point.[46]

Remarks like these should make clear that for Derrida and the other French Nietzscheans, there is no question of eliminating the subject. They should lead us to ask why critics like Ferry and Renaut continue to present this rhetorically charged yet highly inaccurate view of their position.

While Ferry and Renaut have responded primarily to the political implications of contemporary French anti-humanism whose roots they locate in French Nietzscheanism, Vincent Descombes responds primarily to the French Nietzscheans as a philosopher disturbed by their stylistic excesses. In the "Final Remarks" to his survey of French philosophy in the twentieth century, for example, Descombes focuses on the Nietzschean theme of perspectivism and argues that while "the entire generation of 1960 declared itself in favor of perspectivism... the word 'perspective' protests against the use to which it is put."[47] That is to say, while the French Nietzscheans used "perspectivism" to destroy the unity of the phenomenological subject, they failed to recognize the Leibnizian character of Nietzsche's theme. Descombes quotes the *Monadology:*

> And just as a single city, observed from different sides, appears quite different, as if multiplied according to the perspectives, so in the same way by virtue of the infinite multitude of simple substances, there seem to be as many different universes, which are simply the perspectives on a single one, according to the different vantage points of each Monad. (§57)

To which Descombes adds: "French Nietzscheanism claims to overcome the subject when in fact it suppresses the *object* (the city, that object common to those observing it 'from different sides')."[48] Thus, while Nietzschean perspectivism dissolved both subject and object in the infinite diversity of possible perspectives, classical, Leibnizian perspectivism depends on an underlying assumption of identity at the level both of the object upon which perspectives are taken and the subject—the Monad—taking the perspective. And for that reason, Descombes concludes by suggesting that it was not the French Nietzscheans but Merleau-Ponty who used the word "'perspective' in the strict sense," the sense in which "perspectivism is the same thing as phenomenology," the sense in which, "by definition, perspectivism means to find *order* in diversity, *invariables* in change, *identity* in difference."[49]

Descombes's argument here, we should note, is somewhat problematic, for it is not at all clear *why* we must accept perspectivism in its "classical,"

Leibnizian form, rather than its Nietzschean form. As Descombes himself notes, Deleuze recognizes the difference between Leibnizian and Nietzschean perspectivism, but where Deleuze is able to accept different varieties of perspectivism—and ultimately to affirm the Nietzschean variety—Descombes reduces the two versions to the same. In so doing, Descombes overlooks precisely what is *not* Nietzschean about the Leibnizian, classical version of perspectivism—the assumption of a transcendent world "beyond" in which all the individual perspectives are summed as a system of a "*single one.*"[50]

Descombes claimed, in the preface to the English edition of *Objects of All Sorts: A Philosophical Grammar*, the second of his texts to be translated into English, that the constraints imposed on him by his task of providing an introduction to "modern French philosophy" in *Le même et l'autre* barred him "from undertaking a critique of this or that thesis in terms of [his] own choosing." To have brought his own terms to the critique, Descombes continues, would have been "awkward and insensitive." Instead, he contented himself with an "*immanent critique*, the kind that questions a philosophical production on its own ground and measures it by its own standards alone."[51] But he feels no such constraint to "immanent critique" in his contribution to the collection *Pourquoi nous ne sommes pas nietzschéens*. In fact, in "Le moment français de Nietzsche," Descombes picks up precisely where *Le même et l'autre* concluded in terms of a general discussion of contemporary French philosophy as Nietzschean.

The French Nietzscheanism of the 1970s, he claims here, is the third "moment" in which Nietzsche's thought has been mobilized on the French intellectual scene. But unlike the two earlier moments—by writers at the end of the nineteenth century and by certain "nonconformist" intellectuals (most notably those associated with the *Collège de Sociologie* [Bataille, Callois, Klossowski, et al.]) between the two world wars—this third Nietzschean moment in France is distinguished in terms of the primacy of place occupied by philosophers.

This moment of *philosophical* Nietzscheanism nevertheless returns to several of the projects initiated by the earlier Nietzscheans. For example, like its predecessors, Nietzsche's treatment of problems internal to German culture is invoked again in a French context by contemporary Nietzscheanism in order to excite, mobilize, and in general produce *moral* effects in their readers. Similarly, as was the case in the earlier Nietzschean moments, Descombes claims that contemporary Nietzscheans use Nietzsche's critique of political and religious institutions in order to adopt a militant oppositional stance to *all* social and political institutions, the result of which is a kind of social paralysis in which any group political action is felt to be impossible.

While Descombes has little sympathy for these Nietzschean applications, they are not the focus of his critique. Instead, it is to the uniquely *philosophical* faults of the contemporary French Nietzscheans that Descombes qua philosopher turns his critical attention. And the faults he finds on this score are numerous: the Nietzscheans conflate rhetoric and philosophy, they deny rationality, they merely repeat Nietzsche's critique of modern philosophy without adding anything of philosophical merit, and, when they do go beyond Nietzsche's own critique, the Nietzscheans make things worse by failing to recognize that Nietzsche's critique was *philosophical* while their own contributions leave philosophy for a discourse whose rhetorical hyperbole is morally irresponsible and politically dangerous.

The structure of Descombes's account of these faults is fairly simple: he begins with expressions of sympathy for the general points raised by the Nietzscheans. He then proceeds to argue that while the points addressed are important, they were made already quite forcefully by Nietzsche himself; when they reappear in the discourse of the Nietzscheans, however, they are now politicized, taken to extremes, and exaggerated to the point where they become either contradictory, absurd, dangerous, or all three. For example, in discussing the attention to the rhetoric of philosophical argumentation, Descombes acknowledges that there is an important point to be made in distinguishing two senses of the "force" of an argument: the argument's logical force in terms of the strength with which it justifies its conclusions, and the argument's psychological force in terms of its ability to persuade its audience. But in their emphasis on the latter, psychological force, Descombes claims that the French Nietzscheans forget the former; they forget, in other words, that there is in fact a "philosophy of rhetoric"—founded by Aristotle—in which discourses are examined in terms of their ability not just to persuade but to persuade *rationally*. The art of rhetoric can retain its *philosophical* character by refusing to subordinate the logical force (force as "consequence") of philosophical concepts to the genealogical forces (force as historical "effect") at work in the history of ideas. However, by equating effects and consequences, and by historicizing logic as an object for *genealogical* analysis, the French Nietzscheans have lost the point of their initial attention to rhetoric. In so doing, Descombes concludes, they have also lost the ability to discriminate between good and bad arguments, between "well-proved" and "badly-proved" oratory.[52]

This same general strategy appears in the other themes discussed by Descombes. For example, he regards the juncture of Nietzsche, Freud, and Marx as "masters of suspicion," initiated first by Paul Ricoeur[53] and made a foundational axiom of French Nietzscheanism by Foucault in his paper at the Royaumont Colloquium on Nietzsche in 1964, to be a political—and not a philosophical—point. Moreover this political juncture obscures the differences between Marx, Freud, and Nietzsche and it can only be maintained on the basis of establishing an antithesis between the critique of the cogito and the "*critique de la conscience.*" According to Descombes, this opposition makes sense only if one fails to be attentive to the fact that the French language has only one word, '*conscience*,' to translate what, in both German and English, are rendered as two distinct concepts: '*Bewusstsein*' and '*Gewissen*,' 'consciousness' and 'conscience.' The masters of interpretive suspicion can only be united, therefore, by means of erroneously conflating a moral phenomenon (*Gewissen*, conscience) and a metaphysical phenomenon (*Bewusstsein*, consciousness) into the single French word '*conscience*.' Descombes concludes that Nietzsche's critique of the cogito, therefore, was not a matter of suspicion; it was a philosophical critique. And to equate his critique of Descartes with his suspicions concerning bad conscience, as the French Nietzscheans have done (or so Descombes claims!), is bad philosophizing, a rhetorical ploy based upon an equivocation concerning the French word '*conscience*.'[54]

In similar fashion, Descombes locates in Foucault's affirmation of interpretation as an "infinite task" an *excessive* hermeneutics whose genesis lies in Foucault's political reaction to the conservatism of the 1950s:

> Behind the however abstract variations on the theme "Marx, Nietzsche, Freud," one ends up hearing the political terms of the 1950s: *dogmatism, orthodoxy, right to revisionism, exclusion*. Strangely, a particular political experience (that of the cold war and of destalinization) fixes once and for all the meaning of the word *truth*. To use the word *truth*, that would be to give in to dogmatism.[55]

But to sacrifice "truth" to the infinite task of interpretation is, according to Descombes, to fail to distinguish 'to understand' (*comprendre*) from 'to interpret' (*interpréter*). At this point, Descombes in effect challenges the entire post-Heideggerian hermeneutic tradition,[56] as he argues that Foucault here makes a "category mistake" by taking a capacity (the ability to understand) to be an action (the act of interpreting). In making this category mistake, Foucault again exaggerates and obscures the "obvious distinction" between those meanings that are immediately understood and those that are at "first sight" obscure and in need of interpretive explication. And again, Descombes claims that the motivation behind this exaggeration is political, not philosophical, for by making everything subject to interpretation, suspicion can now be cast upon first-person reports. Structuralists like Lévi-Strauss used this strategy to cast suspicion on and ultimately disqualify the reports of indigenous peoples. Descombes concludes that poststructuralists like Foucault go even further than their structuralist predecessors, rendering suspect the reports not only of the "natives" but of the "experts" as well.

In bringing his discussion to a close, Descombes makes clear what is at issue in the politics that underlie the third Nietzschean moment in France. Starting from the assumption that all social relations are relations of forces, the argument of Nietzscheanism proceeds by two stages. The first stage is critical: by generalizing the activity of interpretation, "truth" gets refigured as the received orthodoxy, thereby permitting suspicion to be cast upon all "authorized" beliefs. From this follows the second, positive stage: practical decision-making becomes possible through the assertion of a principle on the basis of which choices can be made among the many competing and relativized beliefs. And the principle to which the Nietzscheans appeal as the foundation of both a personal morality and a line of political conduct is a classical normative principle: the sovereignty of the individual. This principle, Descombes notes, far from being a radical innovation, is in fact an expression of "the most classical French individualism"—the citizen against the powers that be. And contrary to what the Nietzscheans think, although this may in fact be a defensible *moral* principle, as a *political* principle, it is meaningless insofar as it could serve as the legitimating principle of any behavior whatsoever. Which is to say that the development of a politics based on the Nietzschean moral principle of a sovereign individual requires the accompaniment of a philosophy of right or a philosophy of justice, a philosophy that the Nietzscheans have steadfastly refused to provide.[57]

Descombes argues that one sees the dangerous consequences of such a refusal in the interpretation of Nietzsche offered by Deleuze. In his desire to free the sovereign individual from any notion of subjection, Deleuze's interpretation goes beyond Nietzsche's in a way that makes Deleuze's politics even more problematic than Nietzsche's. For Nietzsche could at least advocate a personal morality in which the sovereign individual would be responsible to the laws that he himself imposed, even when these laws obligated the individual to others. In order to eliminate any notion of subjection, however, Deleuze affirms a notion of absolute autonomy and self-legislation that appears to preclude any notion of responsibility to others. But such responsibility, according to Descombes, was the essential feature of Nietzsche's superior, sovereign individual, the individual who, for example, we are told in the second essay of the *Genealogy* had earned "the *right to make promises*" (*GM*, II, 2). Insofar as Deleuze imprudently equates morality with responsibility, Descombes argues that Deleuze has no choice but to interpret the superior individual freed from morality as "irresponsible."[58] And insofar as this freedom from responsibility means that the superior individual will have no responsibility toward others, such a philosophical view "culminates in an apology for tyranny."[59]

From this brief review, the general orientation of Descombes's critique of the French Nietzscheans is clear enough: while he acknowledges the importance of the ideological and cultural problems they confront, he questions whether in going beyond Nietzsche's own solutions to these problems, they don't exaggerate his position to the point of absurdity. While he suggests that we can, therefore, accept the political questions they have posed as worthy of thought, he concludes that we must reject the philosophical answers to these important questions raised by the French Nietzscheans because these answers are "philosophically incoherent," "ill-conceived," and put forward in terms that are "needlessly affected" and "desperately confused."[60]

Postscript to a Postscript: Nietzsche's (Eternal?) Return

> The worst readers are those who behave like plundering troops: they take away a few things they can use, dirty and confound the remainder, and revile the whole.
>
> —NIETZSCHE, *Assorted Opinions and Maxims*

How then should one respond to a critique like Descombes's or Ferry and Renaut's? Writing in the genre of polemic, these writers do not so much want to understand the authors they are reading. Instead, they want to construct a case: like a lawyer, they marshal the evidence in as damaging a way as possible in order to justify their political indictment of "neo-conservatism," "irresponsibility," or "barbarism." To many critics of recent French philosophy who have been awaiting just such an indictment, texts like those we have just examined will be welcomed.[61] But one could of course challenge their interpretation of Nietzsche, or of the French Nietzscheans, offering a more generous, alternative reconstruction of the texts under scrutiny. Or one could try to defend Nietzsche and the French Nietzscheans, answering the criticisms one by one and constructing a defense against the accusations raised.

In the preceding four chapters, I have offered a more generous interpretation, both of Nietzsche and of some of the more important and interesting work that has emerged as part of his French legacy. I have also made, in passing, a few brief remarks in defense of the French Nietzscheans to some of their critics' accusations. But I am not certain that a more lengthy defense is here necessary. This is not to say that I agree with the criticisms raised by recent French (or German, for that matter[62]) anti-Nietzscheans against either Nietzsche or his French descendents. But it is to say that, in a sense, the defense already made, by Derrida among others, in response to the Nazi appropriation of Nietzsche, can be applied as well to readings like those of Descombes, Ferry, and Renaut. While I do not want to suggest in the least that Descombes, Ferry, or Renaut have any connections to or sympathies for Nazi ideology, I do want to note that their readings are *very* selective in terms of what they attend to in the writings of Nietzsche and the French Nietzscheans. For that reason, Derrida's comments seem relevant to their reading practices. One of the points that emerges in the context of Derrida's reading in *Otobiographies* of Nietzsche's 1872 text *On the Future of our Educational Institutions* is that Nietzsche wrote some things that do in fact lend themselves to the sort of use made of his works by the Nazis. As Derrida notes, although it may be contrary to the intention of "the signatories or shareholders in the huge 'Nietzsche Corporation,'... it cannot be entirely fortuitous that the discourse bearing his name in society, in accordance with civil laws and editorial norms, has served as a legitimating reference for ideologues. There is nothing absolutely contingent about the fact that the only political regimen to have *effectively* brandished his name as a major and official banner was Nazi."[63] That is to say, it is not just the result of an unfortunate coincidence or Nietzsche's bad luck that his works, rather than the works of Kant or Leibniz, became linked as they did with National Socialism.

But does this make Nietzsche a Nazi? Of course not. It does, however, say something about his texts and the risks that any writer runs when they allow their works to enter the sphere of public discourse; namely, when they make their writings public, they sanction *de facto* their work being appropriated and grafted into other contexts. These risks become extreme when a writer chooses to write with the hyperbolic rhetoric that one finds in Nietzsche. And one finds this same rhetorical excess in many of the French philosophers discussed in the preceding four chapters, an excess that Ferry and Renaut in particular exploit constantly in their own often rhetorically excessive response to the "Sixties philosophers."[64] But as the wide range of sympathetic commentaries on the work of poststructural French philosophy demonstrates, and as I hope I myself have demonstrated in the previous chapters, one can read the works of Derrida, Foucault, Deleuze, Cixous, et al., far more generously and sympathetically than have the anti-Nietzscheans.

This is not where I want to conclude this study, however. For the fact remains that while one can, and others perhaps will, defend Nietzsche and the French against their readings at the hands of Descombes or Ferry and Renaut, I have chosen to conclude with a discussion of the French anti-Nietzscheans because I want to make the historical observation that Nietzsche no longer plays the role in French intellectual life that he has played for much of the past three decades. Like Jürgen Habermas in *The Philosophical Discourse of Modernity*, Descombes, Ferry, Renaut, and others have chosen to focus on Nietzsche and the Nietzscheanism of poststructuralist French philosophy in order to make what is their fundamentally political rejoinder to the writings of the philosophers whom I have framed in these essays as "Nietzsche's French legacy."[65] This is not to say that the critiques of Habermas, Descombes, and Ferry and Renaut have played a *causal* role in the eclipse of Nietzsche's influence in France. In other words, it is not the force of their critiques that has led to Nietzsche's fall from favor in Parisian intellectual circles. It is more the case that their critiques represent what one might call a sign of the new times in France, and perhaps elsewhere.

As several recent works have shown, Nietzsche's fortunes have played themselves out among both the Left and the Right almost since his texts first appeared.[66] The recent turn to the Right in Europe and the United States, and the resurgence of nationalism often accompanying, if not driving, this turn, has led to new associations between Nietzsche and the Right that should concern those left intellectuals, in the English-speaking world and elsewhere, who will continue to turn to Nietzsche as a philosophical resource. Left-leaning readers of Nietzsche have legitimately criticized those readings that make Nietzsche out to be a "simple" misogynist, or a straight-forwardly anti-Semitic or anti-Enlightenment thinker. But at the same time, there are problems with many of those readings that seek to "save" Nietzsche from charges of misogyny or anti-Semitism or to make him compatible with a leftist or left-leaning liberal-democratic politics. Rather than directly confront and take account of them, many of the readings that seek to package Nietzsche politically as a champion of the Left do so by choosing to overlook as insignificant or momentary lapses Nietzsche's many crudely racist, sexist, or elitist remarks.[67] With a writer whose prose is both as nuanced and as excessive as Nietzsche's, a certain amount of selective inat-tention may be unavoidable. But as philosophical and political centers are shifting to the Right, which appears to be the case as we approach this *fin de millennium*, one will overlook the less progressive remarks of Nietzsche and the Nietzscheans at one's peril.

Does this mean one should give up on Nietzsche, turning, like Lyotard, to a "safer" thinker like Kant or Levinas? I don't believe it does. For many of the themes that first led the French to Nietzsche in the 1960s are worth recalling today—themes like the emphasis on interpretation; the attention to power differentials and the links between relations of power, discursive prac-tices, and knowledge-relations; refusing to see the world as a series of bina-ry, hierarchical oppositions; attending to the interconnections of philo-sophical, cultural, and political institutions; seeing the world in terms of relations and becoming rather than in terms of fixed identities; making judgments—political and ethical as well as aesthetic—without appealing to fixed, formal, or given criteria. And other Nietzschean themes, in particular, the critique of nationalism and the critique of fixed notions of self-identity, while not necessarily a part of the 1960s Parisian landscape, may be more rel-evant today than ever.

As Descombes himself notes, this is not the first time Nietzsche's for-tunes have wavered in France; there have been two prior moments of French Nietzscheanism, and I do not in any way want to imply that the eclipse of the French Nietzsche is total, or final. But it bears noting that, at this historical moment, Nietzsche's *French* legacy is playing itself out more than anywhere else in the *English*-speaking philosophical and critical worlds. That is to say, not only is there a virtual Nietzsche industry producing his-torical and critical studies of his philosophy, particularly in English,[68] but as evidenced in thousands of articles and books written *not* by Nietzsche scholars, Nietzsche has become as important a resource, and as omnipresent a reference, for the cutting edge of critical scholarship in the US and the UK in the 1980s and 1990s as he was for the philosophical-literary avant-garde in Paris in the 1960s and 1970s.

Whether or not this is simply another case of the English-speaking scholarly community operating a decade or two behind the European times, or whether we are witnessing genuinely innovative American and British developments of the poststructural themes that emerged from the French Nietzscheanism of the 1960s and 1970s, is a question that remains to be answered. Similarly, whether the English-speaking critical world will be able to avoid the backlash against Nietzsche's influence that has emerged in recent years in France is another historical question that will have to wait for an answer.[69]

There is, however, reason to be optimistic about the future of Nietzsche's French legacy, especially insofar as the identity politics that has produced ethnic nationalisms in Eastern Europe and Africa calls for a critical response in which the Nietzschean critiques of both identity and nationalism can be of value. For example, while much interpretive work is needed to show Nietzsche as a supporter of democratic pluralism, such work can be done. Consider, in this regard, the following comment from Ernesto Laclau:

> A democratic society is not one in which the "best" content dominates unchallenged but rather one in which nothing is definitely acquired and there is always the possibility of challenge. If we think, for instance, in the resurgence of nationalism and all kinds of ethnic identities in present-day Eastern Europe, then we can easily see that the danger for democracy lies in the closure of these groups around full-fledged identities that can reinforce their most reactionary tendencies and create the conditions for a permanent confrontation with other groups.[70]

This, I would argue, is precisely the sort of leftist political position that a Nietzschean account of—and critique of—nationalism and identity can be used to support.

In fact, a model of such a Nietzschean account might be located in section 475 of *Human, All–Too–Human*, where Nietzsche offers one of his most powerful indictments of nationalism for providing the conditions out of which emerge one of the features of modernity that he finds most deplorable: the contemporary racist and anti-Semitic persecution of the Jews.

Here, in the context of rejecting the artificial and perilous separation of Europe into distinct nations through the "production of *national* hostilities," Nietzsche suggests that it is not the interests of the many but the interests of a few—"certain princely dynasties and certain classes of business and society"—that "impel to this nationalism." It is precisely at this point that Nietzsche situates the origins of modern anti-Semitism: "the entire problem of the Jews," he writes, "exists only in national states." He continues, in a passage that should refute definitively any charge that Nietzsche is straightforwardly anti-Semitic:

> It is here that their energy and higher intelligence, their capital in will and spirit accumulated from generation to generation in a long school of suffering, must come to preponderate to a degree calculated to arouse envy and hatred, so that in almost every nation—and the more so the more nationalist a posture the nation is adopting—there is gaining ground the literary indecency of leading the Jews to the sacrificial slaughter as scapegoats for every possible public or private misfortune. (*HH* 475)

Whether Nietzsche himself may fall victim to an identity politics at the level of culture or ethnicity that his philosophical critique of nationalism should distance him from is, of course, a matter worth addressing. But insofar as he here provides tools for a critique of national identity in favor of the "production of the strongest possible European mixed race," there is reason to look to his critique as a possible resource for criticizing ethnic and cultural identity as well.

In a similar fashion, the Nietzschean critique of dogmatism, grounded as it is on a perspectivist position that calls for multiplying points of view and avoiding fixed and rigid posturings, may be an important voice to heed in constructing a politics that can challenge the panoply of emerging fundamentalisms. At the same time, a thoroughgoing perspectivism can accommodate a notion of radical contingency that seems to be both theoretically desirable and pragmatically necessary at the present moment to many who—from the perspectives of feminism and women's studies, gender studies, queer theory, minoritarian studies, cultural studies, and, in general, from any oppositional perspective—hope to move from theory to action. Which is only to say that seeing the world with more and different eyes (*GM*, III, 12) may become a political necessity if one hopes to succeed, paraphrasing Marx's eleventh Thesis on Feuerbach, in not simply interpreting the world, but changing it as well.

Over a century ago, Nietzsche noted the posthumous character of his work, predicting that a century hence, he would find his rightful heirs, the "philosophers of the future" to whom his works were addressed. To be the sort of reader Nietzsche himself sought, we must recall, means not to receive his words as truths or to follow him as a disciple, two situations he openly tried to forestall. Instead of an aesthetics of reception, Nietzsche's works call for a performative hermeneutics. As someone who considered "every word behind which there does not stand a challenge to action to have been written in vain" (*SE*, p. 184; translation modified slightly), Nietzsche's "rightful readers" will be those incited to action by his works, to the action of transvaluing values.

As I have tried to demonstrate in the preceding chapters, for the past three decades French philosophy has answered Nietzsche's call and responded to his challenge. And I have tried to suggest some of the reasons why I think one might resist the judgment of the French and German anti-Nietzscheans concerning the merits of the responses provided by the French Nietzscheans. But that their responses were intended to be the last word is highly doubtful, as all of the writers examined in the preceding four chapters—and Lyotard belongs with this group as well—are committed to notions of dissemination, difference, repetition, reiteration, endless or interminable interpretation, etc., notions that preclude the possibility of there being a "last word." And if the history of Nietzsche's reception in the twentieth century is any indication, there will be no last word; however one responds to the demon's challenge in *The Gay Science* (*GS*, 341) that everything will return, there seems to be no need to worry about Nietzsche's return. Nietzsche knew his fate; he knew he would be a destiny. And whether directly or indirectly framed by his recent French legacy, Nietzsche's destiny will be to remain forever untimely, "that is to say, acting counter to our time and thereby acting on our time and, let us hope, for the benefits of a time to come" (*H*, p. 60).

Notes

>

Introduction

1. J. M. Kennedy, "Introduction," in Henri Lichtenberger, *The Gospel of Superman: The Philosophy of Friedrich Nietzsche* (Edinburgh: T. N. Foulis, 1910), p. vii. Lichtenberger's text, which was simply titled *La philosophie de Nietzsche*, originally appeared in 1898, published by Félix Alcan, Paris.

2. For a particularly good example of a *bad* reading of recent French philosophy as it pertains to Nietzsche, see Richard L. Howey, "Nietzsche and the 'New' French Philosophers," *International Studies in Philosophy*, Vol. 17, No. 2 (1985): 83–93. See also the hilarious, but nonetheless pointed reply to this essay by "P. A. Chambige" in the same issue, pp. 95–98.

3. See, for example, *BGE*, 253–54; *TI*, "What the Germans Lack," 4; *WS*, 214.

4. See, for example, *BGE*, 253–54; *NCW*, "Where Wagner Belongs."

5. See *BGE*, 246; see also Nietzsche's unpublished note from Fall 1887, where he writes in a draft to a preface: "That it is written in German is, to say the least, untimely: I wish I had written it in French, so that it might not appear to be a confirmation of the aspirations of the German Reich.... (Formerly, I wished I had not written my *Zarathustra* in German)" (*KSA*, 12: 9[188]).

   That this observation is no longer the case is the topic of the final chapter of this study, where I examine some of the works of a new generation of French philosophers who, "having begun their studies in the sixties," seek to separate themselves from the work of their "teachers" by "thinking with Nietzsche against Nietzsche" and by renewing the "ancestral demand of rationality which the relativism of the thinking of difference too easily invited [them] to renounce" (Luc Ferry and Alain Renaut, "Préface," in Alain Boyer, et al. *Pourquoi nous ne sommes pas nietzschéens* [Paris: Grasset, 1991], pp. 7–8).

7. Among the writers who single Nietzsche out in this way, I would include David Carroll, *Paraesthetics: Foucault, Lyotard, Nietzsche* (London: Methuen, 1987); Vincent Descombes, *Modern French Philosophy*, trans. L. Scott–Fox and J. M. Harding (Cambridge: Cambridge University Press, 1980); Luc Ferry and Alain Renaut, *French Philosophy of the Sixties: An Essay on Antihumanism*, trans. Mary Schnackenberg Cattani (Amherst: University of Massachusetts Press, 1990); Jürgen Habermas, *The Philosophical Discourse of Modernity*, trans. Frederick G. Lawrence (Cambridge, MA: MIT Press, 1987); Vincent B. Leitch, *Deconstructive Criticism: An Advanced Introduction* (New York: Columbia University Press, 1983); Allan Megill, *Prophets of Extremity: Nietzsche, Heidegger, Foucault, Derrida* (Berkeley: University of California Press, 1985); Arkady Plotnitsky, *Reconfigurations: Critical Theory and General Economy* (Gainesville: University Press of Florida, 1993); Charles E. Scott, *The Question of Ethics: Nietzsche, Foucault, Heidegger* (Bloomington: Indiana University Press, 1990).

8. Gilles Deleuze, *Nietzsche et la philosophie* (Paris: Presses Universitaires de France, 1962); English translation: *Nietzsche and Philosophy*, trans. Hugh Tomlinson (New York: Columbia University Press, 1983). The importance of Deleuze's study for the French readings of Nietzsche that developed in the 1960s and 1970s has been seriously underestimated by Nietzsche's English–speaking readers, many of whom single out Derrida as the primary figure responsible for initiating the "New Nietzsche." As François Ewald commented recently in the *Magazin Littéraire* special issue on "Les vies de Nietzsche," without Deleuze' two books on Nietzsche, without his text on the reversal of Platonisr (in *Revue de métaphysique et de morale* [1967]), and without h co–organizing the 1964 Royaumont Colloquium, "Nietzsche woul not be what he has become for us today" (François Ewal "Introduction" to Gilles Deleuze, "Mystère d'Ariane," *Magazi Littéraire*, No. 298 [April 1992]: 20). And Sarah Kofman, whc

work is often too quickly and inaccurately situated as a derivative of Derrida's, notes in the opening lines of her second book on Nietzsche that it was Deleuze's work that legitimated Nietzsche as a philosopher (Sarah Kofman, *Nietzsche et la scène philosophique* [Paris: Union Générale d'Éditions, 1979], p. 7). For a brief discussion of Deleuze's impact on French Nietzsche interpretation, see Duncan Large's "Translator's Introduction" in Sarah Kofman, *Nietzsche and Metaphor* (Stanford: Stanford University Press, 1993), pp. x–xiii.

9. The conference at Royaumont, presided over by M. Gueroult, took place July 4–8, 1964, and included papers presented by Henri Birault, Karl Löwith, Jean Wahl, Gabriel Marcel, Giorgio Colli and Mazzino Montinari, Edouard Gaède, Herbert W. Reichert, Boris de Schloezer, Danko Grlic, Michel Foucault, Gianni Vattimo, Pierre Klossowski, Jean Beaufret, Gilles Deleuze, and M. Goldbeck. All but the last of these are collected in *Nietzsche: Cahiers du Royaumont*, Philosophie No. VI (Paris: Éditions de Minuit, 1967). The conference at Cerisy–la–Salle, which took place in July, 1972, saw papers presented by Eugen Biser, Eric Blondel, Pierre Boudot, Eric Clémens, Gilles Deleuze, Jeanne Delhomme, Jacques Derrida, Eugen Fink, Léopold Flam, Edouard Gaède, Danko Grlic, Pierre Klossowski, Sarah Kofman, Philippe Lacoue–Labarthe, Karl Löwith, Jean–François Lyotard, Jean Maurel, Jean–Luc Nancy, Norman Palma, Bernard Pautrat, Jean–Michel Rey, Richard Roos, Paul Valadier, Jean–Noël Vuarnet, and Heinz Wismann. The proceedings of this conference were published in two volumes as *Nietzsche aujourd'hui* (Paris: Union Générale D'Éditions, 1973).

10. David B. Allison, ed., *The New Nietzsche: Contemporary Styles of Interpretation* (New York: Dell, 1977), p. x.

11. There are, of course, many other ways to understand the relationships between existentialism, structuralism, and poststructuralism. For example, we can distinguish these three "movements" in terms of the different ways they appeal to Hegel. Derrida, in fact, points in this direction in his essay "The Ends of Man" in *Margins of Philosophy*, trans. Alan Bass (Chicago: University of Chicago Press, 1982), pp. 109–36. There is much to gain from comparing Sartre or Merleau–Ponty's use of Hegel to Hegel's appearance in the texts of Lacan, Hyppolite, or Althusser, or to Derrida's or Deleuze's critiques of Hegelian dialectics.

12. Heidegger's two–volume work *Nietzsche* was published in Germany in 1961 and translated into French by Pierre Klossowski in 1971 (Paris: Gallimard).

13. Pierre Bourdieu, *Homo Academicus*, trans. Peter Collier (Stanford: Stanford University Press, 1988); see pp. xix–xxv.

14. Bourdieu, p. xix.

15. Bourdieu, p. xxiv.

16. Michel Foucault, "Critical Theory/Intellectual History," trans. Jeremy Harding in *Michel Foucault: Politics, Philosophy, Culture. Interviews and Other Writings 1977–1984*, ed. Lawrence D. Kritzman, (New York: Routledge, 1988), p. 33. See also Gilles Deleuze's comment that it was Nietzsche who allowed him to escape from "a generation... more or less ruined by the history of philosophy" in "Lettre à un critique sévère," reprinted in *Pourparlers* (Paris: Éditions de Minuit, 1990), pp. 14–15.

17. One cannot overestimate the role played here by Pierre Klossowski's work, in particular "Oubli et anamnèse dans l'expérience vécue de l'éternel retour du Même," presented at the Royaumont Conference on Nietzsche in 1964 and published in *Nietzsche: Cahiers du Royaumont*, pp. 227–35, and *Nietzsche et le cercle vicieux* (Paris: Mercure de France, 1969).

18. In their introduction to *Post–structuralism and the Question of History*, Geoff Bennington and Robert Young also make this point, noting that where structuralism sought to efface history, "it could be said that the 'post' of post–structuralism contrives to reintroduce it" (Derek Attridge, Geoff Bennington, and Robert Young, eds., *Post–structuralism and the Question of History*, [Cambridge: Cambridge University Press, 1987], p. 1).

19. I survey the range of these interpretations elsewhere; see my *Nietzsche and the Question of Interpretation: Between Hermeneutics and Deconstruction* (New York: Routledge, 1990), chapter three: "The French Scene," pp. 77–94.

20. The best example here may be the works "on" Nietzsche by Jacques Derrida. Of the three works directed explicitly toward Nietzsche, *Spurs: Nietzsche's Styles* and "Interpreting Signatures (Nietzsche/Heidegger): Two Questions" provide a context for Derrida to challenge both the Heideggerian reading of Nietzsche and Heidegger's philosophy in general, while *Otobiographies* offers Derrida the opportunity to discuss the "politics" of interpretation (Jacques Derrida, *Spurs: Nietzsche's Styles*, trans. Barbara Harlow [Chicago: University of Chicago Press, 1978]; "Interpreting Signatures (Nietzsche/Heidegger): Two Questions," trans. Diane P. Michelfelder and Richard E. Palmer in

Dialogue and Deconstruction: The Gadamer–Derrida Encounter, ed. Diane P. Michelfelder and Richard E. Palmer [Albany: State University of New York Press, 1989], pp. 58–71; *Otobiographies: The Teaching of Nietzsche and the Politics of the Proper Name*, trans. Avital Ronell, in *The Ear of the Other: Otobiography, Transference, Translation*, ed. Christie V. McDonald, trans. Peggy Kamuf [New York: Schocken Books, 1985]). For a detailed analysis of *Spurs* as one of the places in which Derrida most directly challenges Heidegger, see my *Nietzsche and the Question of Interpretation*, chapter four: "Derrida: Nietzsche Contra Heidegger," pp. 95–119.

21. Sarah Kofman cites and discusses several letters from late 1888 in which Nietzsche expresses his desire for two of his last books (*Nietzsche Contra Wagner* and *Ecce Homo*) to be translated into and read in French in the introduction to Sarah Kofman, *Explosion I: De l'"Ecce Homo" de Nietzsche* (Paris: Galilée, 1992); see pp. 15–20.

Chapter One
Derrida: The Critique of Oppositional Thinking and the Transvaluation of Values

1. Jacques Derrida, *Margins of Philosophy*, trans. Alan Bass (Chicago: University of Chicago Press, 1982), p. 305.

2. See, for example, the contrast drawn between Nietzsche and Rousseau in Jacques Derrida, *Of Grammatology*, trans. Gayatri C. Spivak (Baltimore: Johns Hopkins University Press, 1976); and the related contrast between Lévi–Strauss and Nietzsche in "Structure, Sign, and Play in the Discourse of the Human Sciences," in *Writing and Difference*, trans. Alan Bass (Chicago: University of Chicago Press, 1978).

3. My development of this point has benefited from conversations with Jeffrey Nealon.

4. Derrida, "Structure, Sign, and Play in the Discourse of the Human Sciences," p. 292.

5. See my *Nietzsche and the Question of Interpretation: Between Hermeneutics and Deconstruction* (New York: Routledge, 1990), chapter four: "Derrida: Nietzsche contra Heidegger," pp. 95–119.

6. Jacques Derrida, *Otobiographies: The Teaching of Nietzsche and the Politics of the Proper Name*, trans. Avital Ronell, in *The Ear of the*

Other: Otobiography, Transference, Translation, ed. Christie V. McDonald, trans. Peggy Kamuf (New York: Schocken Books, 1985), pp. 1–38.

7. Jacques Derrida, "Interpreting Signatures (Nietzsche/Heidegger): Two Questions," trans. Diane P. Michelfelder and Richard E. Palmer in *Dialogue and Deconstruction: The Gadamer–Derrida Encounter*, ed. Diane P. Michelfelder and Richard E. Palmer (Albany: State University of New York Press, 1989), pp. 58–71.

8. Martin Heidegger, *Nietzsche*, Bd. I (Pfullingen: Verlag Günther Neske, 1961), p. 9.

9. Derrida, "Interpreting Signatures," p. 67.

10. Derrida, *Of Grammatology*, pp. 19–20.

11. See Jacques Derrida, *Of Spirit: Heidegger and the Question*, trans. Geoffrey Bennington and Rachel Bowlby (Chicago: University of Chicago Press, 1989), p. 73.

12. Jacques Derrida, "Nietzsche and the Machine," Interview with Richard Beardsworth in *Journal of Nietzsche Studies*, Vol. 7 (Spring 1994), p. 26. In the second chapter of my *Nietzsche and the Question of Interpretation*, I use the theme of play as part of that Nietzschean reserve to offer such a genealogical reading of Heidegger.

13. Derrida, "Nietzsche and the Machine," p. 53.

14. Hans–Georg Gadamer, "Text and Interpretation," trans. Dennis J. Schmidt and Richard E. Palmer in Michelfelder and Palmer, eds., *Dialogue and Deconstruction*, p. 24.

15. Gadamer, "Text and Interpretation," p. 25.

16. Derrida, *Writing and Difference*, pp. 281–82. See also, for example, "The Ends of Man" in *Margins of Philosophy*, pp. 134–36; and *Of Grammatology*, pp. 19–20.

17. That Derrida also may have come to the meeting with this intention should not be denied. He did, after all, choose to challenge Heidegger's metaphysical "desire" to impose a unitary interpretation on the "totality" of "the history of metaphysics" in terms of Heidegger's supposition of the unity of the proper name "Nietzsche."

18. Derrida, *Writing and Difference*, p. 280.

19. Derrida, *Of Grammatology*, pp. 286–87.

20. Derrida, "The Ends of Man" in *Margins of Philosophy*, p. 136.

21. See Derrida, "Signature, Event, Context" in *Margins of Philosophy*, p.

329.

22. This task is, of course, also profoundly influenced by Heidegger's own "Destruction of the History of Ontology" as outlined in section 7 of *Being and Time*, further problematizing the issue of deciding whether Derrida ever chooses once and for all to privilege Heidegger or Nietzsche in his early works. I am less hesitant to decide this question in Derrida's later works, however, as the importance of and attention to Heidegger and Heideggerian questions in the works that follow *La carte postale* far exceeds the appearance of Nietzsche in these works.

23. Jacques Derrida, *Positions*, trans. Alan Bass (Chicago: University of Chicago Press, 1981), p. 6.

24. See, for example, Heidegger's discussion of Nietzsche's inversion of Platonism in *Nietzsche. Vol. One. The Will to Power as Art*, ed. and trans. David F. Krell (San Francisco: Harper and Row, 1979), pp. 200–20.

25. See, e.g., Jacques Derrida, *Spurs: Nietzsche's Styles*, trans. Barbara Harlow (Chicago: University of Chicago Press, 1979), pp. 117–19.

26. Derrida, *Positions*, p. 42; see also *Margins of Philosophy*, p. 329.

27. See, for example, Derrida, *Of Grammatology*, pp. 179, 215.

28. Jacques Derrida, *Dissemination*, trans. Barbara Johnson (Chicago: University of Chicago Press, 1981), p. 70.

29. Immanuel Kant, *Critique of Pure Reason*, trans. Norman Kemp Smith (New York: St. Martin's Press, 1965), A 761, B 789.

30. Irene E. Harvey, *Derrida and the Economy of Différance* (Bloomington: Indiana University Press, 1986), pp. 1–20.

31. Christopher Norris, *Derrida* (Cambridge: Harvard University Press, 1987), p. 94.

32. Rodolphe Gasché, *The Tain of the Mirror: Derrida and the Philosophy of Reflection* (Cambridge: Harvard University Press, 1986), p. 317.

33. See Harvey, *Derrida and the Economy of Différance*, p. 3.

34. Gasché, *The Tain of the Mirror*, p. 317.

35. Richard Rorty, "Is Derrida a Transcendental Philosopher?" in *Derrida: A Critical Reader*, ed. David Wood (Cambridge: Basil Blackwell, 1992), p. 243.

36. See, for example, his "explication" of "*différance*" in the interviews collected in *Positions* or the following remark from the essay *"Différance"* (albeit *"sous rature"*): "*ce qui rend possible la présentation de l'étant–présent, elle ne se présente jamais comme telle* [what makes

possible the presentation of the being–present, it never presents itself as such]" (*Marges de la philosophie* [Paris: Éditions de Minuit, 1972], p. 6; cf. *Margins of Philosophy*, p. 6).

37. Kant, *Critique of Pure Reason*, A 501, B 529. Emphasis added.

38. Kant, *Critique of Pure Reason*, A 484, B 512.

39. Jacques Derrida, *The Truth in Painting*, trans. Geoff Bennington and Ian McLeod (Chicago: University of Chicago Press, 1987), p. 19.

40. Derrida, *Margins of Philosophy*, p. 329.

41. See, for example, Jacques Derrida, *The Archeology of the Frivolous*, trans. John P. Leavey, Jr. (Pittsburgh: Duquesne University Press, 1980), p. 132: "Philosophy deviates from itself and gives rise to the blows that will strike it nonetheless from the outside."

42. Derrida, *Margins of Philosophy*, p. 17.

43. The peculiarities of Nietzsche's inversion of Platonism is the focus of the concluding chapters of Heidegger's first lecture series on Nietzsche, *Nietzsche. Volume One. The Will to Power as Art*, pp. 151–220. I discuss these chapters elsewhere; see my *Nietzsche and the Question of Interpretation*, pp. 44–50.

44. The genealogical deconstruction of the truth/falsity opposition is a central theme in my *Nietzsche and the Question of Interpretation*; see, in particular, pp. 190–91, where I discuss this critical strategy as it operates in the closing stage of the famous chapter of *Twilight of the Idols* where Nietzsche traces the history of the belief in the "true world."

45. Derrida has also used the term "active interpretation" to distinguish deconstructive reading from the textual doubling of commentary; see *Of Grammatology*, pp. 157–64.

46. See Derrida, *Of Grammatology*, pp. 158ff.

47. See also the following remark: "The separation of the 'deed' from the 'doer,' of the event from someone who produces events, of the process from a something that is not process but enduring, substance, thing, body, soul, etc.—the attempt to comprehend an event as a sort of shifting and place–changing on the part of a 'being,' of something constant: this ancient mythology established the belief in 'cause and effect' after it had found a firm form in the functions of language and grammar" (*KSA*, 12: 2[139]; *WP*, 631).

48. Some of what follows draws from my discussion of Nietzsche's self–deconstruction of his own literary authority in "Reading, Writing, Text: Nietzsche's Deconstruction of Author–ity," *International*

Studies in Philosophy, Vol. 17, No. 2 (1985), pp. 55–64. For an interesting demonstration of Nietzsche's authorial self–deconstruction, see Daniel W. Conway's excellent essay "Nietzsche contra Nietzsche: The Deconstruction of *Zarathustra*" in *Nietzsche as Postmodernist: Essays Pro and Contra*, ed. Clayton Koelb (Albany: State University of New York Press, 1990), pp. 91–110.

49. See Derrida, *The Archeology of the Frivolous*, p. 49.

50. Derrida, *Positions*, p. 49.

51. Derrida, *Margins of Philosophy*, p. 135. Translation altered.

52. Michel Foucault, *The Order of Things* (New York: Random House, 1973), p. 385. Gilles Deleuze makes a similar point, coupling the death of God with the dissolution of the Self, in *Différence et répétition* (Paris: Presses Universitaires de France, 1968), pp. 81ff; English translation: *Difference and Repetition*, trans. Paul Patton (New York: Columbia University Press, 1994), pp. 58ff.

53. See *Margins of Philosophy*, p. 135, and *Spurs*, passim.

54. Jacques Derrida, from the discussion following "Structure, Sign, and Play in the Discourse of the Human Sciences," trans. Richard Macksey in *The Structuralist Controversy*, ed. Richard Macksey and Eugenio Donato (Baltimore: Johns Hopkins University Press, 1970), p. 271. I address more explicitly the question of knowing where the subject comes from in the following two chapters.

55. See *EH*, III, BGE1: "From this moment forward all my writings are fish hooks: perhaps I understand how to fish as well as anyone?... If nothing was *caught*, I am not to blame. *The fish were missing...*"

56. We will return to this quotation in the following chapter when we examine Foucault's repetition of the question "who speaks?"

57. See Derrida, *Margins of Philosophy*, p. 22.

58. Derrida, *Writing and Difference*, pp. 226–27.

59. Derrida, *Writing and Difference*, p. 292.

Chapter Two
Foucault: Genealogy, Power, and the Reconfiguration of the Subject

1. Michel Foucault, "What is an Author?" trans. Josué V. Harari in *The Foucault Reader*, ed. Paul Rabinow (New York: Pantheon Books, 1984), p. 114.

2. Paul Bové, *Intellectuals in Power: A Genealogy of Critical Humanism* (New York: Columbia University Press, 1986), p. 224.

3. Michel Foucault, "Truth and Power," interview conducted in June 1976, translated by Colin Gordon in *Power/Knowledge: Selected Interviews and Other Writings 1972–1977*, ed. Colin Gordon (New York: Pantheon Books, 1977), pp. 122–23.

4. For a general review of some of the literature that relates Foucault to Nietzsche, see Michael Mahon, *Foucault's Nietzschean Genealogy: Truth, Power, and the Subject* (Albany: State University of New York Press, 1992), esp. the section entitled "The Nietzschean Face of Foucault Scholarship," pp. 9–17. Foucault addresses the appeal of Nietzsche in the context of French academic culture and an educational system dominated by phenomenology and Marxism in a number of places. See, for example, "Prison Talk," interview first published in June 1975 and translated by Colin Gordon in *Power/Knowledge*, pp. 52–53; "Critical Theory/Intellectual History," interview first published in Spring 1983 and translated by Jeremy Harding in *Michel Foucault: Politics, Philosophy, Culture. Interviews and Other Writings 1977–1984*, ed. Lawrence D. Kritzman (New York: Routledge, 1988), pp. 23–24; and "Subjectivity and Truth," the first of two lectures at Dartmouth, delivered on November 17 and 24, 1980, ed. Mark Blasius and published under the title "About the Beginning of the Hermeneutics of the Self: Two Lectures at Dartmouth" in *Political Theory*, Vol. 21, No. 2 (May 1993), pp. 201–02.

5. In a 1982 interview with Rux Martin, Foucault comments: "Nietzsche was a revelation to me. I felt that there was someone quite different from what I had been taught. I read him with a great passion and broke with my life, left my job in the asylum, left France: I had the feeling I had been trapped. Through Nietzsche, I had become a stranger to all that. I'm still not quite integrated within French social and intellectual life" ("Truth, Power, Self: An Interview" in *Technologies of the Self: A Seminar with Michel Foucault*, ed. Luther H. Martin, Huck Gutman, and Patrick H. Hutton [Amherst: University of Massachusetts Press, 1988], p. 13). Foucault's remarks should be compared to Deleuze's comments in his 1972 "Lettre à un critique sévère" (Michel Cressole), reprinted in *Pourparlers* (Paris: Éditions de Minuit, 1990), where he credits Nietzsche for pulling him out of "a generation [that was] one of the last generations more or less ruined by the history of philosophy" (pp. 14–15).

6. Foucault, "Truth and Power," p. 115; see also the following: "If I wanted to pose and drape myself in a slightly fictional style, I would say that this has always been my problem: the effects of power and the production of 'truth'" ("Power and Sex," interview first published in March 1977 and translated by David J. Parent in *Michel Foucault: Politics, Philosophy, Culture*, p. 118).

7. Michel Foucault, "On Power," interview conducted in July 1978 and translated by Alan Sheridan in *Michel Foucault: Politics, Philosophy, Culture*, pp. 101–02.

8. Michel Foucault, "Why Study Power: The Question of the Subject" in Hubert L. Dreyfus and Paul Rabinow, *Michel Foucault: Beyond Structuralism and Hermeneutics* (Chicago: University of Chicago Press, 1982), p. 209.

9. Michel Foucault, "On Power," pp. 99–100. Foucault also challenges his being labeled a "philosopher of discontinuity" in "Truth and Power," pp. 111–12.

10. Michel Foucault, *The Use of Pleasure*, trans. Robert Hurley (New York: Random House, 1985), p. 9. See also his remarks about not remaining the same at the end of the Introduction to *The Archaeology of Knowledge*. I thank David Owen for recalling these remarks to me.

11. See, for example, Michel Foucault, *The Order of Things* (New York: Random House, 1973), p. 342: "Perhaps we should see the first attempt at this uprooting of Anthropology—to which, no doubt, contemporary thought is dedicated—in the Nietzschean experience: by means of a philological critique, by means of a certain form of biologism, Nietzsche rediscovered the point at which man and God belong to one another, at which the death of the second is synonymous with the disappearance of the first, and at which the promise of the superman signifies first and foremost the imminence of the death of man." I discuss Nietzsche's appearance in Foucault's early works in *Nietzsche and the Question of Interpretation: Between Hermeneutics and Deconstruction* (New York: Routledge, 1990), pp. 78–81.

12. Michel Foucault, "The Discourse of History," interview first published in June 1967 and translated by John Johnston in *Foucault Live (Interviews, 1966–1984)*, ed. Sylvère Lotringer (New York: Semiotexte, 1989), p. 31.

13. Foucault, *The Order of Things*, p. 305.

14. Foucault, "Truth and Power," p. 133.

15. Foucault, "Truth and Power," p. 133.

16. Michel Foucault, "On the Genealogy of Ethics: An Overview of Work in Progress," interview conducted in April 1983 and published in *The Foucault Reader*, p. 351. This interpretation of his oeuvre is quite similar to his characterization of his work as an analysis of the "three modes of objectification which transform human beings into subjects" at the start of the essay "Why Study Power" (p. 208).

17. Foucault, "On the Genealogy of Ethics," p. 352.

18. Michel Foucault, "What is Enlightenment?" trans. Catherine Porter in *The Foucault Reader*, p. 50.

19. Michel Foucault, "The Confession of the Flesh," interview first published in July 1977 and translated by Colin Gordon in *Power/Knowledge*, p. 198.

20. See Jean–François Lyotard, "An Answer to the Question, What is the Postmodern?" in *The Postmodern Explained: Correspondence 1982–1985*, trans. Don Barry, et al. (Minneapolis: University of Minnesota Press, 1992), p. 15. This essay appeared earlier as an appendix to Lyotard's *The Postmodern Condition: A Report on Knowledge*, trans. Geoff Bennington and Brian Massumi (Minneapolis: University of Minnesota Press, 1984), p. 81.

21. Michel Foucault, *The History of Sexuality, Vol. One: An Introduction*, trans. Robert Hurley (New York: Vintage, 1980), p. 86.

22. Michel Foucault, "How is Power Exercised?", trans. Leslie Sawyer in Dreyfus and Rabinow, *Michel Foucault: Beyond Structuralism and Hermeneutics*, p. 217.

23. This crucial point, that power as such does not exist or that power is its own simulacrum, seems to me to be an important aspect of Foucault's analytics that Jean Baudrillard misses in his critique of Foucault in "Forgetting Foucault," trans. Nicole Dufresne in *Humanities in Society*, Vol. 3, No. 1 (Winter 1980), pp. 87–111, especially pp. 100–11.

24. Foucault, "Critical Theory/Intellectual History," p. 38; see also "How is Power Exercised?" p. 219.

25. Deleuze, *Pourparlers*, p. 159.

26. For Foucault's notion of "governmentality" as a particular form of political rationality, see his essay "Governmentality," trans. Rosi Braidotti in *Ideology and Consciousness*, Vol. 6 (Autumn 1979): 5–21. This translation has been revised and reprinted in *The Foucault Effect:*

Studies in Governmentality, ed. Graham Burchell, Colin Gordon and Peter Miller (Chicago: University of Chicago Press, 1991), pp. 87–104.

27. This was a focal point in Foucault's 1976 lecture series at the Collège de France. See, in particular, his discussion of the first of the five methodological precautions for analyzing power, as put forward in the second lecture, dated January 14, 1976 and published as the second of the "Two Lectures," translated by Kate Soper in *Power/Knowledge*, p. 96.

28. We see this problem in the United States when an institutional head—having become identified as a focal point for the problems of that institution—is removed, with little change to the institution itself. Consider, for example, the removal of Darryl Gates as chief of the Los Angeles Police Department following the beating of Rodney King.

29. Foucault, *The History of Sexuality*, pp. 94–95. This list should be compared to the five methodological precautions of Foucault's "Two Lectures," pp. 96–102.

30. In the following chapter, I examine the way Deleuze's discussion of desire also develops as an analogue to Nietzsche's monism of will to power.

31. See Foucault, "Truth and Power," pp. 118–19.

32. Richard Schacht makes what I take to be much the same distinction in his reconstruction of Nietzsche's "theory of value." See Richard Schacht, *Nietzsche* (New York: Routledge, 1983), pp. 401–02. A further word of clarification is needed in terms of the notion of affirmation at work here. I do not agree with Deleuze's interpretation of eternal recurrence as a selective principle that insures the recurrence of only active forces (see Gilles Deleuze, *Nietzsche and Philosophy*, trans. Hugh Tomlinson [New York: Columbia University Press, 1983], p. 71). Instead, I would argue that to affirm the eternal recurrence requires affirming the recurrence of *all* will to power, both active and reactive. In this context, however, affirmation will have to be understood exclusively in terms of quantity and should not be confused with Nietzsche's *genealogically* based qualitative affirmation of affirmative–active will to power, an act of discriminating affirmation that must be considered apart from the indiscriminate affirmation of eternal recurrence.

33. See Michel Foucault, *Discipline and Punish: The Birth of the Prison*, trans. Alan Sheridan (New York: Random House, 1978), p. 26.

34. See Foucault, *The History of Sexuality*, p. 95.

35. Foucault, *The History of Sexuality*, pp. 100–01.

36. See Foucault, *The Order of Things*, p. 385.

37. Michel Foucault, "Introduction à l'*Anthropologie* de Kant," *thèse complémentaire* for the doctorate of letters, Université de Paris, Faculté des Lettres, 1960, photocopy of typescript, Centre Michel Foucault, p. 128; quoted in James Miller, *The Passion of Michel Foucault* (New York: Simon and Schuster, 1993), p. 142.

38. Foucault addresses this question in *The Order of Things*, p. 305; see also the conclusion of "What Is an Author?" pp. 119–20.

39. Foucault, *The Order of Things*, p. 305.

40. Foucault, *The Order of Things*, p. 304.

41. Michel Foucault, "Nietzsche, Freud, Marx," trans. Alan D. Schrift in *Transforming the Hermeneutic Context: From Nietzsche to Nancy*, ed. Gayle L. Ormiston and Alan D. Schrift (Albany: State University of New York Press, 1990), p. 66.

42. Foucault, *The Order of Things*, pp. 305–06.

43. Foucault, "What Is an Author?" p. 101; see also p. 120. In one of his final interviews (April 25, 1984), Foucault indirectly returned to this point in addressing a question concerning the diverse and sometimes polemically charged readings of his works. In this very pragmatic context, he made several remarks in support of Beckett's response as he speculated on what sort of reading his works might get if they did not appear as the latest work by the famous philosopher at the Collège de France, "Michel Foucault": "it would be better if my books were read for themselves, with whatever faults and qualities they may have" ("An Aesthetics of Existence," interview conducted in April 1984 and translated by Alan Sheridan in *Michel Foucault: Politics, Philosophy, Culture*, p. 53). Interestingly, his remark that the knowledge of an author often stands as a barrier to the reading of their books echoes Nietzsche's comments that a good book "is harmed by its living author if he is celebrated and much is known about him" (*AOM*, 153) and that "as soon as the author announces himself on the title–page, the reader dilutes the [book's] quintessence again with the personality, indeed with what is most personal, and thus thwarts the object of the book" (*AOM*, 156).

44. Foucault, "What Is an Author?" p. 118.

45. See, for example, Michel Foucault, "The Ethic of Care for the Self as a Practice of Freedom," interview conducted in January 1984 and trans-

lated by J. D. Gauthier, S.J., *Philosophy and Social Criticism*, special issue "The Final Foucault," Vol. 12, No. 2–3 (Summer 1987), p. 121.

46. See Foucault, "On the Genealogy of Ethics," p. 351.

47. See Michel Foucault, "Nietzsche, Genealogy, History," trans. Donald F. Bouchard and Sherry Simon in *The Foucault Reader*, pp. 76–100.

48. Foucault, "Nietzsche, Genealogy, History," p. 82.

49. Guilt and the construction of the subject are discussed in detail in the following chapter.

50. Foucault, "Why Study Power: The Question of the Subject," p. 212.

51. Foucault, "How is Power Exercised?", p. 217. Emphasis added.

52. See Foucault, *Discipline and Punish*, p. 29.

53. Foucault, *Discipline and Punish*, pp. 27–28.

54. See Dreyfus and Rabinow, *Michel Foucault: Beyond Structuralism and Hermeneutics*, pp. 143–83.

55. Deleuze, *Pourparlers*, p. 127.

56. Foucault, "An Aesthetics of Existence," pp. 50–51.

57. Foucault, *The Use of Pleasure*, p. 4.

58. Foucault, "Subjectivity and Truth," p. 203.

59. Foucault, "Subjectivity and Truth," p. 204.

60. See Foucault, "Why Study Power: The Question of the Subject," pp. 213–16.

61. See Pierre Bourdieu, *Homo Academicus*, trans. Peter Collier (Stanford: Stanford University Press, 1988), pp. 21–23.

62. This distinction is itself suggested by Foucault in the foreword to the English edition of *The Order of Things*: "I should like to know whether the subjects responsible for scientific discourse are not determined in their situation, their function, their perceptive capacity, and their practical possibilities by conditions that dominate and even overwhelm them" (p. xiv).

63. It should be noted that these institutional matrices function within both the public and private spheres; a man can make the decisions that a "father" has to make within the institution of the family as well as the decisions that an administrator has to make within an academic or corporate institution.

64. I wonder whether we should not locate the failure of the prosecutors in the first trial of the four Los Angeles police officers accused of beating Rodney King in precisely these terms: they failed to anticipate the

transformations that would take place as those twelve empirical individuals became the twelve epistemic individuals who comprised the jury and who were then bound to act in terms of the institutional rules governing judicial directions and the evaluation of evidence.

65. Gilles Deleuze, "What is a *dispositif?*", trans. Timothy J. Armstrong in *Michel Foucault, Philosopher*, ed. Timothy J. Armstrong (New York: Routledge, 1992), p. 164.

66. Deleuze, "What is a *dispositif?*", p. 165.

67. Foucault, "On the Genealogy of Ethics," p. 343. In the original transcript of this interview, dated April 19, 1983, Foucault makes this comment in response to questions from Dreyfus and Rabinow in which they are trying to get Foucault to distinguish his position from that of Richard Rorty, which they frame as a view that accommodates multiple narratives by accepting them all as equally good. It is in this context that Foucault remarks that although he disagrees with Rorty, it isn't because everything is bad, but because everything can be dangerous. The transcript continues: "If everything is dangerous, then we always have something to do. And in this way, I think that Rorty's position, or Rorty's hypothesis, leads to an apathy. And my position leads to a hyper– and pessimistic activism. And I think that's a very great difference." Foucault goes on to remark that our task becomes one of accurately identifying the dangers and "the ethico–political choice we have to make every day [is] to decide which is the main danger" (Centre Michel Foucault, Document D250(5), pp. 22–23).

68. Foucault, "The Ethic of Care for the Self as a Practice of Freedom," p. 129.

69. Judith Butler, *Gender Trouble: Feminism and the Subversion of Identity* (New York: Routledge, 1990), p. 2.

70. Butler, *Gender Trouble*, p. 136.

71. Butler, *Gender Trouble*, p. 145.

72. Butler, *Gender Trouble*, p. 148.

73. Quoted in Butler, *Gender Trouble*, p. 25.

74. Judith Butler, *Bodies That Matter: On the Discursive Limits of "Sex"* (New York: Routledge, 1993), pp. 229–30.

75. See Judith Butler, "Subjection, Resistance, and Resignation: Between Freud and Foucault," *The Question of Identity*, ed. John Rajchman (New York: Routledge, forthcoming).

76. Judith Butler, "Poststructuralism and Postmarxism," *Diacritics*, Vol. 23, No. 4 (Winter 1993), p. 11.

77. Butler, "Poststructuralism and Postmarxism," pp. 10–11.

78. Butler, *Bodies That Matter*, p. 240.

79. It must be noted that in *Bodies That Matter*, Butler herself addresses some of the implications of her theory of performativity for democratic and coalition politics as she responds to interpretations of *Gender Trouble* which make the mistake, mentioned above, of reading "performative" as "performance."

80. Foucault, "The Ethic of Care for the Self," p. 121.

81. Ernesto Laclau and Chantal Mouffe, *Hegemony and Socialist Strategy: Towards a Radical Democratic Politics* (London: Verso, 1985), p. 117.

82. See Laclau and Mouffe, pp. 166–67.

83. See Laclau and Mouffe, pp. 105–07.

84. Laclau and Mouffe, pp. 183–84.

85. Laclau and Mouffe, p. 191.

86. Foucault, *The Order of Things*, p. 387.

Chapter Three

Deleuze: Putting Nietzsche to Work:
Genealogy, Will to Power, and Other Desiring Machines

1. "Intellectuals and Power: A Conversation between Michel Foucault and Gilles Deleuze," trans. Donald F. Bouchard and Sherry Simon in Michel Foucault, *Language, Counter–Memory, Practice*, ed. Donald F. Bouchard (Ithaca: Cornell University Press, 1977), p. 208.

2. Gilles Deleuze, *Nietzsche et la philosophie* (Paris: Presses Universitaires de France, 1962); English translation: *Nietzsche and Philosophy*, trans. Hugh Tomlinson (New York: Columbia University Press, 1983).

3. *David Hume, sa vie, son oeuvre* (Paris: Presses Universitaires de France, 1952). *Empirisme et subjectivité* (Paris: Presses Universitaires de France, 1953); English translation: *Empiricism and Subjectivity: An Essay on Hume's Theory of Human Nature*, trans. Constantin V. Boundas (New York: Columbia University Press, 1991). "Lucrèce et le naturalisme," *Études philosophiques*, No. 1 (January–May 1961): 19–29. *La philosophie critique de Kant* (Paris: Presses Universitaires de France, 1963); English translation: *Kant's Critical Philosophy*, trans. Hugh Tomlinson and Barbara Habberjam (Minneapolis: University of

Minnesota Press, 1984). *Le Bergsonisme* (Paris: Presses Universitaires de France, 1966); English translation: *Bergsonism*, trans. Hugh Tomlinson and Barbara Habberjam (New York: Zone Books, 1988). *Spinoza et le problème de l'expression* (Paris: Minuit, 1968); English translation: *Expressionism in Philosophy: Spinoza*, trans. Martin Joughin (New York: Zone Books, 1990).

4. The anti–Hegelian character of *Nietzsche and Philosophy* is the focus of the second chapter of Michael Hardt's *Gilles Deleuze: An Apprenticeship in Philosophy* (Minneapolis: University of Minnesota Press, 1993), pp. 26–55.

5. See Deleuze, *Nietzsche and Philosophy*, p. 197.

6. Deleuze, *Nietzsche and Philosophy*, p. 180.

7. Deleuze, *Nietzsche and Philosophy*, p. 50.

8. This discussion of *Nietzsche and Philosophy* is a slightly revised and abridged version of my discussion in *Nietzsche and the Question of Interpretation: Between Hermeneutics and Deconstruction* (New York: Routledge, 1990), pp. 82–83.

9. Martin Heidegger, *Nietzsche*, Band I and II (Pfullingen: Verlag Günther Neske, 1961). The French translation, by Pierre Klossowski, was published by Gallimard (Paris, 1971). The English translation was published by Harper and Row (San Francisco) in four volumes: *Nietzsche. Volume One: The Will to Power as Art*, ed. and trans. David Farrell Krell (1979); *Volume Two: The Eternal Recurrence of the Same*, ed. and trans. David Farrell Krell (1984); *Volume Three: The Will to Power as Knowledge and as Metaphysics*, ed. David Farrell Krell, trans. Joan Stambaugh, David Farrell Krell, and Frank A. Capuzzi (1987); *Volume Four: Nihilism*, ed. David Farrell Krell, trans. Frank A. Capuzzi (1982).

10. One of the few critics to discuss this work in the context of French post-structuralism is Vincent P. Pecora, in "Deleuze's Nietzsche and Post–Structuralism," *Sub–Stance*, No. 48 (1986): 34–50. Although largely critical of Deleuze's reading of Nietzsche, Pecora is, I think, correct in indicating the formative role played by Deleuze's replacement of "'*le travail de la dialectique*' by the play of '*différence*'" in the emergence of poststructuralism (p. 36). The importance of Nietzsche in Deleuze's thought and poststructuralist French philosophy is also one of the leading themes of Ronald Bogue's fine introductory text *Deleuze and Guattari* (London and New York: Routledge, 1989); see, in particular, his concluding comments, pp. 156–63.

11. Gilles Deleuze, "Lettre à un critique sévère," (Michel Cressole, 1972) reprinted in *Pourparlers* (Paris: Éditions de Minuit, 1990), pp. 14–15.

12. See Michel Foucault, *L'ordre du discours: Leçon inaugurale au Collège de France prononcée le 2 décembre 1972* (Paris: Gallimard, 1971); English translation by Rupert Swyer as "The Discourse on Language," published as an appendix to Michel Foucault, *The Archaeology of Knowledge* (New York: Harper and Row, 1972), pp. 215–37.

13. Gilles Deleuze and Claire Parnet, *Dialogues*, trans. Hugh Tomlinson and Barbara Habberjam (New York: Columbia University Press, 1987), p. 13. See also Deleuze's remarks in the preface to *Différence et répétition* (Paris: Presses Universitaires de France, 1968), pp. 4–5, on the relation between philosophy and the history of philosophy, where he comments that the ideal writing of the history of philosophy will be both a repetition of and differentiation from its own history.

14. Deleuze and Parnet, *Dialogues*, pp. 14–15; see also *Pourparlers*, p. 14. The phrase "bureaucracy of pure reason" is suggested by Deleuze's concluding remarks in "Nomad Thought," trans. David B. Allison in *The New Nietzsche*, ed. David B. Allison (New York: Dell, 1977), p. 149.

15. A political activist and psychoanalyst at the La borde clinic, Guattari is perhaps best known for coauthoring with Deleuze the two volumes of *Capitalism and Schizophrenia*. Other works written by Guattari include *Psychanalyse et transversalité: essais d'analyse institutionelle* (Paris: Maspero, 1972), *L'inconscient machinique: essais de schizo–analyse* (Fontenay–sous–Bois: Éditions Recherches, 1979) and *Molecular Revolution: Psychiatry and Politics*, trans. Rosemary Sheed (New York: Penguin Books, 1984).

16. See Deleuze and Parnet, *Dialogues*, pp. 46–48. Deleuze and Félix Guattari's *Kafka: Toward a Minor Literature*, trans. Dana Polan (Minneapolis: University of Minnesota Press, 1986) exemplifies what an experimental textual approach can produce by examining how themes function rather than inquiring into what "sense" they might have (see p. 45). We return to this theme later in this chapter.

17. This is a general theme in Gilles Deleuze, "Pensée nomade," in *Nietzsche aujourd'hui I* (Paris: Union Générale d'Éditions, 1973), pp. 159–74; English translation: "Nomad Thought," in Allison, ed. *The New Nietzsche*, pp. 142–49.

18. See, in particular, the chapter "Nietzsche and fragmentary writing" in Maurice Blanchot, *The Infinite Conversation*, trans. Susan Hanson (Minneapolis: University of Minnesota Press, 1993), pp. 151–70.

19. It must be acknowledged that Derrida himself has responded to the facile understanding of this motto as advocating a pan–textualism. In the afterword appended to *Limited Inc* titled "Toward an Ethic of Discussion," Derrida remarks that the "so badly understood" slogan of deconstruction *"il n'y a pas de hors–texte"* means nothing other than "there is nothing outside context" (*Limited Inc*, trans. Samuel Weber [Evanston: Northwestern University Press, 1988], p. 136).

20. Deleuze, "Discussion" following "Pensée nomade," in *Nietzsche aujourd'hui I*, pp. 186–87. While this remark accurately characterizes Deleuze's post–1968 texts, his skill as a "commentator" in his earlier texts (see note 3 to this chapter) should not be undervalued.

21. My formulation of this distinction between Deleuze and Derrida has benefited from the insightful comments of Jeffrey Nealon on an earlier draft of this chapter.

22. Jacques Derrida, "Interpreting Signatures (Nietzsche/Heidegger): Two Questions," trans. Diane P. Michelfelder and Richard E. Palmer in *Dialogue and Deconstruction: The Gadamer–Derrida Encounter*, ed. Diane P. Michelfelder and Richard E. Palmer (Albany: State University of New York Press, 1989), pp. 58–71; and *Otobiographies: The Teaching of Nietzsche and the Politics of the Proper Name*, trans. Avital Ronell in *The Ear of the Other: Otobiography, Transference, Translation*, ed. Christie V. McDonald, trans. Peggy Kamuf (New York: Schocken Books, 1985), pp. 1–38.

23. Jacques Derrida, "Force of Law: The 'Mystical Foundation of Authority,'" trans. Mary Quaintance, *Cardozo Law Review*, Vol. 11, No. 5–6 (1990), p. 959.

24. Gilles Deleuze and Félix Guattari, "Rhizome," trans. Paul Patton in *Ideology and Consciousness*, No. 8 (Spring 1981), pp. 67–68. This version of "Rhizome" was published separately prior to the appearance of *A Thousand Plateaus*, and it differs slightly from the version that introduced the second volume of *Capitalism and Schizophrenia*.

25. See Gilles Deleuze and Félix Guattari, *A Thousand Plateaus*, trans. Brian Massumi (Minneapolis: University of Minnesota Press, 1987), p. 4. Translation altered slightly.

26. Gilles Deleuze, *Cinema 2: The Time–Image*, trans. Hugh Tomlinson and Robert Galeta (Minneapolis: University of Minnesota Press, 1989), pp. 131, 139.

27. Deleuze and Guattari, "Rhizome," p. 56. This image of writing as mapping is one of the many places we can locate the importance of

Foucault's work for Deleuze. See, in this regard, Deleuze's discussion of Foucault's *Discipline and Punish*, entitled "A New Cartographer," in *Foucault*, trans. Seán Hand (Minneapolis: University of Minnesota Press, 1988), pp. 23–44.

28. Deleuze and Guattari, *A Thousand Plateaus*, p. 20.

29. The issue of the transcendental character of Derrida's thinking is a complicated one which I only wish to raise here in order to sharpen the contrast with Deleuze. To be sure, unlike many other transcendental thinkers, Derrida's transcendental "non–concepts" are not foundational. But it seems to me impossible to overlook the transcendental nature of his "explication" of, for example, "*différance*" in the interviews collected in *Positions* as well as in the essay "*Différance*." While I do not want to question the innovative and radical character of Derrida's interventions into the history of philosophy, I do want to note the familiar, indeed traditional transcendental character of remarks like the following, quoted earlier, concerning *différance* being "*ce qui rend possible la présentation de l'étant–présent, elle ne se présente jamais comme telle* [what makes possible the presentation of the being–present, it never presents itself as such]" (*Marges de la philosophie* [Paris: Éditions de Minuit, 1972], p. 6). This issue is discussed in chapter one, see pp. 18–19.

30. Deleuze and Guattari, *A Thousand Plateaus*, pp. 20–21.

31. See Deleuze, *Nietzsche and Philosophy*, pp. 49–55.

32. See Deleuze, *Nietzsche and Philosophy*, p. 220: "Heidegger gives an interpretation of Nietzschean philosophy closer to his own thought than to Nietzsche's.... Nietzsche is opposed to every conception of affirmation which would find its foundation in Being, and its determination in the being of man." I address and criticize Heidegger's interpretation of will to power in some detail in *Nietzsche and the Question of Interpretation*, pp. 53–73.

33. See *Symposium* 200a–d, where Socrates remarks that one who desires something is necessarily in want of that thing. I discuss the Deleuzian critique of "desire as lack" in more detail elsewhere; see my "Spinoza, Nietzsche, Deleuze: An Other Discourse of Desire" in *Philosophy and the Discourse of Desire*, ed. Hugh J. Silverman (New York: Routledge, forthcoming).

34. Deleuze and Parnet, *Dialogues*, p. 91.

35. See the discussion of this point in Gilles Deleuze and Félix Guattari, *Anti–Oedipus*, trans. Robert Hurley, Mark Seem, and Helen R. Lane (Minneapolis: University of Minnesota Press, 1983), p. 348.

36. We might put this point another way and, using Benveniste's distinction, say that desire situates itself as both the subject of the utterance (*sujet d'énonciation*) and the subject of the statement (*sujet d'énoncé*).

37. See Deleuze and Guattari, *Kafka*, p. 57.

38. Deleuze and Guattari, *A Thousand Plateaus*, pp. 238–39.

39. See Deleuze and Guattari, *A Thousand Plateaus*, p. 293.

40. Arthur Danto, *Nietzsche as Philosopher* (New York: Columbia University Press, 1980), pp. 199–200.

41. J. P. Stern, *A Study of Nietzsche* (Cambridge: Cambridge University Press, 1979), p. 117. For an excellent review of the literature concerning the "ideal type" interpretation of the *Übermensch*, see Bernd Magnus, "Perfectibility and Attitude in Nietzsche's *Übermensch*," *Review of Metaphysics* 36 (March 1983): 633–59, and "Nietzsche's Philosophy in 1888: *The Will to Power* and the *Übermensch*," *Journal of the History of Philosophy*, Vol. 24, No. 1 (January 1986): 79–98.

42. Nietzsche's remark continues: "Even the 'hero worship' of that unconscious and involuntary counterfeiter, Carlyle, which I have repudiated so maliciously has been read into it. Those to whom I said in confidence that they should sooner look even for a Cesare Borgia than for a Parsifal, did not believe their own ears" (*EH*, III, 1).

43. Gilles Deleuze, "On the Death of Man and Superman" in *Foucault*, pp. 129–30.

44. See Deleuze and Guattari's comments on the death of God and the death of the Oedipal father in *Anti–Oedipus*, pp. 106ff.

45. Deleuze, *Foucault*, p. 130.

46. And by implication, this also provides an answer to the interpretive question "Is Zarathustra an *Übermensch*?"

47. That the argument in *Anti–Oedipus* follows the same lines as Nietzsche's argument in the *Genealogy* should not obscure the fact that it also follows the outlines of Marx's own historical materialist outline of the socio–economic stages that precede capitalism.

48. Deleuze and Guattari, *Anti–Oedipus*, p. 190. Emphasis added.

49. The connection between Nietzsche's discussion of painful mnemotechnics and Kafka's "In the Penal Colony" should not pass unnoticed.

50. Deleuze and Guattari, *Anti–Oedipus*, pp. 108–12, 269, 332–33. See also Deleuze and Guattari, *A Thousand Plateaus*, p. 154.

NIETZSCHE'S FRENCH LEGACY / 149

51. See Deleuze and Guattari, *Anti–Oedipus*, pp. 64–65.

52. See Deleuze and Guattari, *Anti–Oedipus*, pp. 352–54.

53. Deleuze and Guattari, *Anti–Oedipus*, p. 342.

54. Deleuze and Guattari, *Kafka*, p. 64.

55. Deleuze and Guattari, *Anti–Oedipus*, p. 293. Translation altered slightly.

56. Deleuze and Guattari, *Anti–Oedipus*, p. 343.

57. Gilles Deleuze, "Entretien 1980," in *L'Arc*, No. 49, Second Edition (1980), p. 99. See also *Anti–Oedipus*, p. 55.

58. Deleuze and Guattari, *Anti–Oedipus*, p. 54.

59. Deleuze and Guattari, *Anti–Oedipus*, p. 55. See also Deleuze, "Entretien 1980," p. 99.

60. Deleuze and Guattari, *Anti–Oedipus*, p. 24.

61. Deleuze and Guattari, *Anti–Oedipus*, p. 27.

62. Among other things, this argument is clearly directed against a Marxist philosophy like Sartre's that, in *Critique of Dialectical Reason*, "introduces the notion of scarcity as its initial premise." See the footnote on Maurice Clavel in *Anti–Oedipus*, p. 28.

63. Deleuze and Guattari, *Anti–Oedipus*, p. 28.

64. See Deleuze and Guattari, *Anti–Oedipus*, p. 235.

65. See Wilhelm Reich, *The Mass Psychology of Fascism*, trans. Vincent R. Carfagno (London: Souvenir Press, 1970).

66. See Reich, pp. 63ff.

67. See Deleuze and Guattari, *Anti–Oedipus*, p. 109.

Chapter Four
Cixous: On the Gift–Giving Virtue as Feminine Economy

1. Hélène Cixous, "The Laugh of the Medusa," trans. Keith Cohen and Paula Cohen in *Signs: Journal of Women in Culture and Society*, Vol. 1, No. 4 (Summer 1976): 888. Cixous's remark, which appears in a footnote that did not appear in the original version of "Le Rire de la Méduse" (*L'Arc*, No. 61 [1975]: 39–54), cites incorrectly the title of Derrida's essay; as published in *Nietzsche aujourd'hui I* (Paris: Union Générale d'Éditions, 1973), pp. 235–87, Derrida's essay was titled "La question du style."

2. Jacques Derrida, *Spurs: Nietzsche's Styles*, trans. Barbara Harlow (Chicago: University of Chicago Press, 1979), p. 121; for Derrida's discussion of the gift, see pp. 109–23. Derrida himself has noted in the foreword to his 1991 text *Donner le temps* that the problematic of the gift has been at work in his texts "wherever it is a question of the *proper* (appropriation, expropriation, exappropriation), economy, the trace, the name, and especially the *rest*, of course, which is to say more or less constantly" (Jacques Derrida, *Given Time*, trans. Peggy Kamuf [Chicago: University of Chicago Press, 1992] p. ix). More specifically, I would say that the gift was a largely unrecognized but central and recurrent Derridean theme in his texts of the 1970s ranging from *Spurs*, in which the giving of woman is joined to Heidegger's question of the proper, property, and the gift of Being, through *Glas* and *Truth in Painting*, about which Derrida remarks that the theme of the gift plays a "more organizing role" (p. ix), to *La carte postale*, in which Derrida addresses issues surrounding giving and the gift in terms of *envois* and their failure to arrive at their destinations, the giving and return of the *fort/da* in Freud, the giving/theft of the letter in Poe, and the *es gibt* of *Sein* and *Ereignis* in Heidegger.

3. In addition to Derrida's *Spurs*, the reader interested in discussions of Nietzsche as or as not a misogynist is referred to Christine Allen, "Nietzsche's Ambivalence about Women," in *The Sexism of Social and Political Theory*, ed. Lorenne M. G. Clark and Lynda Lange (Toronto: University of Toronto Press, 1979): 117–33; Elizabeth Berg, "The Third Woman," *Diacritics*, Vol. 12: *Cherchez La Femme: Feminist Critique/Feminine Text* (Summer 1982): 11–20; Debra B. Bergoffen, "On the Advantage and Disadvantage of Nietzsche for Women," in *The Question of the Other*, ed. Arleen B. Dallery and Charles E. Scott (Albany: State University of New York Press, 1989): 77–88; Peter J. Burgard, ed., *Nietzsche and the Feminine* (Charlottesville: University of Virginia Press, 1994); Jacques Derrida, "Choreographies," trans. Christie V. McDonald in *Diacritics*, Vol. 12: *Cherchez La Femme: Feminist Critique/Feminine Text* (Summer 1982): 66–76; Luce Irigaray, *Amante marine de Friedrich Nietzsche* (Paris: Éditions de Minuit, 1980) [English translation: *Marine Lover of Friedrich Nietzsche*, trans. by Gillian C. Gill (New York: Columbia University Press, 1991)]; Sarah Kofman, *Nietzsche et la scène philosophique* (Paris: Union Générale d'Éditions, 1979), especially chapter eight: "Baubô: Perversion théologique et Fétichisme," pp. 263–304 [a translation of this chapter by Tracy B. Strong appears in Strong and Michael Allen Gillespie, eds., *Nietzsche's New Seas: Explorations in*

Philosophy, Aesthetics, and Politics (Chicago: University of Chicago Press, 1988), pp. 175–202]; David Farrell Krell, *Postponements: Woman, Sensuality, and Death in Nietzsche* (Bloomington: Indiana University Press, 1986); Kelly Oliver, *Womanizing Nietzsche: Philosophy's Relation to the "Feminine"* (New York: Routledge, 1994); Gayle L. Ormiston, "Traces of Derrida: Nietzsche's Image of Women," *Philosophy Today* (Summer 1984): 178–88; Paul Patton, ed., *Nietzsche, Feminism and Political Theory* (New York: Routledge, 1993); R. Hinton Thomas, "Nietzsche, Women, and the Whip," *German Life and Letters*, Vol. 34, No. 1 (October 1980): 117–25.

4. Gilles Deleuze and Félix Guattari, *Anti–Oedipus*, trans. Robert Hurley, Mark Seem, and Helen R. Lane (Minneapolis: University of Minnesota Press, 1983), p. 190.

5. Nietzsche does acknowledge, on occasion, an "instinct for repayment [*Instinkt der Vergeltung*]" in the noble soul, but this instinct has its place only among equals; see *BGE*, 265.

6. Although Nietzsche fails to do so, one could here make a connection between Nietzsche's idea that a community shows its strength in terms of its capacity for generosity and the ideals of the welfare state. One would, of course, have to deflate Nietzsche's rhetoric concerning the squandering of excess resources in order to support parasites, but the basic idea of distributing excess wealth in order to satisfy minimal needs is, as the sentiment in *Daybreak* 202 clearly shows, compatible with Nietzsche's notion of the strong or healthy community. I thank Johanna Meehan for first bringing this connection to my attention.

7. Marcel Mauss, *Essai sur le don: Forme et raison de l'échange dans les sociétés archaïques*, in the *Année sociologique* (1923–1924), pp. 30–186; English translation: *The Gift: The Form and Reason for Exchange in Archaic Societies*, trans. W. D. Halls (New York: W. W. Norton, 1990). While little has been written that brings Mauss and Nietzsche together, it is perhaps more than just a coincidence that Mauss's famous little essay "Gift–Gift" was written for inclusion in *Mélanges offerts à Charles Andler par ses amis et ses élèves* (Strasbourg: Istra, 1924), a collection of offerings by students and friends of Charles Andler, one of the leading French Nietzscheans of the early twentieth century and the author of one of the first significant interpretations of his work: *Nietzsche, sa vie et sa pensée* (Paris: Gallimard, 1920).

8. See Georges Bataille, *The Accursed Share: An Essay on General Economy, Volume I: Consumption*, trans. Robert Hurley (New York:

Zone Books, 1988), Part One. For an earlier discussion of his concept of "expenditure," see "The Notion of Expenditure," in Georges Bataille, *Visions of Excess: Selected Writings, 1927–1939*, ed. and trans. Allan Stoekl (Minneapolis: University of Minnesota Press, 1985): 116–29. A good introduction to Bataille's work as it relates to the question of the gift is Michèle H. Richman's *Reading Georges Bataille: Beyond the Gift* (Baltimore: Johns Hopkins University Press, 1982). For a provocative discussion of general economy that continually relates Bataille and Nietzsche (and Derrida), see Arkady Plotnitsky, *Reconfigurations: Critical Theory and General Economy* (Gainesville: University Press of Florida, 1993).

9. This remark should be compared with the following description of the genius: "The genius—in work, in deed, is necessarily a squanderer [*Verschwender*]: his greatness lies in the fact *that he expends himself* [*dass es sich ausgiebt*]. The instinct of self–preservation is as it were suspended; the overwhelming pressure of the energies which emanate from him forbids him any such care and prudence. One calls this 'sacrifice'; one praises his 'heroism' therein, his indifference to his own interests, his devotion to an idea, a great cause, a fatherland: all misunderstandings.... He flows out, he overflows, he uses himself up, he does not spare himself—..." (*TI*, "Expeditions," 44; translation altered).

10. Although Nietzsche was quite hostile to what he understood to be the goals of socialism, the position that I am characterizing here as a noble economy is not far from the ideal expressed by Marx in *Critique of the Gotha Program* when he writes that on the banner of the higher phase of communist society will be inscribed: "From each according to his ability, to each according to his needs!"

11. I can only note here the importance of forgetting in Derrida's discussion of the gift. For Derrida, "forgetting would be in the *condition of the gift* and the gift in the *condition of forgetting*" (*Given Time*, p. 18), which is to say that the gift cannot be (a gift) unless its having been given can be forgotten. Without this forgetting, the gift will stand as a debt to be repaid rather than as a generous donation. The link between giving, gifts, and forgetting allows Derrida to move the discussion to Heidegger insofar as for Heidegger the event (*Ereignis*) of the gift (of Being)—the *es gibt* of *Sein*—has been forgotten, and the recollection of this event, which is to say, the appropriate reception of this gift, which is to say, the overcoming of this forgetfulness is now, at present, the task of thinking.

12. An important exception here is Gary Shapiro, who focuses attention on the thematic of the gift in *Thus Spoke Zarathustra* in his excellent study *Alcyone: Nietzsche on Gifts, Noise, and Women* (Albany: State University of New York Press, 1991).

13. On a number of occasions, Derrida has drawn attention to the gift as a *pharmakon*, often in the context of a comment on Mauss. One of the first occasions is in "Plato's Pharmacy," where he cites Mauss's call to examine the etymology of "gift," which comes from the Latin *dosis*, Greek δόσις, a dose of poison (*Dissemination*, trans. Barbara Johnson [Chicago: University of Chicago Press, 1981], pp. 131–32). More recently, he discusses the gift as *pharmakon* in *Given Time*, chapter two: "The Madness of Economic Reason: A Gift without Present," pp. 34–70; see esp. pp. 36ff.

14. Georges Bataille, *The Accursed Share*, Vol. 3, trans. Robert Hurley (New York: Zone Books, 1991), p. 370.

15. Nietzsche's prefiguration of both Derridean dissemination and Deleuzian experimentation should here be noted.

16. In the following discussion of Cixous, I will for the most part refrain from qualifying "economy" with either of the adjectives "textual," "libidinal," or "political." As I read Cixous, she sees these three economies working in terms of the same principles and what is true of one will be true of the others. When I choose to use one of these adjectives, it will be to emphasize that particular economy in the context of what I am discussing at that moment, but should not be understood to isolate that economy from the others.

17. This is, of course, one of the central themes in Irigaray's critique of Nietzsche in *Marine Lover*; see esp. pp. 42–45, 82–87.

18. That Cixous's discussion of the *"Empire du Propre"* is, in part, a rejoinder to Jacques Derrida's raising the *"question du propre"* with respect to the questions of style/woman in Nietzsche is clear. I discuss Derrida's *"question du propre"* in some detail in my *Nietzsche and the Question of Interpretation: Between Hermeneutics and Deconstruction* (New York: Routledge, 1990), pp. 104–06, 117.

19. Hélène Cixous and Catherine Clément, *The Newly Born Woman*, trans. Betsy Wing (Minneapolis: University of Minnesota Press, 1986), p. 78.

20. Cixous and Clément, *The Newly Born Woman*, p. 80.

21. Hélène Cixous, "Castration or Decapitation?" trans. Annette Kuhn, *Signs: Journal of Women in Culture and Society*, Vol. 7, No. 1 (1981): 50.

22. Hélène Cixous, "An exchange with Hélène Cixous," trans. Verena Andermatt Conley in Conley, *Hélène Cixous: Writing the Feminine* (Lincoln: University of Nebraska Press, 1984), p. 129.

23. Hélène Cixous, "Extreme Fidelity," trans. Ann Liddle and Susan Sellers in *Writing Differences: Readings from the seminar of Hélène Cixous*, ed. Susan Sellers (New York: St. Martin's Press, 1988), p. 15.

24. Cixous and Clément, *The Newly Born Woman*, p. 85.

25. Cixous and Clément, *The Newly Born Woman*, pp. 80–81.

26. See Derrida, *Given Time*, esp. pp. 11–15. To cite one remark, out of context to be sure, of Derrida's articulation of the gift's impossibility, I offer (as a gift?) the following: "if there is no gift, there is no gift, but if there is gift held or beheld *as* gift by the other, once again there is no gift; in any case the gift does not *exist* and does not *present* itself. If it presents itself, it no longer presents itself" (p. 15).

In this chapter, I will only be able to touch the surface of these divergent logics of gift–giving. For a sense of the range of reflection on the diverse logics of gift–giving, see the essays in my anthology *The Logic of the Gift: Toward an Ethic of Generosity* (New York: Routledge, forthcoming). Although I am not able to do so here, a full treatment of these divergent logics would have to be pursued not only, or even primarily, within Derrida's texts but also, and perhaps more importantly, within the domain of anthropology insofar as this issue has been at the forefront of anthropological research since, to quote Gayle Rubin, Lévi–Strauss, in chapter five of *The Elementary Structures of Kinship* (Boston: Beacon Press, 1969), added "to the theory of primitive reciprocity the idea that marriages are a most basic form of gift exchange, in which it is women who are the most precious of gifts" (Gayle Rubin, "The Traffic in Women," in *Toward an Anthropology of Women*, ed. Rayna R. Reiter [New York and London: Monthly Review Press, 1975], p. 173). Any serious analysis of gift–giving would, at the very least, have to consult and address the work of a wide range of recent feminist and feminist–inspired reappraisals of the effects of gender on exchange relations including, among others, Daryl K. Feil, *Ways of Exchange: The Enga 'tee' of Papua New Guinea* (St. Lucia: University of Queensland Press, 1984); Renée Hirschon, ed., *Women and Property, Women as Property* (London: Croom Helm, 1984); Lisette Josephides, *The Production of Inequality: Gender and Exchange among the Kewa* (London: Tavistock Publications, 1985); Marilyn Strathern, *The Gender of the*

Gift: Problems with Women and Problems with Society in Melanesia (Berkeley: University of California Press, 1988); J. Van Baal, *Reciprocity and the Position of Women* (Amsterdam: Van Gorcum, 1975); and Annette B. Weiner, *Women of Value, Men of Renown: New Perspectives on Trobriand Exchange* (Austin: University of Texas Press, 1976) and *Inalienable Possessions: The Paradox of Keeping–While–Giving* (Berkeley: University of California Press, 1992).

27. Cixous, "Castration or Decapitation?" p. 48.

28. Making much the same point, Irigaray locates Nietzsche's highest *ressentiment* in his having received the gift of his life—a gift that cannot be repaid—from a woman; see *Marine Lover*, pp. 42–43.

29. Cixous, "Castration or Decapitation?" p. 48. Nietzsche himself recognizes this point as he notes that deep within the noble soul resides an "instinct for repayment" that is uncomfortable with clemency (*Gnade*) among equals (*BGE*, 265).

30. Hélène Cixous, "The Laugh of the Medusa," p. 893. The English translation mistakenly reads "two non–masters ≠ two dead." Cf. "Le Rire de la Méduse," p. 54.

31. Cixous and Clément, *The Newly Born Woman*, p. 87. Translation altered.

32. Cixous, in Conley, p. 158.

33. Cixous and Clément, *The Newly Born Woman*, p. 87.

34. Although he is skeptical about many of my conclusions in this chapter, I owe a debt of thanks to Jeffrey Nealon for suggesting this way of putting the point.

35. Cixous, in Conley, p. 137.

36. C. A. Gregory, *Gifts and Commodities* (London: Academic Press, 1982), p. 41. Lewis Hyde develops the same distinction between gift and commodity in *The Gift: Imagination and the Erotic Life of Property* (New York: Vintage Books, 1979). Hyde goes on to further distinguish the giving of gifts from the selling of commodities by claiming, in a way that raises as many questions as it answers, that while a commodity has a quantifiable "value," a gift has "worth" to which no price can be attached (p. 60).

37. Virginia Held has explored a similar distinction in the context of feminism and moral theory, and she moves in a direction close to Cixous when she argues that it is the relationship between "mother or mothering person and child" and not "contractual relationships" that is

"most central or fundamental to society and morality" (Virginia Held, "Feminism and Moral Theory" in *Women and Moral Theory*, ed. Eva Feder Kittay and Diana T. Meyers [Totowa, NJ: Rowman and Littlefield, 1987], p.114).

38. Bataille, *Visions of Excess*, p. 120.

39. Cixous and Clément, *The Newly Born Woman*, p. 90.

40. Cixous and Clément, *The Newly Born Woman*, p. 95.

41. Cixous and Clément, *The Newly Born Woman*, p. 90.

42. Cixous and Clément, *The Newly Born Woman*, p. 81. The appeal to maternity, maternal language and maternal images in French feminist writing is frequently an object of criticism by other, especially American, feminists; see, for example, Domna Stanton, "Difference on Trial: A Critique of the Maternal Metaphor in Cixous, Irigaray, and Kristeva" in *The Thinking Muse: Feminism and Modern French Philosophy*, ed. Jeffner Allen and Iris Marion Young (Bloomington: Indiana University Press, 1989), pp. 156–79.

43. Ironically, Cixous comes both closest to and furthest from Nietzsche when she approaches essentialism—closest to the Nietzsche who sees woman's essential function in terms of the capacity to bear children (and give birth to the *Übermensch*); furthest from the Nietzsche who, as the philosopher of self–overcoming and the "dangerous maybe," resists all essentializing attributes of identity.

44. Cixous, "Extreme Fidelity," p. 18.

45. Hélène Cixous, *Reading with Clarice Lispector*, ed. and trans. Verena Andermatt Conley (Minneapolis: University of Minnesota Press, 1990), p. 156.

46. I am grateful to Paula Smith for first suggesting this point to me.

47. Cixous, "The Laugh of the Medusa," p. 888.

48. Cixous and Clément, *The Newly Born Woman*, p. 92.

49. Cixous, in Conley, p. 137.

50. Pierre Bourdieu, *Outline of a Theory of Practice*, trans. Richard Nice (Cambridge: Cambridge University Press, 1977), p. 5.

51. Bourdieu, *Outline*, pp. 5–6; see also p. 171. Bourdieu also recognizes two different economies that are distinguished along gender lines: "The opposition between the two 'economies' is so marked that the expression *err arrtal*, also used to express the taking of revenge, means the *returning of a gift*, an exchange, in the men's speech, whereas it means 'giving back a loan' when used by the women" (p.

62). He goes on to note that "loan conduct" is more common among women than is gift–exchange, which he takes to indicate that although less socially prestigious, "economic truth… is closer to the surface in female exchanges" (p. 63).

52. Cixous, "Castration or Decapitation?" p. 53.

53. Cixous and Clément, *The Newly Born Woman*, p. 86.

54. Cixous and Clément, *The Newly Born Woman*, p. 83.

55. Theodor Adorno, *Minima Moralia*, trans. E. F. N. Jephcott (London: New Left Books, 1974), p. 42.

56. Cixous and Clément, *The Newly Born Woman*, p. 72.

57. This point has been made forcefully by Kelly Oliver in her reading of Luce Irigaray's *Marine Lover* in "The Plaint of Ariadne," in *The Fate of the New Nietzsche*, ed. Keith Ansell–Pearson and Howard Caygill (Aldershot, England: Avebury, 1993), pp. 211–28; see also chapter four in Oliver's *Womanizing Nietzsche*, pp. 102–43.

58. As indicated in note 28 above, Irigaray situates Nietzsche's hostility to women in part as a manifestation of *ressentiment* for having received the gift of being born of a woman.

59. Cixous and Clément, *The Newly Born Woman*, p. 96.

60. Cf. *Z*, "On the Vision and the Riddle." This chapter benefited from the careful reading and thoughtful suggestions of several people, including Caroline Gebhard, Paula Smith, Johanna Meehan, Jill Schrift, Aletta Biersack, Debra Bergoffen, Maura Strassberg, Kelly Oliver and Marcia Stephenson. Although most of these readers no doubt still have questions concerning my approach to the issues raised in this chapter, I thank them for the generous gift of their time and their criticisms, which made this discussion of gendered economies better than it would otherwise have been.

Chapter Five
Why the French Are No Longer Nietzscheans

1. Sarah Kofman, *Explosion I: De l'"Ecce Homo" de Nietzsche* (Paris: Galilée, 1992); *Explosion II: Les enfants de Nietzsche* (Paris: Galilée, 1993).

2. This gesture—setting up "Nietzsche" as a battlefield on which to take one's stand against or to challenge the ideas of one's intellectual predecessors or rivals—is remarkably common in the twentieth century.

As I argue in my *Nietzsche and the Question of Interpretation: Between Hermeneutics and Deconstruction* (New York: Routledge, 1990), this is what in part underlies Derrida's reading of Nietzsche in *Spurs: Nietzsche's Styles;* see chapter four: "Derrida: Nietzsche contra Heidegger," pp. 95–119. One can also locate this gesture in Heidegger's reading of Nietzsche as a response to the vitalist/racist readings of Oehler and Bäumler; Adorno and Horkheimer's reading as a response to Heidegger; Deleuze's reading as a response to the French Hegelians; Derrida and Gadamer debating each other at the Paris Goethe House encounter in terms of their readings of Nietzsche vis–à–vis Heidegger. The list could continue but the point should be clear: there is something about "Nietzsche" that makes him a desirable site for such polemics.

3. Vincent Descombes, *Le même et l'autre: Quarante–cinq ans de philosophie française (1933–1978)* (Paris: Éditions de Minuit, 1979); English translation: *Modern French Philosophy*, trans. L. Scott–Fox and J. M. Harding (Cambridge: Cambridge University Press, 1980).

4. Luc Ferry and Alain Renaut, *La pensée 68: Essai sur l'anti–humanisme contemporain* (Paris: Gallimard, 1985); English translation: *French Philosophy of the Sixties: An Essay on Antihumanism*, trans. Mary Schnackenberg Cattani (Amherst: University of Massachusetts Press, 1990).

5. Alain Boyer, et al., *Pourquoi nous ne sommes pas nietzschéens* (Paris: Éditions Grasset et Fasquelle, 1991). In addition to essays by Descombes, and Ferry and Renaut, this collection includes essays by Alain Boyer, André Comte–Sponville, Robert Legros, Philippe Raynaud, and Pierre–André Taguieff.

6. Luc Ferry and Alain Renaut, "Préface" in *Pourquoi nous ne sommes pas nietzschéens*, p. 7.

7. See, for example, Vincent Descombes, "Le moment français de Nietzsche," in *Pourquoi nous ne sommes pas nietzschéens*, p. 103. Lyotard's paper at the Cerisy conference was titled "Notes sur le retour et le capital," *Nietzsche aujourd'hui I* (Paris: Union Générale d'Éditions, 1973), pp. 141–57.

8. Jean–François Lyotard, *Économie libidinale* (Paris: Éditions de Minuit, 1974); English translation: *Libidinal Economy*, trans. Iain Hamilton Grant (Bloomington: Indiana University Press, 1993).

9. Peter Dews, *Logics of Disintegration: Post–Structuralist Thought and the Claims of Critical Theory* (London: Verso, 1987), p. 216. In a recent

interview, Lyotard challenges this characterization, remarking that it is Deleuze and Guattari, and not himself, who take their inspiration from Nietzsche, adding "Re–reading *Libidinal Economy*, I note that Nietzsche is referred to perhaps twice. He is not really present in this text: *Libidinal Economy* is predominantly a struggle with Freud" ("Nietzsche and the Inhuman," Interview with Richard Beardsworth in *Journal of Nietzsche Studies*, Vol. 7 [Spring 1994], p. 80). Whether one should measure the impact of Nietzsche's thinking on a text in terms of the number of times his name appears is, of course, highly questionable and Lyotard's text may in fact be far more Nietzschean than he now cares to admit.

10. *Socialisme ou Barbarie* was founded in 1949 and dominated intellectually by Cornelius Castoriadis and Claude Lefort. Lyotard worked with this group between 1955 and 1963, publishing several articles in the group's journal. Some of these articles, especially concerning Algeria, have been translated by Bill Readings and Kevin Paul in Lyotard's *Political Writings* (Minneapolis: University of Minnesota Press, 1993). For a general account of this group and their journal, see Castoriadis's "General Introduction" in his collection *Political and Social Writings*, 2 Vols., ed. and trans. David Ames Curtis (Minneapolis: University of Minnesota Press, 1988).

11. Jean–François Lyotard and Jean–Loup Thébaud, *Just Gaming*, trans. Wlad Godzich (Minneapolis: University of Minnesota Press, 1985), p. 17.

12. Lyotard and Thébaud, p. 17.

13. Dews, p. 219.

14. See Lyotard and Thébaud, p. 90.

15. Lyotard and Thébaud, p. 18; see also p. 98.

16. Jean–François Lyotard, *The Differend: Phrases in Dispute*, trans. Georges Van Den Abbeele (Minneapolis: University of Minnesota Press, 1988), p. 135; see also Lyotard and Thébaud, *Just Gaming*, p. 59.

17. Lyotard and Thébaud, p. 17.

18. Lyotard and Thébaud, p. 93.

19. Lyotard and Thébaud, p. 94.

20. Lyotard and Thébaud, p. 94. Emphasis added.

21. Lyotard and Thébaud, p. 95.

22. Lyotard and Thébaud, p. 100.

23. Lyotard and Thébaud, p. 100.

24. Lyotard and Thébaud, p. 105.
25. Lyotard, *The Differend*, §164; Levinas Notice §1.
26. Lyotard, *The Differend*, §176.
27. See Søren Kierkegaard, *Fear and Trembling*, Problema III: "Was it Ethically Defensible for Abraham to Conceal his Undertaking from Sarah, from Eliezer, and from Isaac?"
28. Lyotard, *The Differend*, Levinas Notice §2.
29. Lyotard, *The Differend*, §155. Emphasis added.
30. Lyotard, *The Differend*, Kant Notice 2, §5.
31. Lyotard, *The Differend*, Kant Notice §6.
32. Lyotard, *The Differend*, Kant Notice §6, p. 127.
33. Lyotard, *The Differend*, §192.
34. Lyotard, *The Differend*, §206.
35. Lyotard, The *Differend*, §197.
36. See, for example, the critical references to Lyotard in Ferry and Renaut, "Le sujet en process," in *Tod des Subjekts?*, ed. Herta Nagl–Docekal and Helmuth Vetter (Vienna: R. Oldenbourg Verlag, 1987), pp. 117–18; and *French Philosophy of the Sixties*, pp. xxiii–xxiv, 17.
37. See Lyotard's remark in the preface to *The Differend*, under the heading "Pretext," in which he notes that the legacy of Kant's *Critique of Judgment* and Wittgenstein's *Philosophical Investigations*—the two "epilogues to modernity and prologues to an honorable postmodernity" that prompt his text—"ought to be relieved of [their] cumbersome debt to anthropomorphism" (xiii). On this point and elsewhere in my discussion of Lyotard, I have profited from several conversations with Rudi Visker, as well as from his excellent paper "DISSENSUS COMMUNIS: How to Keep Silent 'after' Lyotard," forthcoming in *DISSENSUS COMMUNIS: Between Ethics and Politics*, ed. Philippe Van Haute and Peg Birmingham (Kampen, The Netherlands: J. H. Kok, forthcoming).
38. See, for example, Luc Ferry and Alain Renaut, *68–86: Itinéraires de l'individu* (Paris: Gallimard, 1987), especially chapter three: "Foucault et Deleuze: le vitalisme contre le droit," pp. 75–108; "Le sujet en process," pp. 108–19; and their contribution to *Pourquoi nous ne sommes pas nietzschéens*: "'Ce qui a besoin d'être démontré ne vaut pas grand–chose,'" pp. 129–52.
39. Ferry and Renaut, *French Philosophy of the Sixties*, p. 13.

40. Ferry and Renaut, *French Philosophy of the Sixties*, p. 14.

41. Ferry and Renaut, *French Philosophy of the Sixties*, p. 120. Ferry and Renaut reiterate this point in the concluding pages of *Political Philosophy 3: From the Rights of Man to the Republican Idea*, trans. Franklin Philip (Chicago: University of Chicago Press, 1992), pp. 126–28.

42. See Ferry and Renaut, *68–86: Itinéraires de l'individu*, pp. 79–86.

43. See the conclusion of Ferry and Renaut, "Le Sujet en Process," p. 119.

44. Ferry and Renaut, *Political Philosophy 3*, pp. 127–28.

45. Jacques Derrida, from the discussion following "Structure, Sign, and Play in the Discourse of the Human Sciences," trans. Richard Macksey in *The Structuralist Controversy*, ed. Richard Macksey and Eugenio Donato (Baltimore: Johns Hopkins University Press, 1970), p. 271.

46. "'Eating Well,' or the Calculation of the Subject: An Interview with Jacques Derrida," trans. Peter Connor and Avital Ronell in *Who Comes After the Subject?*, ed. Eduardo Cadava, Peter Connor, and Jean–Luc Nancy (New York: Routledge, 1991), pp. 96–97.

47. Descombes, *Modern French Philosophy*, p. 187.

48. Descombes, *Modern French Philosophy*, p. 189. The passage from Leibniz's *Monadology* also appears on p. 189.

49. Descombes, *Modern French Philosophy*, p. 188.

50. Descombes, *Modern French Philosophy*, pp. 188–190.

51. Vincent Descombes, *Objects of All Sorts: A Philosophical Grammar*, trans. Lorna Scott–Fox and Jeremy Harding (Baltimore: Johns Hopkins University Press, 1986), p. 2.

52. Descombes, "Le moment français de Nietzsche," pp. 103–07.

53. See Paul Ricoeur, *Freud and Philosophy: An Essay on Interpretation*, trans. Denis Savage (New Haven: Yale University Press, 1970), pp. 32–36.

54. That the French Nietzscheans do, in fact, link conscience as a moral phenomenon with consciousness as a metaphysical phenomenon, is clear. But far from being a mistake, this linkage is one of the central ideas they take from their reading of Nietzsche's *On the Genealogy of Morals*. The link between conscience/consciousness and the subject is addressed at length above in my discussions of Foucault and Deleuze in chapters two and three, where I argue that rather than "bad philosophizing," this linkage is "good interpretation."

55. Descombes, "Le moment français de Nietzsche," pp. 112–13.
56. For an account of this tradition, see the readings collected together in Gayle L. Ormiston and Alan D. Schrift, eds., *Transforming the Hermeneutic Context: From Nietzsche to Nancy* (Albany: State University of New York Press, 1990).
57. Descombes, "Le moment français de Nietzsche," pp. 118–19.
58. Descombes, "Le moment français de Nietzsche," p. 121.
59. Descombes, "Le moment français de Nietzsche," p. 126.
60. Descombes, "Le moment français de Nietzsche," p. 107.
61. That there is an audience for such criticisms can be seen in the appearance of a new series titled "New French Thought," edited by Thomas Pavel and Mark Lilla for Princeton University Press. Their editorial "mission statement" offers a clear expression of their intentions: "The aim of this series is to bring to a cultivated public the best of recent French writing in the humanities in clear, accessible translations. The series focuses on the younger generation of philosophers, historians, and social commentators who represent the new, liberal, humanistic bent of French intellectual life." The perspective of the editors is made more clear, perhaps, in Lilla's introduction to one of their first editions, *New French Thought: Political Philosophy*, where he writes that "the almost universal abandonment of the Hegelian, Marxist, and structuralist dogmas" on the French intellectual scene in the last fifteen years has "also signaled the demise of a certain conception of the intellectual himself, as a 'master thinker' whose philosophy of history or theory of power licensed him to deliver ex cathedra judgments on the political events of the day. This image of the French *philosophe* may still have its admirers in certain airless corners of American and British universities, but it has virtually disappeared in France" (Mark Lilla, "The Legitimacy of the Liberal Age," in *New French Thought: Political Philosophy*, ed. Mark Lilla [Princeton: Princeton University Press, 1994], p. 15). Whether this last comment is wishful thinking on Lilla's part is worth questioning, especially in terms of the continuing attention paid to Derrida and Foucault and the increasing interest in Deleuze's work. The publication of Foucault's four–volume *Dits and écrits* (Paris: Gallimard, 1994) was perhaps the major publishing "event" in France in 1994, and in addition to a twice–monthly television show on France's cultural station (Arte) that has aired excerpts from a lengthy conversation with Deleuze, a number of new books have recently appeared in France which address Deleuze's work. Lilla's conclusion that the presence of the philosophers known as "poststructuralist" has "virtually disappeared" in

France is, therefore, highly suspect.

62. See, for example, Jürgen Habermas, *The Philosophical Discourse of Modernity*, trans. Frederick G. Lawrence (Cambridge, MA: MIT Press, 1987) and Manfred Frank, *What is Neostructuralism?*, trans. Sabine Wilke and Richard Gray (Minneapolis: University of Minnesota Press, 1989).

63. Jacques Derrida, *Otobiographies: The Teaching of Nietzsche and the Politics of the Proper Name*, trans. Avital Ronell in *The Ear of the Other: Otobiography, Transference, Translation*, ed. Christie V. McDonald and trans. Peggy Kamuf (New York: Schocken Books, 1985), pp. 30–31.

64. For example, in reaction to Lyotard's question in *Libidinal Economy*: "What was Marx's left hand doing while he wrote *Capital?*" Ferry and Renaut write: "We consider it fortunate that, in spite of the marginalization of philosophical activity by the ambient technopolitics of the '68 period, the discovery of these traces of what passed for thought at the time means that the need for historians to try to reconstruct texts that would otherwise have been regarded as caricature can be permanently avoided" (*French Philosophy of the Sixties*, pp. 17–18). Their text is littered with such examples.

65. While there are, to be sure, substantive issues involved here, one should perhaps also note that complex issues concerning professional jealousies and Parisian academic politics are also at work in the backlash against the French Nietzscheans.

66. Nietzsche's cultural and political reception in Germany is discussed in a number of recent works, including Steven E. Aschheim, *The Nietzsche Legacy in Germany 1890–1990* (Berkeley: University of California Press, 1992), and Seth Taylor, *Left–Wing Nietzscheans: The Politics of German Expressionism 1910–1920* (Berlin: Walter de Gruyter, 1990). An earlier and more narrowly focused discussion of Nietzsche's reception by the German Left is to be found in R. Hinton Thomas, *Nietzsche in German Politics and Society 1890–1918* (Manchester: Manchester University Press, 1983).

67. An example of the sort of reading called for, which does take account of the complexity of Nietzsche's position, has been provided by Sarah Kofman in her recent work *Le mépris des Juifs: Nietzsche, les Juifs, l'antisémitisme* (Paris: Galilée, 1994). By examining his remarks in context, Kofman is able to defend many of Nietzsche's comments about the Jews against the accusation that they are obviously and crudely anti–Semitic. But Kofman refuses to apologize for all of Nietzsche's

remarks, leaving the reader better informed about what might have motivated many of Nietzsche's remarks while providing a detailed account of the complexity of his position on "the Jews."

68. A bibliography of "Nietzsche Scholarship in English (1968–1992)," compiled by B. Bryan Hilliard and distributed through the North American Nietzsche Society, lists 1,912 publications. In addition, the Nietzsche–werkgroep at the Katholieke Universiteit Nijmegen, directed by Paul van Tongeren, lists 1,050 titles, and reviews over 100 books (many, but not all, in English) on or about Nietzsche published between 1986 and 1992 in "Kroniek van Recente Nietzsche–Literatuur (II)," *Tijdschrift voor Filosofie*, No. 4 (December 1993): 694–720.

69. Signs of this backlash have already started to appear in the United States as Nietzsche's name, alone or in conjunction with many of the French Nietzscheans, is often mentioned in politically motivated attacks on the "Left's" supposed "control" of the American academy. The most widely discussed example is, of course, Allan Bloom's *Closing of the American Mind* (New York: Simon and Schuster, 1987). But in the popular press's reporting of "The Heidegger Affair" and "The DeMan Affair," it was not uncommon to loosely link Heidegger's and/or DeMan's reported Nazi sympathies back to Nietzsche and forward to Derrida and deconstruction. While these links usually are incapable of standing up to close critical scrutiny, they seem often to take hold in the imagination of the popular audience. For a good example of this sort of rhetorical ploy, see Dinesh D'Souza's *Illiberal Education: The Politics of Race and Sex on Campus* (New York: Macmillan, Inc., 1991), pp. 191–93, where he moves on one page from J. Hillis Miller, Geoffrey Hartmann, and Jacques Derrida to DeMan's writings to Hitler's *Mein Kampf* to DeMan's *Allegories of Reading* before closing with a non sequitur misquote from Nietzsche: "men would rather believe in nothingness than believe in nothing" (p. 192).

70. Ernesto Laclau, "Power and Representation," in *Politics, Theory, and Contemporary Culture*, ed. Mark Poster (New York: Columbia University Press, 1993), p. 292.

Bibliography

➢

Adorno, Theodor. *Minima Moralia*. Translated by E. F. N. Jephcott. London: New Left Books, 1974.

Allen, Christine. "Nietzsche's Ambivalence about Women." In *The Sexism of Social and Political Theory*. Edited by Lorenne M. G. Clark and Lynda Lange. Toronto: University of Toronto Press, 1979. Pp. 117–33.

Allison, David B., editor. *The New Nietzsche: Contemporary Styles of Interpretation*. New York: Dell, 1977.

Andler, Charles. *Nietzsche, sa vie et sa pensée*. Paris: Gallimard, 1920.

Aschheim, Steven E. *The Nietzsche Legacy in Germany 1890–1990*. Berkeley: University of California Press, 1992.

Attridge, Derek, Geoff Bennington, and Robert Young, editors. *Post–structuralism and the Question of History*. Cambridge: Cambridge University Press, 1987.

Bataille, Georges. *The Accursed Share: An Essay on General Economy, Volume I: Consumption*. Translated by Robert Hurley. New York: Zone Books, 1988.

_____. *The Accursed Share: An Essay on General Economy, Volumes II and III*. Translated by Robert Hurley. New York: Zone Books, 1991.

_____. *Sur Nietzsche*. Paris: Gallimard, 1945. [English translation: *On Nietzsche*. Translated by Bruce Boone. New York: Paragon House, 1992.]

_____. "The Notion of Expenditure." In *Visions of Excess: Selected Writings, 1927–1939.* Translated and edited by Allan Stoekl. Minneapolis: University of Minnesota Press, 1985. Pp. 116–29.

Baudrillard, Jean. "Forgetting Foucault." Translated by Nicole Dufresne. *Humanities in Society,* Vol. 3, No. 1 (Winter 1980): 87–111.

Berg, Elizabeth. "The Third Woman." *Diacritics,* Vol. 12: *Cherchez La Femme: Feminist Critique/Feminine Text* (Summer 1982): 11–20.

Bergoffen, Debra B. "On the Advantage and Disadvantage of Nietzsche for Women." In *The Question of the Other.* Edited by Arleen B. Dallery and Charles E. Scott. Albany: State University of New York Press, 1989. Pp. 77–88.

Blanchot, Maurice. *The Infinite Conversation.* Translated by Susan Hanson. Minneapolis: University of Minnesota Press, 1993.

Bloom, Allan. *The Closing of the American Mind.* New York: Simon and Schuster, 1987.

Bogue, Ronald. *Deleuze and Guattari.* London and New York: Routledge, 1989.

Bourdieu, Pierre. *Homo Academicus.* Translated by Peter Collier. Stanford: Stanford University Press, 1988.

_____. *Outline of a Theory of Practice.* Translated by Richard Nice. Cambridge: Cambridge University Press, 1977.

Bové, Paul. *Intellectuals in Power: A Genealogy of Critical Humanism.* New York: Columbia University Press, 1986.

Boyer, Alain, et al. *Pourquoi nous ne sommes pas nietzschéens.* Paris: Éditions Grasset et Fasquelle, 1991.

Burchell, Graham, Colin Gordon, and Peter Miller, editors. *The Foucault Effect: Studies in Governmentality.* Chicago: University of Chicago Press, 1991.

Burgard, Peter J., editor. *Nietzsche and the Feminine.* Charlottesville: University of Virginia Press, 1994.

Butler, Judith. *Bodies That Matter: On the Discursive Limits of "Sex".* New York: Routledge, 1993.

_____. *Gender Trouble: Feminism and the Subversion of Identity.* New York: Routledge, 1990.

_____. "Poststructuralism and Postmarxism." *Diacritics,* Vol. 23, No. 4 (Winter 1993): 3–11.

_____. "Subjection, Resistance, and Resignation: Between Freud and Foucault." In *The Question of Identity*. Edited by John Rajchman. New York: Routledge, forthcoming.

Carroll, David. *Paraesthetics: Foucault, Lyotard, Nietzsche.* London: Methuen, 1987.

Castoriadis, Cornelius. *Political and Social Writings.* 2 Vols. Edited and translated by David Ames Curtis. Minneapolis: University of Minnesota Press, 1988.

Cixous, Hélène. "Castration or Decapitation?" Translated by Annette Kuhn. *Signs: Journal of Women in Culture and Society*, Vol. 7, No. 1 (1981): 41–55.

_____. "An exchange with Hélène Cixous." Translated by Verena Andermatt Conley. In Conley, *Hélène Cixous: Writing the Feminine.* Lincoln: University of Nebraska Press, 1984. Pp. 129–61.

_____. "Extreme Fidelity." Translated by Ann Liddle and Susan Sellers. In *Writing Differences: Readings from the Seminar of Hélène Cixous.* Edited by Susan Sellers. New York: St. Martin's Press, 1988. Pp. 9–36.

_____. *Reading with Clarice Lispector.* Edited and translated by Verena Andermatt Conley. Minneapolis: University of Minnesota Press, 1990.

_____. "Le Rire de la Méduse." *L'Arc*, No. 61 (1975): 39–54. [English translation: "The Laugh of the Medusa." Translated by Keith Cohen and Paula Cohen. *Signs: Journal of Women in Culture and Society*, Vol. 1, No. 4 (Summer 1976): 875–93.]

Cixous, Hélène, and Catherine Clément. *The Newly Born Woman.* Translated by Betsy Wing. Minneapolis: University of Minnesota Press, 1986.

Conway, Daniel W. "Nietzsche contra Nietzsche: The Deconstruction of *Zarathustra*." In *Nietzsche as Postmodernist: Essays Pro and Contra.* Edited by Clayton Koelb. Albany: State University of New York Press, 1990. Pp. 91–110.

Danto, Arthur. *Nietzsche as Philosopher.* New York: Columbia University Press, 1980.

Deleuze, Gilles. *Le Bergsonisme.* Paris: Presses Universitaires de France, 1966. [English translation: *Bergsonism.* Translated by Hugh

Tomlinson and Barbara Habberjam. New York: Zone Books, 1988.]

_____. *Cinema 2: The Time–Image*. Translated by Hugh Tomlinson and Robert Galeta. Minneapolis: University of Minnesota Press, 1989.

_____. *David Hume, sa vie, son oeuvre*. Paris: Presses Universitaires de France, 1952.

_____. *Différence et répétition*. Paris: Presses Universitaires de France, 1968. [English translation: *Difference and Repetition*. Translated by Paul Patton. New York: Columbia University Press, 1994.]

_____. *Empirisme et subjectivité*. Paris: Presses Universitaires de France, 1953. [English translation: *Empiricism and Subjectivity: An Essay on Hume's Theory of Human Nature*. Translated by Constantin V. Boundas. New York: Columbia University Press, 1991.]

_____. "Entretien 1980." *L'Arc*, No. 49, Second Edition (1980): 99–102.

_____. *Foucault*. Translated by Seán Hand. Minneapolis: University of Minnesota Press, 1988.

_____. "Lucrèce et le naturalisme." *Études philosophiques*, No. 1 (January–May 1961): 19–29.

_____. *Nietzsche et la philosophie*. Paris: Presses Universitaires de France, 1962. [English translation: *Nietzsche and Philosophy*. Translated by Hugh Tomlinson. New York: Columbia University Press, 1983.]

_____. "Pensée nomade." In *Nietzsche aujourd'hui I*. Paris: Union Générale d'Éditions, 1973. Pp. 159–74. [English translation: "Nomad Thought." Translated by David B. Allison. In *The New Nietzsche: Contemporary Styles of Interpretation*. Edited by David B. Allison. New York: Dell, 1977. Pp. 142–49.]

_____. *La philosophie critique de Kant*. Paris: Presses Universitaires de France, 1963. [English translation: *Kant's Critical Philosophy*. Translated by Hugh Tomlinson and Barbara Habberjam. Minneapolis: University of Minnesota Press, 1984.]

_____. *Pourparlers*. Paris: Éditions de Minuit, 1990.

_____. *Spinoza et le problème de l'expression*. Paris: Éditions de Minuit, 1968. [English translation: *Expressionism in Philosophy: Spinoza*. Translated by Martin Joughin. New York: Zone Books, 1990.]

_____. "What is a *dispositif*?" Translated by Timothy J. Armstrong. In *Michel Foucault, Philosopher*. Edited by Timothy J. Armstrong. New York: Routledge, 1992. Pp. 159–68.

Deleuze, Gilles, and Félix Guattari. *Anti-Oedipus*. Translated by Robert Hurley, Mark Seem, and Helen R. Lane. Minneapolis: University of Minnesota Press, 1983.

————. *Kafka: Toward a Minor Literature*. Translated by Dana Polan. Minneapolis: University of Minnesota Press, 1986.

————. "Rhizome." Translated by Paul Patton. *Ideology and Consciousness*, No. 8 (Spring 1981): 49–71.

————. *A Thousand Plateaus*. Translated by Brian Massumi. Minneapolis: University of Minnesota Press, 1987.

Deleuze, Gilles and Claire Parnet. *Dialogues*. Translated by Hugh Tomlinson and Barbara Habberjam. New York: Columbia University Press, 1987.

Derrida, Jacques. *The Archeology of the Frivolous*. Translated by John P. Leavey, Jr. Pittsburgh: Duquesne University Press, 1980.

————. *La carte postale: De Socrate à Freud et au–delà*. Paris: Flammarion, 1980. [English translation: *The Post Card: From Socrates to Freud and Beyond*. Translated by Alan Bass. Chicago: University of Chicago Press, 1987.]

————. "Choreographies." Translated by Christie V. McDonald. *Diacritics*, Vol. 12: *Cherchez La Femme: Feminist Critique/Feminine Text* (Summer 1982): 66–76.

————. *Dissemination*. Translated by Barbara Johnson. Chicago: University of Chicago Press, 1981.

————. *Donner le temps*. Paris: Éditions Galilée, 1991. [English translation: *Given Time*. Translated by Peggy Kamuf. Chicago: University of Chicago Press, 1992.]

————. "'Eating Well' or the Calculation of the Subject: An Interview with Jacques Derrida." Translated by Peter Connor and Avital Ronell. In *Who Comes After the Subject?* Edited by Eduardo Cadava, Peter Connor, and Jean–Luc Nancy. New York: Routledge, 1991. Pp. 96–119.

————. "Force of Law: The 'Mystical Foundation of Authority'." Translated by Mary Quaintance. *Cardozo Law Review*, Vol. 11, No. 5–6 (1990): 920–1045.

————. "Interpreting Signatures (Nietzsche/Heidegger): Two Questions." Translated by Diane P. Michelfelder and Richard E.

Palmer. In *Dialogue and Deconstruction: The Gadamer–Derrida Encounter.* Edited by Diane P. Michelfelder and Richard E. Palmer. Albany: State University of New York Press, 1989. Pp. 58–71.

_____. *Limited Inc.* Translated by Samuel Weber. Evanston: Northwestern University Press, 1988.

_____. *Marges de la philosophie.* Paris: Éditions de Minuit, 1972. [English translation: *Margins of Philosophy.* Translated by Alan Bass. Chicago: University of Chicago Press, 1982.]

_____. "Nietzsche and the Machine." Interview with Richard Beardsworth. *Journal of Nietzsche Studies,* Vol. 7 (Spring 1994): 7–66.

_____. *Of Grammatology.* Translated by Gayatri C. Spivak. Baltimore: Johns Hopkins University Press, 1976.

_____. *Of Spirit: Heidegger and the Question.* Translated by Geoffrey Bennington and Rachel Bowlby. Chicago: University of Chicago Press, 1989.

_____. *Otobiographies: The Teaching of Nietzsche and the Politics of the Proper Name.* Translated by Avital Ronell. In *The Ear of the Other: Otobiography, Transference, Translation.* Edited by Christie V. McDonald. Translated by Peggy Kamuf. New York: Schocken Books, 1985. Pp. 1–38.

_____. *Positions.* Translated by Alan Bass. Chicago: University of Chicago Press, 1981.

_____. *Spurs: Nietzsche's Styles.* Translated by Barbara Harlow. Chicago: University of Chicago Press, 1978.

_____. "Structure, Sign, and Play in the Discourse of the Human Sciences." Translated by Richard Macksey. In *The Structuralist Controversy: The Languages of Criticism and the Sciences of Man.* Edited by Richard Macksey and Eugenio Donato. Baltimore: Johns Hopkins University Press, 1970. Pp. 247–72.

_____. *The Truth in Painting.* Translated by Geoff Bennington and Ian McLeod. Chicago: University of Chicago Press, 1987.

_____. *Writing and Difference.* Translated by Alan Bass. Chicago: University of Chicago Press, 1978.

Descombes, Vincent. *Le même et l'autre: Quarante–cinq ans de philosophie française (1933–1978).* Paris: Éditions de Minuit, 1979. [English translation: *Modern French Philosophy.* Translated by L. Scott–Fox and J. M. Harding. Cambridge: Cambridge University Press, 1980.]

_____. "Le moment français de Nietzsche." In Boyer, Alain, et al. *Pourquoi nous ne sommes pas nietzschéens.* Paris: Éditions Grasset et Fasquelle, 1991. Pp. 99–128.

_____. *Objects of All Sorts: A Philosophical Grammar.* Translated by Lorna Scott–Fox and Jeremy Harding. Baltimore: Johns Hopkins University Press, 1986.

Dews, Peter. *Logics of Disintegration: Post–Structuralist Thought and the Claims of Critical Theory.* London: Verso, 1987.

Dreyfus, Hubert L., and Paul Rabinow. *Michel Foucault: Beyond Structuralism and Hermeneutics.* Chicago: University of Chicago Press, 1982.

D'Souza, Dinesh. *Illiberal Education: The Politics of Race and Sex on Campus.* New York: Macmillan, 1991.

Ewald, François. "Introduction" to Gilles Deleuze, "Mystère d'Ariane." *Magazine Littéraire,* No. 298 (April 1992): 20.

Feil, Daryl K. *Ways of Exchange: The Enga 'tee' of Papua New Guinea.* St. Lucia: University of Queensland Press, 1984.

Ferry, Luc, and Alain Renaut. "'Ce qui a besoin d'être démontré ne vaut pas grand–chose'." In Boyer, Alain, et al. *Pourquoi nous ne sommes pas nietzschéens.* Paris: Éditions Grasset et Fasquelle, 1991. Pp. 129–52.

_____. *La pensée 68: Essai sur l'anti–humanisme contemporain.* Paris: Gallimard, 1985. [English translation: *French Philosophy of the Sixties: An Essay on Antihumanism.* Translated by Mary Schnackenberg Cattani. Amherst: University of Massachusetts Press, 1990.]

_____. *Political Philosophy 3: From the Rights of Man to the Republican Idea.* Translated by Franklin Philip. Chicago: University of Chicago Press, 1992.

_____. *68–86: Itinéraires de l'individu.* Paris: Gallimard, 1987.

_____. "Le Sujet en Process." In *Tod des Subjekts?* Edited by Herta Nagl–Docekal and Helmuth Vetter. Vienna: R. Oldenbourg Verlag, 1987. Pp. 108–19.

Foucault, Michel. "An Aesthetics of Existence." Interview conducted in April 1984. Translated by Alan Sheridan. In *Michel Foucault: Politics,*

Philosophy, Culture. Interviews and other Writings 1977–1984. Edited by Lawrence D. Kritzman. New York: Routledge, 1988. Pp. 47–53.

————. *The Archaeology of Knowledge.* Translated by A. M. Sheridan Smith. New York: Harper Colophon Books, 1972.

————. "The Confession of the Flesh." Interview first published in July 1977. Translated by Colin Gordon. In *Power/Knowledge: Selected Interviews and Other Writings 1972–1977.* Edited by Colin Gordon. New York: Pantheon Books, 1977. Pp. 194–228.

————. "Critical Theory/Intellectual History." Interview first published in spring 1983. Translated by Jeremy Harding. In *Michel Foucault: Politics, Philosophy, Culture. Interviews and Other Writings 1977–1984.* Edited by Lawrence D. Kritzman. New York: Routledge, 1988. Pp. 17–46.

————. *Discipline and Punish: The Birth of the Prison.* Translated by Alan Sheridan. New York: Random House, 1978.

————. "The Discourse of History." Interview first published in June 1967. Translated by John Johnston. In *Foucault Live (Interviews, 1966–1984).* Edited by Sylvère Lotringer. New York: Semiotexte, 1989. Pp. 11–33.

————. *Dits and écrits.* 4 Vols. Paris: Gallimard, 1994.

————. "The Ethic of Care for the Self as a Practice of Freedom." Interview conducted in January 1984. Translated by J. D. Gauthier, S.J. *Philosophy and Social Criticism.* Special issue "The Final Foucault," Vol. 12, No. 2–3 (Summer 1987): 112–31.

————. *Foucault Live (Interviews, 1966–1984).* Edited by Sylvère Lotringer. New York: Semiotexte, 1989.

————. *The Foucault Reader.* Edited by Paul Rabinow. New York: Pantheon Books, 1984.

————. "The Functions of Literature." Interview conducted in June 1975. Translated by Alan Sheridan. In *Michel Foucault: Politics, Philosophy, Culture. Interviews and Other Writings 1977–1984.* Edited by Lawrence D. Kritzman. New York: Routledge, 1988. Pp. 307–13.

————. "Governmentality." Translated by Rosi Braidotti. *Ideology and Consciousness,* Vol. 6 (Autumn 1979): 5–21.

————. *The History of Sexuality. Vol. One: An Introduction.* Translated by Robert Hurley. New York: Vintage, 1980.

_____. "How is Power Exercised?" Translated by Leslie Sawyer. In Dreyfus, Hubert L. and Paul Rabinow. *Michel Foucault: Beyond Structuralism and Hermeneutics*. Chicago: University of Chicago Press, 1982. Pp. 216–26.

_____. "Intellectuals and Power: A Conversation between Michel Foucault and Gilles Deleuze." Translated by Donald F. Bouchard and Sherry Simon. In *Language, Counter–Memory, Practice*. Edited by Donald F. Bouchard. Ithaca: Cornell University Press, 1977. Pp. 205–17.

_____. "Introduction à l'*Anthropologie* de Kant." *Thèse complémentaire* for the doctorate of letters, Université de Paris, Faculté des Lettres, 1960, photocopy of typescript, Centre Michel Foucault.

_____. *Language, Counter–Memory, Practice*. Translated by Donald F. Bouchard and Sherry Simon. Edited by Donald F. Bouchard. Ithaca: Cornell University Press, 1977.

_____. *Michel Foucault: Politics, Philosophy, Culture. Interviews and Other Writings 1977–1984*. Edited by Lawrence D. Kritzman. New York: Routledge, 1988.

_____. "Nietzsche, Freud, Marx." In *Nietzsche: Cahiers du Royaumont, Philosophie*, No. VI. Paris: Éditions de Minuit, 1967. Pp. 183–200. [English translation by Alan D. Schrift. In *Transforming the Hermeneutic Context: From Nietzsche to Nancy*. Edited by Gayle L. Ormiston and Alan D. Schrift. Albany: State University of New York Press, 1990. Pp. 59–67.]

_____. "Nietzsche, Genealogy, History." Translated by Donald F. Bouchard and Sherry Simon. In *The Foucault Reader*. Edited by Paul Rabinow. New York: Pantheon Books, 1984. Pp. 76–100.

_____. "On the Genealogy of Ethics: An Overview of Work in Progress." Interview conducted in April 1983. In *The Foucault Reader*. Edited by Paul Rabinow. New York: Pantheon Books, 1984. Pp. 340–72.

_____. "On Power." Interview conducted in July 1978. Translated by Alan Sheridan. In *Michel Foucault: Politics, Philosophy, Culture. Interviews and Other Writings 1977–1984*. Edited by Lawrence D. Kritzman. New York: Routledge, 1988. Pp. 96–109.

_____. *The Order of Things*. New York: Random House, 1973.

_____. *L'ordre du discours: Leçon inaugurale au Collège de France*

prononcée le 2 décembre 1972. Paris: Gallimard, 1971. [English translation: "The Discourse on Language." Translated by Rupert Swyer and published as an appendix to *The Archaeology of Knowledge*. New York: Harper and Row, 1972. Pp. 215–37.]

_____. *Power/Knowledge: Selected Interviews and Other Writings 1972–1977*. Translated and edited by Colin Gordon. New York: Pantheon Books, 1977.

_____. "Power and Sex." Interview first published in March 1977. Translated by David J. Parent. In *Michel Foucault: Politics, Philosophy, Culture. Interviews and Other Writings 1977–1984*. Edited by Lawrence D. Kritzman. New York: Routledge, 1988. Pp. 110–24.

_____. "Prison Talk." Interview first published in June 1975. Translated by Colin Gordon. In *Power/Knowledge: Selected Interviews and Other Writings 1972–1977*. Edited by Colin Gordon. New York: Pantheon Books, 1977. Pp. 37–54.

_____. "Subjectivity and Truth." Edited by Mark Blasius and published under the title "About the Beginning of the Hermeneutics of the Self: Two Lectures at Dartmouth." *Political Theory*, Vol. 21, No. 2 (May 1993): 198–227.

_____. "Truth and Power." Interview conducted in June 1976. Translated by Colin Gordon. In *Power/Knowledge: Selected Interviews and Other Writings 1972–1977*. Edited by Colin Gordon. New York: Pantheon Books, 1977. Pp. 109–33.

_____. "Truth, Power, Self: An Interview." In *Technologies of the Self: A Seminar with Michel Foucault*. Edited by Luther H. Martin, Huck Gutman, and Patrick H. Hutton. Amherst: University of Massachusetts Press, 1988. Pp. 9–15.

_____. "Two Lectures." Lectures delivered at the Collège de France, January 7 and 14, 1976. Translated by Kate Soper. In *Power/Knowledge: Selected Interviews and Other Writings 1972–1977*. Edited by Colin Gordon. New York: Pantheon Books, 1977. Pp. 78–108.

_____. *The Use of Pleasure*. Translated by Robert Hurley. New York: Random House, 1985.

_____. "What Is an Author?" Translated by Josué V. Harari. In *The Foucault Reader*. Edited by Paul Rabinow. New York: Pantheon Books, 1984. Pp. 101–20.

_____. "What is Enlightenment?" Translated by Catherine Porter. In *The Foucault Reader*. Edited by Paul Rabinow. New York: Pantheon Books, 1984. Pp. 32–50.

_____. "Why Study Power: The Question of the Subject." In *Michel Foucault: Beyond Structuralism and Hermeneutics*. Dreyfus, Herbert L. and Paul Rabinow. Chicago: University of Chicago Press, 1982. Pp. 208–16.

Frank, Manfred. *What is Neostructuralism?* Translated by Sabine Wilke and Richard Gray. Minneapolis: University of Minnesota Press, 1989.

Gadamer, Hans-Georg. "Text and Interpretation." Translated by Dennis J. Schmidt and Richard E. Palmer. In *Dialogue and Deconstruction: The Gadamer–Derrida Encounter*. Edited by Diane P. Michelfelder and Richard E. Palmer. Albany: State University of New York Press, 1989. Pp. 221–51.

Gasché, Rodolphe. *The Tain of the Mirror: Derrida and the Philosophy of Reflection*. Cambridge: Harvard University Press, 1986.

Gregory, C. A. *Gifts and Commodities*. London: Academic Press, 1982.

Guattari, Félix. *L'inconscient machinique: essais de schizo–analyse*. Fontenay–sous–Bois: Éditions Recherches, 1979.

_____. *Molecular Revolution: Psychiatry and Politics*. Translated by Rosemary Sheed. New York: Penguin Books, 1984.

_____. *Psychanalyse et transversalité: essais d'analyse institutionelle*. Paris: Maspero, 1972.

Habermas, Jürgen. *The Philosophical Discourse of Modernity*. Translated by Frederick G. Lawrence. Cambridge, MA: MIT Press, 1987.

Hardt, Michael. *Gilles Deleuze: An Apprenticeship in Philosophy*. Minneapolis: University of Minnesota Press, 1993.

Harvey, Irene E. *Derrida and the Economy of Différance*. Bloomington: Indiana University Press, 1986.

Heidegger, Martin. *Nietzsche*. Band I and II. Pfullingen: Verlag Günther Neske, 1961.

_____. *Nietzsche. Volume One: The Will to Power as Art*. Edited and translated by David F. Krell. San Francisco: Harper and Row, 1979.

_____. *Nietzsche. Volume Two: The Eternal Recurrence of the Same*. Edited and translated by David F. Krell. New York: Harper and Row, 1984.

_____. *Nietzsche. Volume Three: The Will to Power as Knowledge and Metaphysics.* Edited by David F. Krell. Translated by Joan Stambaugh, David F. Krell, and Frank A. Capuzzi. New York: Harper and Row, 1987.

_____. *Nietzsche. Volume Four: Nihilism.* Edited by David F. Krell. Translated by Frank A. Capuzzi. San Francisco: Harper and Row, 1982.

_____. *The Question of Being.* Translated by William Kluback and Jean T. Wilde. New York: Twayne, 1958.

Held, Virginia. "Feminism and Moral Theory." In *Women and Moral Theory.* Edited by Eva Feder Kittay and Diana T. Meyers. Totowa, NJ: Rowman and Littlefield, 1987. Pp. 111–28.

Hirschon, Renée, editor. *Women and Property, Women as Property.* London: Croom Helm, 1984.

Howey, Richard L. "Nietzsche and the 'New' French Philosophers." *International Studies in Philosophy,* Vol. 17, No. 2 (1985): 83–93.

Hyde, Lewis. *The Gift: Imagination and the Erotic Life of Property.* New York: Vintage Books, 1979.

Irigaray, Luce. *Amante marine de Friedrich Nietzsche.* Paris: Éditions de Minuit, 1980. [English translation: *Marine Lover of Friedrich Nietzsche.* Translated by Gillian C. Gill. New York: Columbia University Press, 1991.]

Josephides, Lisette. *The Production of Inequality: Gender and Exchange among the Kewa.* London: Tavistock, 1985.

Kant, Immanuel. *Critique of Pure Reason.* Translated by Norman Kemp Smith. New York: St. Martin's Press, 1965.

Kennedy, J. M. "Introduction." In Henri Lichtenberger. *The Gospel of Superman: The Philosophy of Friedrich Nietzsche.* Edinburgh: T. N. Foulis, 1910.

Klossowski, Pierre. *Nietzsche et le cercle vicieux.* Paris: Mercure de France, 1969.

_____. "Oubli et anamnèse dans l'expérience vécue de l'éternel retour du Même." In *Nietzsche: Cahiers du Royaumont, Philosophie* No. VI. Paris: Éditions de Minuit, 1967. Pp. 227–35.

Kofman, Sarah. "Baubô: Theological Perversion and Fetishism." Translated by Tracy B. Strong. In *Nietzsche's New Seas: Explorations in*

Philosophy, Aesthetics, and Politics. Edited by Tracy B. Strong and Michael Allen Gillespie. Chicago: University of Chicago Press, 1988. Pp. 175–202.

_____. *Explosion I: De l'"Ecce Homo" de Nietzsche.* Paris: Galilée, 1992.

_____. *Explosion II: Les enfants de Nietzsche.* Paris: Galilée, 1993.

_____. *Le mépris des Juifs: Nietzsche, les Juifs, l'antisémitisme.* Paris: Galilée, 1994.

_____. *Nietzsche and Metaphor.* Translated by Duncan Large. Stanford: Stanford University Press, 1993.

_____. *Nietzsche et la scène philosophique.* Paris: Union Générale d'Éditions, 1979.

Krell, David Farrell. *Postponements: Woman, Sensuality, and Death in Nietzsche.* Bloomington: Indiana University Press, 1986.

Krell, David Farrell, and David Wood, editors. *Exceedingly Nietzsche: Aspects of Contemporary Nietzsche Interpretation.* London: Routledge and Kegan Paul, 1988.

Laclau, Ernesto. "Power and Representation." In *Politics, Theory, and Contemporary Culture.* Edited by Mark Poster. New York: Columbia University Press, 1993. Pp. 277–96.

Laclau, Ernesto, and Chantal Mouffe. *Hegemony and Socialist Strategy: Towards a Radical Democratic Politics.* London: Verso, 1985.

Large, Duncan. "Translator's Introduction." In Sarah Kofman, *Nietzsche and Metaphor.* Stanford: Stanford University Press, 1993. Pp. vii–xiv.

Leitch, Vincent B. *Deconstructive Criticism: An Advanced Introduction.* New York: Columbia University Press, 1983.

Lévi–Strauss, Claude. *The Elementary Structures of Kinship.* Translated by James Harle Bell and John Richard von Sturmer. Boston: Beacon Press, 1969.

Lichtenberger, Henri. *La philosophie de Nietzsche.* Paris: Félix Alcan, 1898.

Lilla, Mark. "The Legitimacy of the Liberal Age." In *New French Thought: Political Philosophy.* Edited by Mark Lilla. Princeton: Princeton University Press, 1994. Pp. 3–34.

Lyotard, Jean–François. *The Differend: Phrases in Dispute.* Translated by Georges Van Den Abbeele. Minneapolis: University of Minnesota Press, 1988.

_____. *Économie libidinale*. Paris: Éditions de Minuit, 1974. [English translation: *Libidinal Economy*. Translated by Iain Hamilton Grant. Bloomington: Indiana University Press, 1993.]

_____. "Nietzsche and the Inhuman." Interview with Richard Beardsworth. *Journal of Nietzsche Studies*, Vol. 7 (Spring 1994): 67–130.

_____. "Notes sur le retour et le capital." In *Nietzsche aujourd'hui I*. Paris: Union Générale d'Éditions, 1973. Pp. 141–57.

_____. *Political Writings*. Translated by Bill Readings and Kevin Paul. Minneapolis: University of Minnesota Press, 1993.

_____. *The Postmodern Condition: A Report on Knowledge*. Translated by Geoff Bennington and Brian Massumi. Minneapolis: University of Minnesota Press, 1984.

_____. *The Postmodern Explained: Correspondence 1982–1985*. Translated by Don Barry, et al. Minneapolis: University of Minnesota Press, 1992.

Lyotard, Jean–François, and Jean–Loup Thébaud. *Just Gaming*. Translated by Wlad Godzich. Minneapolis: University of Minnesota Press, 1985.

Magnus, Bernd. "Nietzsche's Philosophy in 1888: *The Will to Power* and the *Übermensch*." *Journal of the History of Philosophy*, Vol. 24, No. 1 (January 1986): 79–98.

_____. "Perfectibility and Attitude in Nietzsche's *Übermensch*." *Review of Metaphysics*, Vol. 36 (March 1983): 633–59.

Mahon, Michael. *Foucault's Nietzschean Genealogy: Truth, Power, and the Subject*. Albany: State University of New York Press, 1992.

Mauss, Marcel. *Essai sur le don: Forme et raison de l'échange dans les sociétés archaïques*. *Année sociologique*. (1923–1924): 30–186. [English translation: *The Gift: The Form and Reason for Exchange in Archaic Societies*. Translated by W. D. Halls. New York: W. W. Norton, 1990.]

_____. "Gift–Gift." First published in *Mélanges offerts à Charles Andler par ses amis et ses élèves*. Strasbourg: Istra, 1924. Reprinted in Marcel Mauss. *Oeuvres. 3. Cohésion social et divisions de la sociologie*. Edited by Victor Karady. Paris: Éditions de Minuit, 1969. Pp. 46–51. [English translation: "Gift–Gift." Translated by Koen Decoster. In *The Logic of the Gift: Toward an Ethic of Generosity.* Edited by Alan D. Schrift. New York: Routledge, forthcoming.]

Megill, Allan. *Prophets of Extremity: Nietzsche, Heidegger, Foucault, Derrida.* Berkeley: University of California Press, 1985.

Michelfelder, Diane P., and Richard E. Palmer, editors. *Dialogue and Deconstruction: The Gadamer–Derrida Encounter.* Albany: State University of New York Press, 1989.

Miller, James. *The Passion of Michel Foucault.* New York: Simon and Schuster, 1993.

Nehamas, Alexander. *Nietzsche: Life as Literature.* Cambridge: Harvard University Press, 1985.

Nietzsche. Cahiers du Royaumont. Philosophie No. VI. Paris: Éditions de Minuit, 1967.

Nietzsche aujourd'hui. 2 Vols. Paris: Union Générale D'Éditions, 1973.

Nietzsche, Friedrich. *Beyond Good and Evil.* Translated by Walter Kaufmann. New York: Random House, 1966.

_____. *The Birth of Tragedy. The Case of Wagner.* Translated by Walter Kaufmann. New York: Random House, 1967.

_____. *Daybreak.* Translated by R. J. Hollingdale. Cambridge: Cambridge University Press, 1982.

_____. *The Gay Science.* Translated by Walter Kaufmann. New York: Random House, 1974.

_____. *Human, All–Too–Human. Volumes One and Two [Assorted Opinions and Maxims. The Wanderer and His Shadow].* Translated by R. J. Hollingdale. Cambridge: Cambridge University Press, 1986.

_____. *On the Genealogy of Morals. Ecce Homo.* Translated by Walter Kaufmann. New York: Random House, 1967.

_____. *Sämtliche Werke. Kritische Studienausgabe.* Edited by Giorgio Colli and Mazzino Montinari. Berlin: Walter de Gruyter, 1980.

_____. *Thus Spoke Zarathustra. Twilight of the Idols. The Antichrist. Nietzsche Contra Wagner.* In *The Viking Portable Nietzsche.* Translated and edited by Walter Kaufmann. New York: The Viking Press, 1967.

_____. *Twilight of the Idols. The Antichrist.* Translated by R. J. Hollingdale. Middlesex, England: Penguin Books, 1968.

————. *Untimely Meditations: David Strauss, the Confessor and the Writer; On the Uses and Disadvantages of History for Life; Schopenhauer as Educator; Richard Wagner in Bayreuth*. Translated by R. J. Hollingdale. Cambridge: Cambridge University Press, 1983.

————. *The Will to Power*. Translated by Walter Kaufmann and R. J. Hollingdale. New York: Random House, 1968.

Norris, Christopher. *Derrida*. Cambridge: Harvard University Press, 1987.

Oliver, Kelly. "The Plaint of Ariadne." In *The Fate of the New Nietzsche*. Edited by Keith Ansell–Pearson and Howard Caygill. Aldershot, England: Avebury, 1993. Pp. 211–28.

————. *Womanizing Nietzsche: Philosophy's Relation to the "Feminine."* New York: Routledge, 1994.

Ormiston, Gayle L. "Traces of Derrida: Nietzsche's Image of Women." *Philosophy Today* (Summer 1984): 178–88.

Ormiston, Gayle L., and Alan D. Schrift, editors. *Transforming the Hermeneutic Context: From Nietzsche to Nancy*. Albany: State University of New York Press, 1990.

Patton, Paul, editor. *Nietzsche, Feminism and Political Theory*. New York: Routledge, 1993.

Pecora, Vincent P. "Deleuze's Nietzsche and Post–Structuralism." *Sub–Stance*, No. 48 (1986): 34–50.

Plotnitsky, Arkady. *Reconfigurations: Critical Theory and General Economy*. Gainesville: University Press of Florida, 1993.

Reich, Wilhelm. *The Mass Psychology of Fascism*. Translated by Vincent R. Carfagno. London: Souvenir Press, 1970.

Richman, Michèle H. *Reading Georges Bataille: Beyond the Gift*. Baltimore: Johns Hopkins University Press, 1982.

Ricoeur, Paul. *Freud and Philosophy: An Essay on Interpretation*. Translated by Denis Savage. New Haven: Yale University Press, 1970.

Rorty, Richard. "Is Derrida a Transcendental Philosopher?" In *Derrida: A Critical Reader*. Edited by David Wood. Cambridge: Basil Blackwell, 1992. Pp. 235–46.

Rubin, Gayle. "The Traffic in Women." In *Toward an Anthropology of Women*. Edited by Rayna R. Reiter. New York and London: Monthly Review Press, 1975. Pp. 157–210.

Schacht, Richard. *Nietzsche*. New York: Routledge, 1983.

Schrift, Alan D. *Nietzsche and the Question of Interpretation: Between Hermeneutics and Deconstruction*. New York: Routledge, 1990.

_____. "Reading, Writing, Text: Nietzsche's Deconstruction of Author–ity," *International Studies in Philosophy*, Vol. 17, No. 2 (1985), pp. 55–64.

_____. "Reconfiguring the Subject: Foucault's Analytics of Power." In *Reconstructing Foucault: Essays in the Wake of the 80s*. Edited by Ricardo Miguel–Alfonso and Silvia Caporale–Bizzini. Amsterdam: Rodopi, 1995. Pp. 185–99.

_____. "Spinoza, Nietzsche, Deleuze: An Other Discourse of Desire." In *Philosophy and the Discourse of Desire*. Edited by Hugh J. Silverman. New York: Routledge, forthcoming.

Schrift, Alan D., editor. *The Logic of the Gift: Toward an Ethic of Generosity*. New York: Routledge, forthcoming.

Scott, Charles E. *The Question of Ethics: Nietzsche, Foucault, Heidegger*. Bloomington: Indiana University Press, 1990.

Shapiro, Gary. *Alcyone: Nietzsche on Gifts, Noise, and Women*. Albany: State University of New York Press, 1991.

Stanton, Domna. "Difference on Trial: A Critique of the Maternal Metaphor in Cixous, Irigaray, and Kristeva." In *The Thinking Muse: Feminism and Modern French Philosophy*. Edited by Jeffner Allen and Iris Marion Young. Bloomington: Indiana University Press, 1989. Pp. 156–79.

Stern, J. P. *A Study of Nietzsche*. Cambridge: Cambridge University Press, 1979.

Strathern, Marilyn. *The Gender of the Gift: Problems with Women and Problems with Society in Melanesia*. Berkeley: University of California Press, 1988.

Strong, Tracy B., and Michael Allen Gillespie, editors. *Nietzsche's New Seas: Explorations in Philosophy, Aesthetics, and Politics*. Chicago: University of Chicago Press, 1988.

Taylor, Seth. *Left–Wing Nietzscheans: The Politics of German Expressionism 1910–1920*. Berlin: Walter de Gruyter, 1990.

Thomas, R. Hinton. *Nietzsche in German Politics and Society 1890–1918*. Manchester: Manchester University Press, 1983.

_____. "Nietzsche, Women, and the Whip." *German Life and Letters.* Vol. 34, No. 1 (October 1980): 117–25.

Tongeren, Paul van. "Kroniek van Recente Nietzsche–Literatuur (II)." *Tijdschrift voor Filosofie,* No. 4 (December 1993): 694–720.

Van Baal, J. *Reciprocity and the Position of Women.* Amsterdam: Van Gorcum, 1975.

Veyne, Paul. "The Final Foucault and His Ethics." Translated by Catherine Porter and Arnold I. Davidson. *Critical Inquiry,* Vol. 20 (Autumn 1993): 1–9.

Visker, Rudi. "DISSENSUS COMMUNIS: How to Keep Silent 'after' Lyotard." In *DISSENSUS COMMUNIS: Between Ethics and Politics.* Edited by Philippe Van Haute and Peg Birmingham. Kampen, The Netherlands: J. H. Kok, forthcoming.

Weiner, Annette B. *Inalienable Possessions: The Paradox of Keeping–While–Giving.* Berkeley: University of California Press, 1992.

_____. *Women of Value, Men of Renown: New Perspectives on Trobriand Exchange.* Austin: University of Texas Press, 1976.

Index

➤